Equality, Participation, Transition

Equality, Participation, Transition

Essays in Honour of Branko Horvat

Edited by

Vojmir Franičević
Professor of Economics
University of Zagreb
Croatia

and

Milica Uvalić
Professor of Economics
University of Perugia
Italy

Foreword by Benjamin Ward

First published in Great Britain 2000 by
MACMILLAN PRESS LTD
Houndmills, Basingstoke, Hampshire RG21 6XS and London
Companies and representatives throughout the world

A catalogue record for this book is available from the British Library.

ISBN 0-333-77640-2

 First published in the United States of America 2000 by
ST. MARTIN'S PRESS, INC.,
Scholarly and Reference Division,
175 Fifth Avenue, New York, N.Y. 10010

ISBN 0-312-23225-X

Library of Congress Cataloging-in-Publication Data
Equality, participation, transition : essays in honour of Branko Horvat / edited by
Milica Uvalic and Vojmir Franicevic.
   p. cm.
Includes bibliographical references and index.
ISBN 0-312-23225-X (cloth)
1. Comparative economics. 2. Social justice. 3. Horvat, Branko. I. Uvalic, Milica.
II. Franicevic, Vojmir.

HB90 .E69   2000
330—dc21
                                                              99-086196

Selection, editorial matter and Introduction © Vojmir Franičević and Milica Uvalić 2000
Foreword © Benjamin Ward 2000
Chapters 1–11 © Macmillan Press Ltd 2000

All rights reserved. No reproduction, copy or transmission of this publication may be made without written permission.

No paragraph of this publication may be reproduced, copied or transmitted save with written permission or in accordance with the provisions of the Copyright, Designs and Patents Act 1988, or under the terms of any licence permitting limited copying issued by the Copyright Licensing Agency, 90 Tottenham Court Road, London W1P 0LP.

Any person who does any unauthorised act in relation to this publication may be liable to criminal prosecution and civil claims for damages.

The authors have asserted their rights to be identified as the authors of this work in accordance with the Copyright, Designs and Patents Act 1988.

This book is printed on paper suitable for recycling and made from fully managed and sustained forest sources.

10 9 8 7 6 5 4 3 2 1
09 08 07 06 05 04 03 02 01 00

Printed and bound in Great Britain by
Antony Rowe Ltd, Chippenham, Wiltshire

Contents

List of Tables	vii
List of Figures	viii
Foreword by Benjamin Ward	ix
Acknowledgements	xi
Notes on the Contributors	xii
Introduction: Branko Horvat – Beyond the Mainstream	xx
Branko Horvat: Select Bibliography	xxxii
1 Ideas and Ideals: Horvat's Contributions to Twentieth-Century Economic and Social Theory *Howard M. Wachtel*	1
2 Individual Initiative, Entry and Economic Democracy *Jaroslav Vanek*	16
3 Egalitarianism On Its Own *Samuel Bowles* and *Herbert Gintis*	27
4 Determinants of Cross-Country Income Inequality: An 'Augmented' Kuznets Hypothesis *Branko Milanović*	48
5 Illyrian Theories of Cooperative Rent-Sharing and Their Application in Real Life *Dinko Dubravčić*	80
6 Employee Participation in Enterprise Control and Returns: Patterns, Gaps and Discontinuities *Mario Domenico Nuti*	91
7 Employee Involvement and the Modern Firm *Tea Petrin* and *Aleš Vahčič*	102
8 Uneasy Symbiosis of a Market Economy and Democratic Centralism: Emergence and Disappearance of Market Socialism and Yugoslavia *Jože Mencinger*	118

9 Self-Management, Employee Ownership and
   Transition   145
   Saul Estrin

10 Privatization and Enterprise Performance:
   Evidence from Estonia   162
   Derek C. Jones and *Niels Mygind*

11 Growth Theory and Transition Economies   184
   Ivo Bićanić

Index   201

List of Tables

4.1 Summary Statistics for the Five Regions	54
4.2 The Regressions: Dependent Variable GINI	62
4.3 Factors Explaining the Difference in Inequality Compared to OECD Countries (in Gini Points)	65
4.4 The Role of Social Choice Variables	67
6.1 Traditional Typology of Employee Ownership According to Control and Return Rights and Examples	93
8.1 The Main Performance Indicators of the Yugoslav Economy, 1946–88	130
8.2 Performance of the Yugoslav Economy in the 1980s	136
9.1 Methods of Privatization for Medium-Size and Large Enterprises in Seven Transition Economies	150
9.2 Mass Privatization Programmes in Central and Eastern Europe and the Commonwealth of Independent States	152
9.3 Ownership Consequences of Privatization	153
9.4 Dominant Owner Type in Russia, 1994	154
9.5 State Ownership in Ukraine, 1996	155
10.1 Performance Regressions: Privatization and Majority Ownership	172
10.2 Performance Regressions: Majority and Minority Ownership	174
10.3 Performance Regressions: Majority Ownership and Changes in Ownership	175
11.1 The Economic Lag of Transitioning Economies	187

List of Figures

2.1	First Law of Optimal Participation	19
2.2	Second Law of Optimal Participation	23
3.1	The Evolution of Cooperation in a Dynamic Setting	38
4.1	(4.1a) Relationship Between GINI and STATE	56
	(4.1b) Relationship Between GINI and TRANS	56
	(4.1c) Relationship Between GINI and INCOME	57
4.2	Residuals from Equation 1.0 as a function of INCOME	58
4.3	The Residuals:	64
	(4.3a) From Equation (1)	64
	(4.3b) From Equation (7)	64
4.4	Predicted and Actual GINIs	66
6.1	An Alternative View of Employee Participation in Enterprise Control and Returns	98
9.1	Privatization Options for State Sector	148
11.1	Convergency 'Scenarios' of Different Growth Model Specifications	194

Foreword

One of the twentieth century's most important and least discussed transformations has been the regionalization of class. Roughly speaking, the most affluent four fifths of Americans could fit into the top fifth of the Third World's income distribution, and vice versa for the world's poor. This geographic concentration of economic well-being and security has gone hand in hand with geographic concentration of technical change, population growth, and transportation and communication modes, and a distinct geographic bias in the spread of healthcare techniques. Though causation is complex and controversial, these are undisputed facts, and in combination they clearly display the entirely new world of class structure that has emerged over the decades of our century.

This is a world in which Branko Horvat is at home though not at ease. A product of the developing world, educated at home and in the United Kingdom, he has served as a planner as well as a professor of economics in Yugoslavia, and has taught, lectured and served as a research fellow at a great variety of institutions around the world. Our world is no village, and Horvat's experience of it is uniquely broad and clearly evident in his work. His work runs the gamut from mathematical modeling through empirical analysis to the appraisal of broad historical forces. However, his focus has always been on understanding the ways in which developing economies operate and interact with the rest of the world's economies and polities.

Horvat is an independent thinker and his work has generated a lot of controversy; in fact he and I have gone at it from time to time. No doubt some of that criticism is justified, but not all of it has passed the test of time. For example, thirty years ago he presented a model of economic growth whose main result was that it was possible, with the right policies, for an economy to combine rapid economic growth with a steady growth in per capita consumption. It was roundly criticized, but in hindsight it looks like it was not a bad metaphor for what happened in much of East Asia in the couple of decades after his work was published, a time in which foreign trade and investment were not a major constraint on the economic growth of many countries of that part of the world.

A central feature of Horvat's work has been his emphasis on the role of institutions in shaping economies and their markets. And the institution most dear to Horvat's heart has been worker management. I believe most of the contributors to this volume share Horvat's belief that some form of industrial democracy can be found that can be made to work. This is not a widely popular view these days and I am among those who have been critical of the forms that it has taken in the former Yugoslavia. However, the ten years that I spent at the beginning of my worklife as a merchant seaman gave me some sense of its problems and possibilities at a practical level, and that has left me with a fixed desire to keep this option open. Perhaps most important was this: when I moved from the sea to academia I found my new colleagues to be far more articulate than my old shipmates; but I found no increase in wisdom.

Horvat has made some efforts to try and meld central ideas of Marxism with those of neoclassical political economy. For many these days, including myself, Marxism is clearly a spent intellectual force. But in our century, Marxism has been the only intellectual force that has been anchored firmly in an attempt to understand and defend the interests of the wretched of the earth. The latter, this underclass, is probably larger today than it has ever been, and it will acquire a voice. Those interested in developing that voice can do no better than to build on the humane, informed, analytic, and committed elements provided by the works and career of Branko Horvat.

Berkeley, California BENJAMIN WARD

Acknowledgements

The editors and publishers would like to thank the Egon Sohmen Foundation for having permitted the use, in Jaroslav Vanek's contribution to this volume, of section 2 of Egon-Sohmen-Lecture 'Welfare State: Bandaid or Full Cure?' (Vienna, 15 October 1996). They would also like to thank the World Bank for having authorized the reproduction of Table 9.1 *Methods of privatization for medium-size and large enterprises in seven transition economies* (published in *From Plan to Market – World Development Report 1996*) in Saul Estrin's contribution. Similarly, they thank Blackwell Publishers for having authorized the reproduction of Table 6.1 *Typology of employee ownership* (published in A. Ben-Ner and D. Jones, 'Employee participation, ownership and productivity', *Industrial Relations*, 34(4)) in Mario Nuti's contribution to this volume.

Notes on the Contributors

Ivo Bićanić is Professor in the Faculty of Economics, Zagreb, and Recurrent Visiting Professor at the Central European University, Budapest. He obtained his PhD from the Faculty of Economics in Zagreb (1983) and was a former Fellow of the Woodrow Wilson Center in Washington DC. He has published a number of articles on economic inequality, the unofficial economy, privatization, and on various other issues concerned with the transition to market economy in Croatia and in other Southeastern European economies. His current research is concerned with growth theory and growth prospects of transition economies. Recent publications include 'The Economic Divergence of Yugoslavia's Successor States' in *Problems of Economic and Political Transformation in the Balkans*, edited by Ian Jeffries (Pinter, 1996), 'Differing Approaches to Transition to Post-Socialist Development in Newly Formed Balkan States', with M. Škreb, in B. Dallago (ed) (1995), *Integrationary and Disintegrationary Process in the European Economy*. He has also published in *East European Politics and Society, Communist Economies and Economic Transformation, Osteuropa Wirtschaft*, and he regularly contributes to *Oxford Analitica* and *FRE/RL Research Reports*. He is member of EACES, of the International Economic History Association, and of the Editorial Boards of *Economic Analysis – Journal of Enterprise and Participation*, and of *Acta Economica Historiae*.

Samuel Bowles and Herbert Gintis, Professors of Economics at the University of Massachusetts at Amherst, are now entering their fourth decade of fruitful collaboration. They received doctorates in Economics in 1965 and 1969 respectively from Harvard University, where they taught Economics before moving to the University of Massachusetts. They wrote *Schooling in Capitalist America: Educational Reform and the Contradictions of Economic Life* (Basic Books, 1976), *Democracy and Capitalism: Community, Property, and the Contradictions of Modern Social Thought* (Basic Books, 1986), as well as numerous scholarly essays in economics, philosophy, sociology, history, public policy and political science. They are currently pursuing research on the sources and consequences of inequality and the evolution of preferences and values.

More recently, they wrote (edited by Erik Olin Wright) *Recasting Egalitarianism: New Rules for Markets, States, and Communities* (Verso,

1999). Samuel Bowles is also co-editor (with Kenneth Arrow and Steven Durlauf) of *Meritocracy and Economic Inequality* (Princeton University Press, 1999), and Herbert Gintis is author of *Game Theory Evolving* (Princeton University Press, 1999).

Dinko Dubravčić graduated in Chemical Engineering and in Economics, and obtained a PhD in Economics from the University of Zagreb (1965). Among positions held are a Postdoctoral Fellowship at the LSE, London (1968–9), Guest Researcher at the Vienna Institute for Comparative Studies (1971–3), Fulbright Professor at Barnard College, Columbia University (1986). He also held various posts in industry in Zagreb, and was a researcher at the Institute of Economics in Zagreb, with several years of teaching at the University of Zagreb. Main fields of interest include industrial and regional development, entrepreneurial aspects of the labour-managed economy and of privatization processes during transition, structure of investment in socialist economies, monetary economics. He has published articles in *Economica, Economic Analysis and Workers' Management, Europe–Asia Studies*. Among his recent publications are 'Economic Causes and Political Context of the Dissolution of a Multinational Federal State: The Case of Yugoslavia', *Communist Economies and Economic Transformation*, 5(3), 1993, and 'Entrepreneurial Aspects of Privatisation in Transition Economies', *Europe–Asia Studies*, 1995, 47(2). He is a member of EACES and contributor to its conferences in Urbino, Verona, Groningen and Budapest.

Saul Estrin is Professor of Economics and Deputy Dean (Faculty and Academic Planning) at the London Business School, where he is also Director of the CIS-Middle Europe Centre. He has worked for many years on privatization and restructuring of state-owned firms in Central and Eastern Europe. His recent publications include the widely cited edited volume *Privatisation in Central and Eastern Europe* (Longmans, 1994) and the co-edited book *Foreign Direct Investment into Transitional Economics: A Case Study Approach* (Cassell, 1997). He has written numerous articles for scholarly journals including the *Quarterly Journal of Economics, European Economic Review, Journal of Public Economics, Economica*, as well as for practitioner journals such as *Business Strategy Review*, and the *Financial Times*. He has been consultant to the OECD, the World Bank, the European Communities, as well as to a variety of international companies and banks. His current research interests include privatization and enterprise restructuring in Central and Eastern Europe, EU enlargement, and foreign direct investment. He is member of the Editorial Board of *Economic Analysis – Journal of Enterprise and Participation*.

Vojmir Franičević is Professor of Economics in the Faculty of Economics, University of Zagreb. He received his PhD in economics from the Faculty of Economics in Zagreb (1983) with a thesis 'Radical Political Economy in the USA' (published in 1986 with major revisions). He was a visiting Fulbright scholar at the UC Berkeley from 1990–1 and a visiting professor at the Faculty of Economics in Ljubljana in 1993–4. His research in the 1990s has been mostly concerned with privatization, entrepreneurship, small business policies, business networking, unofficial economy, the role of institutions and state. His recent publications include 'Markets, hierarchies, networks and small firms', *Zbornik radova*, (Rijeka: Faculty of Economics, 1995); 'The Trade-Off: Problems of Accumulation and Legitimation of Emerging Capitalism', in J. Hersh and J. D. Schmidt (eds) (1996), *The Aftermath of 'Real Existing Socialism' in Eastern Europe, Vol.1* (London: Macmillan); 'Institutions and Entrepreneurial Behavior: Privatization and Competition in Croatia', in: *Enterprise in Transition* (Split: Faculty of Economics, 1997); 'Croatia's economy after stabilizaion' (with Evan Kraft), *Europe–Asia Studies* (1997); 'Privatization in Croatia: legacies and context', *Eastern European Economics* (1999), 'Political Economy of the Unofficial Economy: The State and Regulation', in E. Feige and K. Ott (eds.) (1999), *Underground Economies in Transition: Unrecorded Activity, Tax Evasion, Corruption and Organized Crime* (Aldershot: Ashgate).

Derek C. Jones is James L. Ferguson Professor of Economics, Hamilton College, Clinton (NY). He undertook some of the first empirical analyses of long established workers' cooperatives, with publications in the *Economic Journal, Economica, Journal of Economic Literature*. With Jan Svejnar he edits the research series *Advances in the Economic Analysis of Participatory and Labor Managed Firms*. His current research investigates employee ownership around the world, with an article on Japan (*American Economic Review*, 1995), privatization in the former command economies, and the economic effects of the new forms of ownership and other organizational innovations. Countries studied include Bulgaria, with a recent volume co-edited with Jeffrey Miller, *The Bulgarian Economy: Lessons from Reform During Early Transition* (Avebury, 1997), and an article in the *Journal of Comparative Economics* (Sept. 1998); Russia (*Comparative Economic Studies*, summer 1998); and the Baltic States. He is a member of editorial boards of various journals including *Economic Analysis – Journal of Enterprise and Participation* and *Annals of Public and Cooperative Economy*.

Jože Mencinger is Professor of Economics and Director of the Economics Institute at the Law School, University of Ljubljana, and Rector of the University of Ljubljana (since 1998). He obtained his degree in Law at the University of Ljubljana (1964), MA in Economics at the University of Belgrade (1966), and PhD in Economics at the University of Pennsylvania (1975, with a thesis *A Quarterly Econometric Model of the Yugoslav Economy*). He is a former Visiting Professor at the Universities of Zagreb, Maribor, and Pittsburgh, and Visiting Scholar at ICER, Torino, and Institute for Social Studies, Vienna. He has written numerous articles on economic systems, economic policy, labour markets, exchange rates, transition and privatization in Yugoslavia and in Slovenia, published in various journals including *Economic Analysis, Empirica, Annals of Public and Cooperative Economy, Est-Ovest, Transit, Europpaische Rundshau, Nationalities Papers, Communist Economies and Economic Transformation, Weltwirtschaftlisches Review*. He served as Deputy Prime Minister and Minister for Economic Affairs of Slovenia (1990–1); as member of the Board, Bank of Slovenia (1991–97); as adviser to UNDP for Bosnia, Vienna (1996–7). He is Editor of the monthly *Gospodarska gibanja* (since 1987), member of the European Academy of Arts and Sciences in Salzburg (since 1995), and member of the Editorial Board of *Economic Analysis – Journal of Enterprise and Participation*.

Branko Milanović is Principal Economist in the World Bank Research Department and Adjunct Professor at the School for Advanced International Studies, Johns Hopkins University, Baltimore. He obtained his PhD in Economics (1987) from Belgrade University (Yugoslavia), with a dissertation on income inequality in Yugoslavia (*Ekonomska nejednakost u Jugoslaviji*, Ekonomika & Institute of Economic Sciences, Belgrade, 1990). He is the author of numerous articles on income distribution methodology, poverty, and social policy in Eastern Europe and the former Soviet Union, including 'Cash Social Transfers, Direct Taxes and Income Distribution in Late Socialism' (*Journal of Comparative Economics*, 1994). His most recent publication, *Income, Inequality, and Poverty during the Transition from Planned to Market Economy* (World Bank, 1998), is the first book to discuss, in a unified framework, what happened to real incomes and their distribution, and poverty in eighteen transition economies since 1989.

Niels Mygind is Associate Professor and Director of the Center for East European Studies (CEES) at the Copenhagen Business School. He has done research on employee ownership and economic performance in transition economies, particularly in the Baltic States. The transition to a market economy in Eastern Europe is analyzed from a general point of view in his book *Societies in Transition* (1994), which can be downloaded from the CEES-homepage (www.econ.cbs.dk/cees). His core research areas include privatization, corporate governance, and enterprise restructuring in Eastern Europe. Among recent research is empirical evidence on enterprise performance in the Baltic countries, based on a longitudinal study of a large number of enterprises (some results of this research can be found on the CEES-homepage). He is member of EACES and of the Editorial Board of *Economic Analysis – Journal of Enterprise and Participation*.

Mario Domenico Nuti is Professor of Comparative Economic Systems, University of Rome (since 1993), Visiting Professor and Director of Research, CIS and Middle Europe Centre, London Business School. He has a Degree in Law, *summa cum laude*, Rome University (1962) and a PhD in Economics, Cambridge (1970). Previously, he has held academic positions at King's College, Cambridge; at the Faculty of Economics and Politics, Cambridge University; at the University of Birmingham, where he was Director of the Centre for Russian and East European Studies; and at the European University Institute, Florence. He was Economic Adviser to the European Commission, Brussels (1990–3); Consultant to the World Bank, IMF, ILO, NATO, UNDP, OECD; Specialist Adviser to the House of Lords (1993–4); Economic Adviser to the Polish Government (1994–7), and to President Lukashenko of Belarus, under World Bank sponsorship (1998). He was editor of *Socialist Economics* (with Alec Nove; Penguin 1972, 1974, 1977) and of V.K. Dmitriev's *Value, Competition and Utility* (CUP, 1974); main author of the World Bank *Report on Poland* (1988); co-author of *Transformation and Integration: Shaping the Future of Central Eastern Europe*, (IPPR, London, 1995) and *Not Just Another Accession – Political Economy of EU Enlargement to the East* IPPR, London (1997); and of numerous other publications on the reform of centrally planned economies and their transition to capitalism.

Tea Petrin is Professor of Economics and Business and Head of the Graduate Program on Entrepreneurship Studies in the Faculty of Economics, University of Ljubljana. She obtained her BA in Economics from the University of Ljubljana, MA in Economics from Louisiana State University (New Orleans), and PhD in Economics from the University of Ljubljana. She has served as Advisor to the Government of Slovenia on small business development, entrepreneurship, and restructuring. She is a former Fulbright Professor, University of California at Berkeley, and Visiting Professor, UMASS at Amherst and Lowell. She also served as Regional Officer for rural development through entrepreneurship for Europe at UN-FAO, Rome. Publications include 'Promoting entrepreneurship in Eastern Europe' (co-authors L. D'Andrea Tyson and R. Halsey), *Small Business Economics* (1994); *Industrial Policy Supporting Economic Transition in Central-Eastern Europe, Lessons from Slovenia*, Institute of International Studies, University of California at Berkeley, 1995; and 'Industrial policy and the restructuring of firms in post-socialist Slovenia', *Review of Industrial Organization*, 1996.

Milica Uvalić is Professor of Economics in the Faculty of Political Sciences, University of Perugia. She obtained her BA (1975) and MA (1979) in Economics from the University of Belgrade, and a PhD in Economics (1988) from the European University Institute, Florence, where she was Research Fellow before moving to the University of Perugia in 1992. She has been Consultant to the Commission of the European Communities both for former Yugoslavia (1991) and for Employee Participation in Western Europe (1991–2), and more recently to the ILO (1994–6) and to Governor Avramović of the National Bank of Yugoslavia (1996), for privatization. She is author of *Investment and Property Rights in Yugoslavia – The Long Transition to a Market Economy* (CUP, 1992) and of *The PEPPER Report* (European Communities, 1992); co-editor of *Impediments to the Transition in Eastern Europe* (EUI Florence, 1992), *Privatization Surprises in Transition Economics* (Edward Elgar, 1997, reprinted in March 1999); *The Balkans and the Challenge of Economic Integration* (Longo Editore, 1997); and *Advances in the Economic Analysis of Participatory and Labor Managed Firms, Volume 6* (1998). Together with Will Bartlett, she edits the journal *Economic Analysis – The Journal of Enterprise and Participation* (Carfax, starting from 1998). Since 1993, she has been coordinator of the Economics Group of Experts of the *International Network Europe and the Balkans* based at the University of Bologna.

Aleš Vahčič is Professor of Economics and Business and Head of the Statistical Data Service in the Faculty of Economics, University of Ljubljana. He obtained his BA in Economics from the University of Ljubljana, MA in Economics from Louisiana State University (New Orleans), and PhD in Economics from Cornell University. He has served as Advisor to the Government of Slovenia for small business development and entrepreneurship. He was founder and co-founder of several enterprises in Slovenia, including GEA College, a successful private entrepreneurship training institution. He has been a consultant for enterprise restructuring in Slovenia, Hungary, and Moldova. His publications include 'Financial System for Restructuring the Yugoslav Economy' (co-author T. Petrin) in *Financial Reform in Socialist Economies* (1989), 'Privatization Controversies in the East and West' (co-authors D. Ellerman and T. Petrin) in *Communist Economies and Economic Transformation* (1991), *SMEs and Job Creation in Slovenia* (1998, co-authors M. Glas and T. Petrin), ESBC Seminar, Vienna.

Jaroslav Vanek, born in Prague, has lived and worked in the United States since 1955, teaching in the Faculty of Economics of Harvard and Cornell Universities. At Cornell, he founded and directed for twenty years the Program on Participation and Labor Managed Systems (PPLMS) and is now Professor Emeritus at Cornell University. He is the author of several books and many articles on international economics and economic democracy, including the *General Theory of Labor-Managed Market Economies* (Cornell University Press, 1970) and *Self-Management, Economic Liberation of Man* (Penguin, 1975). More recently, he has developed simple solar energy technologies for the STEVEN Foundation, and invented an all-wheel-drive bicycle, the 'Vanek Superbike'.

Howard M. Wachtel is Acting Dean of the College of Arts and Sciences at American University in Washington, DC. He did his dissertation on Yugoslavia (where he lived in 1967–8), in association with Branko Horvat in Belgrade at the Institute for Economic Sciences. The first of his three books, *Workers' Management and Workers' Wages in Yugoslavia* was followed by *Labor and the Economy* and *The Money Mandarins*. He was a correspondent for the journal *Economic Analysis and Workers' Management* throughout its existence and published many articles in the journal. His work extends beyond the economies of central and eastern Europe and encompasses labour studies, globalization and finance, and the new global economy. He has published more than 30 articles in leading academic journals, as well as in such media as the *New York Times*, *Le Monde Diplomatique*, *International Herald Tribune*, *The Guardian* (London) and *Excelsior*. He is a Fellow of the Transnational Institute (Amsterdam) and has held visiting faculty appointments at the London School of Economics, Cambridge University, the American University in Paris, and Cornell University, and has lectured in many countries.

Benjamin Ward took his degrees at University of California at Berkeley. He has taught at Stanford University, the Chinese University of Hong Kong, and University of California at Berkeley, where he was until his retirement in 1992. His main research interests were comparative economics, development, and national security studies. What can probably be considered his most famous work is the article 'The Firm in Illyria – Market Syndicalism' published in the *American Economic Review* 48(4), in 1958, which had been inspired by the Yugoslav ('Illyrian') system of self-management. This article marked the beginning of an important new area of economic theory and comparative economic systems, namely the theory of the labour-managed firm, and as such inspired an enormous literature on the subject appearing in the following decades. Among his other more important publications are *The Socialist Economy* (1967), *What is Wrong with Economics* (1972), *Greek Regional Development* (1962) and *The Ideal Worlds of Economics* (1979).

Introduction: Branko Horvat – Beyond the Mainstream

Milica Uvalić and Vojmir Franičević

This book is dedicated to Branko Horvat. It is a collective tribute for his 70th birthday, with which we intend to celebrate a lifetime of dedicated work. In this brief introduction preceding the eleven essays in his honour, we would like to recall some of the most essential features of this rather unique economist and unconventional personality. After a brief biographical note and presentation of Horvat as an economist (sections 1 and 2), we will introduce the readers to the rich and multifaceted world of Branko Horvat (section 3), as he has not been simply an academic. This will be followed by an outline of the essays contributed in this book (section 4).

1 The life and work of Branko Horvat

Born in a small town of Petrinja in Croatia in 1928, Branko Horvat spent his youth in Slavonska Požega. He was raised in a middle-class family of intellectuals. As a 16-year old, he joined the Yugoslav partisans' resistance movement – something that he always so proudly stresses – which undoubtedly influenced his future life and work, especially his 'ideas and ideals' (see Wachtel, Chapter 1 below).

After the end of the war, he enrolled at the University of Zagreb where he initially studied engineering but very soon decided to switch to economics. He graduated in 1952 and received his first Ph.D. in Economics from the University of Zagreb in 1955, and his second Ph.D. from the University of Manchester in 1959, with a thesis that was published soon after (*Towards a Theory of a Planned Economy*, Belgrade 1961, New York 1964). During this whole period, he was actively studying other disciplines as well, including philosophy and sociology.

His career as professional researcher started in Zagreb, at the Petroleum Institute (1952–3) and the Institute of Economics (1954–5), which resulted in the publication of several books related to the petroleum industry. After returning from his studies in modern economics in Manchester in 1958, he joined the Federal Planning Bureau in Belgrade as Chief Methodologist. Within the Bureau he established the Economic Research Department (which in 1963 would become the Institute of Economic Sciences) whose Director he remained until 1970.

At the Institute of Economic Sciences, Horvat developed a wide range of research projects and educational activities, including the most distinguished postgraduate school in Economics in former Yugoslavia. During this period, he also taught at the University of Belgrade (1962–3) and the University of Ljubljana (1967–9). He returned to Zagreb in 1975, and was Professor of Economics at the University until his retirement in 1992. While in Zagreb, he taught a number of undergraduate and postgraduate courses in economic theory and various other economic disciplines. The high quality of his graduate program is known to have attracted the best and most promising students from the whole of Yugoslavia. His teaching activities led to the publication of a number of textbooks introducing students to contemporary economic theories and methodologies.

While at the Institute of Economic Sciences in Belgrade, in 1967 Horvat founded the journal *Economic Analysis and Workers' Management* which he edited for twenty-seven years. In 1978 *Economic Analysis* became the official journal of the International Association for the Economics of Self-management, which became the International Association for the Economics of Participation (IAFEP) in 1994. Horvat was one of the founding members and today he is life Honorary President of IAFEP. A few years after Horvat's retirement, a new series of his journal was launched with a somewhat different subtitle: *Economic Analysis – Journal of Enterprise and Participation* (Carfax Publishing). In addition to his very active editorial work for *Economic Analysis*, Horvat has also been member of the editorial boards (at different times) of *European Economic Review, World Development, Journal of Comparative Economics, Economic and Industrial Democracy, Scientia Yugoslavica*.

Internationally known and respected at an early stage of his career, Horvat has been Visiting, Distinguished, and UNESCO Professor at numerous universities, including the University of Michigan (1968); University of Florida (1970), American University, Washington (1970, 1972, 1974), Catholic University of Chile (1972), University of Stockholm (1973–4), University of Dar Es Salaam (1975), University of Notre

Dame (1978), University of Paris (1978), Yale University (1984–5), Cambridge University (1986), University of Southern California (1987), University of California at Berkeley (1993). He has also delivered numerous lectures at a number of universities around the world.

Since Horvat also became one of the widely recognized experts in self-management, planning and development, he has been consultant, at different periods of his life, to various governments. In addition to advising his own government, he has advised the governments of Peru, Brazil, Bangladesh, Turkey and Ukraine.

During his long career, Horvat has published an astounding number of books, contributions to edited volumes, journal articles, papers in conference proceedings, and articles in weekly and daily press. A large part of his publications has been published in many foreign languages throughout the world (see Select Bibliography).

2 Horvat the economist

Branko Horvat has been undoubtedly one of the most important and most well-known economists of former Yugoslavia, and nowadays of Croatia. He belongs to a category of economists which is usually described as heterodox, though his heterodoxy has a number of distinct features. Among these, three merits should be particularly emphasized: his specific approach to Marxism (which led Benjamin Ward to coin the term Marxism–Horvatism); his specific critique of neoclassical economics; and his pronounced inclination towards inter-disciplinary research, which received full expression in his masterpiece, *The Political Economy of Socialism* (1982).

His research interests cover a great number of areas and topics, not only in economics but also in political science, sociology, and philosophy. In what follows, however, we will try to single out some of Horvat's most important contributions to economic science. Most of these contributions fall within four broad areas: growth theory and economic cycles, theory of the labour-managed firm, political economy of modern societies, and 'pure' economic theory.

In the 1950s, at a time when a number of economists were focusing their interest on economic growth, development, and inequality in income distribution, Horvat was looking for optimal solutions for a new economic system. Contrary to the prevailing view at that time, that the volume of investment is determined by the willingness of consumers to decrease the level of consumption, he proposed an optimal rate of investment which would assure the highest rate of growth – consumption included. In his two classic articles in the *Economic Journal* (1958, 1965), he emphasized the direct link between the limited absorptive capacity of an economy and the optimal rate of growth, stressing the importance of determining the optimal rate of investment for a given economy. If an economy tries to realize a higher than optimal rate of investment, rather than achieving faster economic growth, the rate of growth will be reduced. Related to this work is his research on business cycles in Yugoslavia, which enabled him to provide valuable advice to Yugoslav policy makers in the 1960s.

Perhaps even more important are Horvat's contributions to the theory of the labour-managed firm. After the pioneering work of Benjamin Ward (1958) on the firm in Illyria, and later, the appearance of Jaroslav Vanek's *General Theory of Labor-managed Market Economy* (1971), the theoretical literature on the labour-managed firm blossomed, producing a whole new school of thought. Horvat has made a number of important contributions to this literature, proposing how to correct the alleged inefficiency and perverse behavior of the labour-managed firm (see Wachtel's and Dubravčić's contribution to this volume, Chapters 1 and 5). He showed that the theory, as developed by Ward, Vanek, Domar and other scholars, is not applicable to the real world labour-managed firm, since the basic assumptions of Ward's model do not correspond to its actual behaviour. The observed practice in Yugoslavia led him to suggest that instead of maximizing income per worker, the Yugoslav firm sets the total wage fund *ex ante*, and the actual wages distributed to the workers at the end of the period depend directly on obtained results.

Horvat has never been an economist of narrow views and approaches but has been a true political economist. Very early in his life, he realized the importance of institutions for an economically efficient, politically democratic, and just, socialist society. This is what led him towards an indepth critique of capitalism and of 'etatism' (what, in his opinion, 'real socialism' actually was) and his endeavour to construct a theory of socialism built on premises of economic and political democracy. His work on socialist economic theory produced what probably can be considered his greatest work, *The Political Economy of Socialism* (1982). As he himself commented in the Foreword, 'The present book is an exploration into this uncharted territory, intended to meet Robert Heilbroner's request to convert economics into an instrument of social science...an exercise in system design.'

Being a Marxist but well trained in neoclassical economics, Horvat's growing dissatisfaction with logical fundamentals of the neoclassical theory led him to try and build a theoretical system around the labour theory of value. He made his first contribution to this field while still a third-year undergraduate, with a paper that in 1950 won a prize at his University. Much later, as a mature theorist, he found the neo-Ricardian critique particularly helpful. While he found the neo-Ricardian argument against the neoclassical theory valid, he felt that the positive reconstruction of the economic theory was missing, which is what he tried to address in his two recent books. In the first one, *The Theory of Value, Capital and Interest* (1995), he applies the theory of systems to economics, arguing that macroeconomics cannot be based on micro foundations, but rather that it must be the other way round. Since the book focused on a closed economy, he felt the need to expand it to an open economy, which led to the second book, *The Theory of International Trade* (1999). In this book he extends the argument of the previous book to the theory of international trade, criticizing the logic and fundamentals of mainstream neoclassical trade theory (primarily the Heckscher-Ohlin theory). Both books again confirm Horvat's unconventional treatment of fundamental issues in economic theory.

3 The many facets of Branko Horvat

But Horvat has not been *only* an important economist. During his rich professional life as distinguished scientist, he has also been a social engineer, a pedagogue, a controversial political activist. Thanks to his broad educational background, his writings display a truly multidisciplinary scholar. Being a convinced but critical Marxist, he has always insisted on the need to develop simultaneously economic and sociopolitical theory, stressing that one cannot study economics without exploring social relations and politics. Not surprisingly, therefore, the term 'political economy' has a special meaning for him, representing, as he himself put it, 'a fusion of economic and political theory into one single social theory' (see Foreword, in Horvat, 1982, *Political Economy of Socialism*).

Throughout his life, Horvat has been a committed socialist activist and a great supporter of socialist values, and socialism has undoubtedly always been his predominant concern. He wanted to design and implement a better social system than the one he lived in, but as he clearly recognized, social design is immensely more complex than design in natural sciences: he was well aware of how difficult a task he had given himself. In line with such an approach to social change, he has always been highly critical of the social and political environment in which he has been living. While supportive of the general trust of the Yugoslav system of self-management, he often criticized it for falling short of providing a truly efficient economic and politically democratic system. Similarly, today he is one of the harshest critics of various aspects of emerging capitalism in Croatia. Such a generally critical attitude has, on a number of occasions, brought him to the margin of being a dissident, though he never really became one.

Horvat has been a convinced advocate of the system of self-management and other forms of economic and industrial democracy. For him, socialism as practiced in 'real socialism' countries, in reality, was equivalent to 'etatism' because of the lack of political and economic democracy. This is the main reason why he strongly supported the Yugoslav way to socialism, namely self-managed market socialism. He has been convinced of the desirability of workers' control through self-management, and of the superiority and necessity of a more diffused application of this social form. Although he built his theories in a rigorous way, he also always tried to put them in the function of real life problems and relate them to reality, with the objective of changing and improving the existing political, economic and social system he lived in. That is why he has also been very critical, on various occasions, of the actual institutional set-up in former Yugoslavia, as well as specific economic policies applied by the Yugoslav government which, in his view, fell short of both the ideas of economic rationality and efficiency, and the ideals of equality and justice. Thus, for example, he strongly criticized the breaking-up of enterprises into 'organizations of associated labor', whereby the market was introduced into enterprises, while the outside market was left intact, functioning in a poor and unsatisfactory way.

Another important facet of Branko Horvat concerns his work as pedagogue. He has educated whole generations of economists in former Yugoslavia, many of whom are today professors at universities, or occupying top positions in government in countries of former Yugoslavia or in international organizations and institutions all over the world. Being well aware of the importance of discussion and criticism, in the 1980s he established a forum of mostly younger scholars from universities and research institutes from all over Yugoslavia, the so-called 'JUNASET' group, which met regularly to present their work and discuss both the newest economic theories and current economic problems. Horvat has also had students from many countries around the world. We believe all his students have benefited from his frequently severe, though friendly, criticism, as he tried to keep the right balance between encouragement and critique.

Throughout his life, Horvat has also been a political activist. Starting from his partisan days, he has not remained indifferent in front of important developments on the political scene in his country. He was close to a number of critical social scientists in former Yugoslavia and with them participated in various interdisciplinary research projects and discussions. He openly and usually very critically, sometimes provoking major public controversies and strong reactions from official politicians, raised his voice regarding poorly designed institutional changes or major crises in Yugoslavia: for example, on the occasion of the 1965 economic reform or the 1971 Constitutional amendments; or still later, in the early 1980s, motivated by the worsening of the crisis in Kosovo, he felt the need to investigate key problems in this region, which resulted in the publication of a book on the problem of Kosovo (*Kosovsko pitanje*, 1988).

With the worsening of the political and economic crisis in Yugoslavia in the 1980s, Horvat became one of the harshest and most open critics of nationalism, its ideologues and political leaders. While strongly opposed to such political options, which in his view led to an undemocratic and overcostly resolution of the Yugoslav crisis, he actively tried to promote an alternative political agenda: a democratic reconstruction of Yugoslavia. Such activities, very much opposed by the prevailing political climate, made him an active participant of numerous public debates.

After the introduction of multi-party democracy in Croatia in the early 1990s, he founded (and has been leading) a new political party, the Social Democratic Union, which promotes the concept of full democracy – including political democracy, social democracy and economic democracy – as one of its basic principles. However, he has left a much stronger impact as an outspoken critic of the course that transition and privatization in Croatia (and elsewhere) have taken, than as a leader of this rather marginalized political party.

Horvat has been, and remains, a controversial – for some, even eccentric – scholar, an economist beyond the mainstream. Yet he has always been fully consistent as a theorist, and has remained faithful to himself and to his 'ideas and ideals' which he defended throughout his rich and fruitful life. Being committed from his early youth to socialist values of economic and political democracy and social justice, he has never shied away from the normative side of economic theory. This combination of rigorous reasoning and strong convictions place

Horvat among those rare social thinkers who actively tried to transform their ideas into reality.

Being beyond the mainstream has not brought Horvat praise and the merited recognition. He has perhaps been more often criticized than praised, and very often not understood at all. That is why we believe the following statement, made almost twenty years ago by Benjamin Ward (who also kindly contributed the Foreword to the present book), is still valid today: 'Horvat has offered an integrated and thoroughgoing theory of social movement in contemporary state capitalist and socialist society. His ideas have not yet been subjected to a systematic appraisal within the body of radical literature ... Such an appraisal is very much needed' (Ward, *The Ideal Worlds of Economics: The Radical Economic World View* 1980: 126).

4 Contributions to this volume

Scholars invited to contribute an essay to this volume were asked to focus on one of the areas in which Horvat has worked during his long professional career. Our request produced three groups of essays: a first group focusing on broad themes related to socialism and socialist values; a second group dealing with workers' self-management and employee participation; and a third, dedicated to problems of the transition to a market economy in Central and Eastern Europe.

The first group of papers (Chapters 1–4) is dedicated to issues dealing with socialism, democracy, egalitarianism and income inequality. Howard Wachtel (Chapter 1) discusses 'Ideas and Ideals', namely Horvat's contributions to this century's economic and social theory, in particular his quest for a new theory of society that integrates ideas and ideals: the ideas deriving from economic and political theory, while the ideals, from the twentieth century fusion of democracy and socialism. These issues are addressed in the framework of the four cells of economic theory – capital accumulation and growth, class consequences, economic efficiency and economic justice. Wachtel considers 'associationist socialism', the theory of the worker-managed firm (Horvat's sharpest departure from conventional economics), and examines its implications for the labour market, technology and investment. A proper assessment of the theory of the worker-managed firm involves an excursus through Yugoslavia's economic history, where he concludes that the failure of Yugoslavia's experiment is not due to the supposed economic irrationalities thrown at it by western economists.

The second paper, by Jaroslav Vanek, dedicated to individual initiative, entry and economic democracy (Chapter 2), is a search for an optimal socio-economic system. Vanek outlines the theoretical framework of what he calls 'a unified theory of social systems', whereby the degree of optimality or misery in a society depends on the degree of involvement and participation. Vanek formulates what he calls the two laws of optimal participation. To attain optimum, the first law requires the maximal degree of participation, and decisional participation proportional to the intensity of involvement, while the second law requires that participation be governed also by the nature and quality of involvement. If applied, these laws could promise to be a major step in the direction of a better, happier and more just society. Applying the two laws to entrepreneurship, two trajectories are identified: one emanating from the entrepreneur *qua* human spirit, the other from the entrepreneur *qua* Mammon-developer capitalist, with implications of the two trajectories obviously being very different. Vanek concludes that the first trajectory (though optimal) has been rejected, while the second (though suboptimal) has prevailed, thus leading to the continuous worsening of the labour contract.

Sam Bowles and Herb Gintis, in 'Egalitarianism on Its Own' (Chapter 3), argue in favour of recasting egalitarianism, through a radical reconsideration of both the goals and the means for achieving it. Their paradigm is based on three constitutional desiderata governing the nature and assignment of property rights and other rights of governance, which reflect their understanding of how individuals interact with the rules of the game structuring economic and other social interactions. Discussing the main sources of the demoralization of the egalitarian project, Bowles and Gintis stress the need to design egalitarian policies that affirm and evoke widely held moral sentiments. They argue in favour of *Homo reciprocans*, somebody with a propensity to cooperate and share, who is neither the unconditional altruist of socialist theory nor the hedonistic sociopath of neoclassical economics, but rather a conditional cooperator who has strong instincts for sharing. The model of *Homo reciprocans* supports the authors' optimism concerning the possibility of egalitarian redistribution, as they believe that an egalitarian society could be built on the basis of these norms.

Branko Milanović (Chapter 4) takes us to concrete problems of worldwide income inequality between countries and provides new evidence on its determinants. The author seeks to explain why income inequality differs between countries, by considering the role of certain social choice variables such as social transfers and state sector employment, as an alternative to the traditional hypothesis advanced by Kuznets (therefore calling his own thesis an 'augmented' Kuznets' hypothesis). The hypothesis is tested econometrically using data from the 1980s and a cross-sectional sample of 80 countries, including OECD countries, all former socialist countries, and 50 countries from Africa, Asia and Latin America. The results of the regressions are rather straightforward: the social choice variables, jointly with the purely economic variables included in the standard formulation of the Kuznets' hypothesis, do determine economic inequality, having a significant negative impact on it.

Papers in the second group (Chapters 5–7) are all dedicated to issues of economic democracy, whether employee participation, labour-management, or other themes which have been at the core of Horvat's writings. Dinko Dubravčić (Chapter 5) goes back to the Illyrian theories of the labour-managed firm. Having identified rent-sharing as one of the most essential characteristics of this type of enterprise, he compares rent-sharing in the labour-managed firm with rent appropriation by organized labour in Western economies, reaching some interesting conclusions. Dubravčić tries to evaluate the possible application of Illyrian theories to new domains, such as the acquisition of capital by joint-stock companies, or immigration policies of modern states, but his conclusions about the relevance of these theories today are rather sceptical.

Mario Nuti (Chapter 6) reviews and attacks the standard classification of enterprise types by degree of employee participation in enterprise returns and control rights, exemplified in a recent article by Avner Ben-Ner and Derek Jones. An alternative approach is developed in which a number of key concepts, such as returns or control, are specified differently. Contrary to Ben-Ner's and Jones's continuous spectrum of combinations of different degrees of the two forms of participation, this alternative approach reveals classification discontinuities and gaps. This also has significant implications for the impact of participation on productivity, thus substantially weakening, if not altogether destroying, the case for public policy support of participation.

Tea Petrin and Aleš Vahčič (Chapter 7) discuss employee involvement in the modern firm. Workers' involvement in different forms has not only survived, but is increasingly becoming one of the key factors determining the success of companies. In this sense, the authors note, Horvat's analysis of the prospects of self-management proved to be correct. While discussing the economist's approach to economic welfare, Petrin and Vahčič suggest that much can be learned from other disciplines such as management, political science, or sociology, and therefore point to some possible applications. Throughout the paper, lessons are drawn from the experience with self-management in both former Yugoslavia and Slovenia.

The last group of papers (Chapters 8–11) addresses systemic change, whether in past attempts of fundamental economic reform or the most recent historical example, namely the 1990s transition to a market economy in Central and South Eastern Europe. The first of these papers, by Jože Mencinger (Chapter 8), discusses the emergence and disappearance of both market socialism and Yugoslavia. He analyzes in detail the various economic reforms undertaken in Yugoslavia from the 1950s onwards, evaluating their scope, nature and limitations. Mencinger also discusses Yugoslavia's economic performance, and points to the key factors and main developments which led to the collapse of the country in the early 1990s. The numerous attempts of systemic change in Yugoslavia remained half-hearted, primarily because they failed to delimit political from economic power.

Saul Estrin (Chapter 9) focuses on self-management and employee ownership in transition economies. The 1990s economic reforms and the transition from plan to market have created unprecedented opportunities for the development of a significant employee owned sector, primarily through the privatization of state-owned enterprises using the method of sale, or free distribution of shares, to employed workers. In this context, Estrin tries to evaluate the opportunities for labour-management in transition economies, and discusses what the most appropriate policies for employee owned firms would be, particularly in areas such as investment, incentives and productivity, and enterprise restructuring. However, in spite of the diffusion of employee ownership in many transition economies, labour-management has not, for a number of reasons, emerged as a significant form. The most serious problems that arise in cases of substantial employee ownership are also discussed.

Derek Jones and Niels Mygind (Chapter 10) present privatization results in Estonia. The paper provides fresh empirical evidence of the effects of different forms of private ownership upon economic performance, based on a new and large panel, representative of the whole economy. Models which worked well for the Visegrad countries, surprisingly, had low overall explanatory power in Estonia, consistent with the hypothesis that the key factor influencing performance may not necessarily be ownership (being thus in line with Horvat's views). Part of the results give mild support for the view that some attention might be paid to the ownership trajectory that the firm has followed. On balance, it seems that for Estonian firms it is difficult to draw definite conclusions as to whether private ownership does or does not deliver improved performance.

The last paper, by Ivo Bićanić (Chapter 11), is dedicated to growth theory and growth prospects in transition economies. The author criticizes the dominant paradigm of transition, in both theory and policy, based on the notions of linearity and optimism, and presents a rather critical evaluation of some existing growth models, primarily stressing their overemphasis of optimism and linearity in development. The varied historical experience with growth and the implications of modern growth theory clearly cast a shadow on the optimistic and linear approach, suggesting that growth and catching up are not the only, inevitable option. Moreover, the variety of transition paths in transition economies clearly runs against transition linearity, and therefore alternative approaches need to be developed. Bićanić expects that the variety of transition paths is likely to increase even further in the forthcoming period, during the second stage of transition.

While all the eleven essays and the Foreword to this volume, offered as a sign of recognition and esteem for Branko Horvat, are to be judged for their own merit, we as editors very much hope that this book will lead towards a further and deeper appraisal and understanding of Branko Horvat's work and his contributions to economic and social sciences. We believe he certainly deserves it.

Branko Horvat: Select Bibliography

Horvat's complete bibliography contains more than 650 entries. The present list excludes numerous papers in journals, conference papers, interviews, reviews and newspaper articles, mostly written in Croatian or some other language that is not widely accessible. Books are all listed.

I Books

1. *Distribucija nafte (Oil Distribution)*, Zagreb: Ekonomski institut, 1956.
2. *Ekonomska teorija planske privrede (Towards a Theory of Planned Economy)*, Beograd: Kultura, 1961. First English edition by the Yugoslav Institute of Economic Research, Belgrade, 1964; 2nd printing by International Arts and Science Press, New York, 1975. Spanish edition: *Teoria de la planificaciòn econòmica*, Barcelona: Oikos Tau, 1970. German edition: *Die Arbeiter Selbstverwaltung*, München: Nymphenburger Verlag, 1973.
3. *Ekonomski modeli (Economic Models)*, Zagreb: Ekonomski institut, 1962.
4. *Ekonomika jugoslavenske naftne privrede (Economics of Yugoslav Oil Industry)*, Beograd: Tehnička knjiga, 1962.
5. *Medjusektorska analiza (Interindustrial analysis)*, Zagreb: Narodne novine, 1962.
6. *Proizvodnja nafte (Oil Production)*, Beograd: Institut ekonomskih nauka, 1965.
7. *Prerada nafte (Oil Refining)*, Beograd: Institut ekonomskih nauka, 1965.
8. *Ekonomska nauka i narodna privreda (Economic Science and National Economy)*, Zagreb: Naprijed, 1968.
9. *Ogled o jugoslavenskom društvu (An Essay on Yugoslav Society)*, Zagreb: Mladost, 1969. English edition by International Arts and Sciences Press, New York, 1969. German edition: *Die Jugoslawische Gesellschaft*, Frankfurt: Suhrkamp, 1972. Also translated into Korean, 1984.
10. *Privredni ciklusi u Jugoslaviji (Business Cycles in Yugoslavia)*, Beograd: Institut ekonomskih nauka, 1969. English edition by International Arts and Sciences Press, New York, 1971.
11. *Integrirani sistem društvenog računovodstva za jugoslavensku privredu (An Integrated System of National Accounting for the Yugoslav Economy)*, Beograd: Institut ekonomskih nauka, 1969.
12. *Privredni sistem i ekonomska politika Jugoslavije (Economic System and Economic Policy of Yugoslavia)*, Beograd: Institut ekonomskih nauka, 1970.
13. *Ekonomska analiza (Economic Analysis)*, Beograd: Oeconomica, 1972.
14. *Socialismo y economia en Yugoslavia*, Buenos Aires: Ediciones periferia, 1974.
15. *Self Governing Socialism: A Reader* (edited together with R. Supek and M. Marković), New York: International Arts and Sciences Press, 1975.
16. *Ekonomska politika stabilizacije (Economic Policy of Stabilisation)*, Zagreb: Naprijed, 1976.
17. *The Yugoslav Economic System*, New York: International Arts and Sciences Press, 1976 (1979, 1983).

18 *The Political Economy of Socialism*, New York: Sharpe, Oxford: Martin Robertson, 1982. Croatian edition: *Politička ekonomija socijalizma*, Zagreb: Globus, 1984.
19 *Jugoslavenska privreda 1965–1983 (Yugoslav Economy 1965–1983)*, Zagreb: Cankarjeva Založba, 1984.
20 *Društvena kriza u Jugoslaviji (Social Crisis in Yugoslavia)*, Zagreb: Globus, 1985.
21 *Radna teorija cijena i drugi neriješeni problemi Marxove ekonomske teorije (Labour Theory of Prices and Some Unresolved Problems in Marx's Economic Theory)*, Beograd: Rad, 1986.
22 *Kosovsko pitanje (The Kosovo Question)*, Zagreb: Globus, 1988 (2nd enlarged ed 1989).
23 *ABC jugoslavenskog socijalizma (ABC of Yugoslav Socialism)*, Zagreb: Globus, 1989.
24 *Poduzetništvo i tržišna transformacija 'društvenog' vlasništva (Entrepreneurship and Market Transformation of 'Social' Ownership)*, Zagreb: Institut za javne financije, 1990.
25 *The Theory of Value, Capital and Interest*, Aldershot: Elgar, 1995. Macedonian edition, 1998.
26 *The Theory of International Trade*, London: Macmillan, 1999.

II Papers published in edited books, conference proceedings, major encyclopedias and similar volumes (in foreign languages)

1 'The Conceptual Background of Social Product', *Income and Wealth*, Series IX, London: Bowes & Bowes, 1961, pp. 234–52.
2 'Planning in Yugoslavia', *Development Plans and Programmes*, Paris: OECD, 1964, pp. 149–66.
3 'Planning and the Market: The Yugoslav Experience', in S .H. Robock and L. M. Solomon, *International Development*, New York: Oceana Publications, 1966, pp. 71–82.
4 'Der Markt als Instrument der Planung', in K. Wessely (ed.), *Probleme zentraler Wirtschaftsplanung*, Wien, 1967, pp. 107–16.
5 'Yugoslav System of Self-Management and the Import of Foreign Private Capital', in *Joint Business Ventures of Yugoslav Enterprises and Foreign Firms*, Beograd: IMPP, 1968, pp. 83–96.
6 'The Gap between the Rich and the Poor Nations from the Socialist Viewpoint', in Ranis G. (ed.), *The Gap between the Rich and the Poor Nations*, London: Macmillan, 1972, pp. 96–112.
7 'Planning in Yugoslavia', in M. Faber and D. Seers (eds.), *The Crisis in Planning*, vol. 2, London: Sussex University Press, 1972, pp. 193–206.
8 'Arbeiterselbstverwaltung im Betrieb', in P. Hemicke (ed.), *Probleme des Sozialismus und der übergangsgesellschaften*, Frankfurt: Suhrkamp, 1973, pp. 243–56.
9 'Autogestion et économie', in R. Supek (ed.), *Etatisme et autogestion*, Paris: Anthropos, 1973, pp. 177–210.
10 'On the Political Economy of Socialism', in E. Pusić (ed.), *Participation and Self-Management*, Vol. 6, Zagreb: Institute for Social Research, 1973, pp. 99–112.

11 'Market versus Nonmarket Output and Implicit Grants in a Socialist Economy', in M. Pfaff (ed.), *Grants and Exchange*, Amsterdam: North Holland, 1976, pp. 118–23.
12 'Plan de socialisation progressive du capital', in S. C. Kolm (ed.), *Solutions socialistes*, Paris: Ramsay, 1978, pp. 159–84.
13 'Op weg haar arbeiderszelfbestur', in G. Hofstede (ed.), *De toekomst van ons werk*, Leiden: Stenfert-Kozrese, 1978, pp. 131–44.
14 'Paths of Transition to Workers' Self-Management in the Developed Capitalist Countries', in T. Burns, L. E. Karlsson and V. Rus, *Work and Power*, London: SAGE, 1979, pp. 49–80.
15 'Comparative Organization and Efficiency of Social Systems', in U. Gärtner and J. Kosta (eds.), *Wirschaft und Gesellschaft*, Berlin: Dunker & Humblot, 1979, pp. 31–58.
16 'The Delegitimation of Old and the Legitimation of New Social Relations in Late Capitalist Societies', in B. Denitch (ed.), *Legitimation of Regimes*, London: SAGE, 1979, pp. 81–101.
17 'La gestione dei lavoratori', in D. Cuszi and R. Stefanelli (eds), *Il sistema Jugoslavo*, Bari: De Donato, 1980, pp. 28–46.
18 'L'Economie politique du socialisme autogestionnaire', 'Autogestion, efficacité et théorie neoclassique', 'Critique de la théorie de la firme autogerée', in A. Dumas (ed.), *L'Autogestion, un système économique?*, Paris: Dunod, 1981, pp. 26–44, 229–36, 310–17.
19 'Socialist Planning – The Problem of Co-ordination and Autonomy', in U. Himmelstrand (ed.) *Spontaneity and Planning in Social Development*, London: SAGE, 1981, pp. 1953–64.
20 'Establishing Self-governing Socialism in a Less Developed Country', in Ch. Wilber and K. Jameson (eds), *Socialist Models of Development*, Oxford; Pergamon, 1982, pp. 951–64.
21 'Labour-managed Firms and Social Transformations', in F. H. Stephen (ed.), *The Performance of Labour Managed Firms*, London: Macmillan, 1982, pp. 249–64.
22 'Wirtschaftssysteme: Jugoslawien', in *Handwörterbuch der Wirtschaftswissenschaft*, Bd 9, Stuttgart: Fischer, 1982, pp. 370–82.
23 'Establishing Self-Governing Socialism in a Less Developed Country', in Ch. K. Wilber (ed.), *The Political Economy of Underdevelopment*, 3rd ed., New York: Random House, 1984, pp. 504–21.
24 'La fijacion de precios de los factores da producion', in J. Hocevar (ed.), *Socialismo Autogestionario en Marcha*, Mérida: Universidad de los Andes, 1984, pp. 231–41.
25 'Efficiencia de los gastos del sector publico', in *El desarrollo financero de America Latina y el Caribe*, Caracas: Instituto Interamericano de Mercados de Capital, 1985, pp. 341–54.
26 'Marx's Contribution to Social Science and His Errors', in B. Chavance (ed.), *Marx en perspective*, Paris: École des hautes études en sciences sociales, 1985, pp. 459–74.
27 'Political Economy', *Social Science Encyclopedia*, London: Routledge & Kegan, London, 1985, pp. 611–12.
28 'The Prospects for Disalienation of Work', in B. Gustavson, J. Karlsson and C. Röftegard (eds), *Work in 1980s*, Aldershot: Gower,1985, pp. 235–40.

29 'Workers' Management and the Market', in J. Stiglitz and F. Mattewson (eds), *New Developments in the Analysis of Market Structure*, Cambridge, Mass.: MIT University Press, 1986, pp. 297–310.
30 'Labour-managed Economies', in *The New Palgrave*, London: Macmillan, 1987, pp. 79–84. Also in: J. Eatwell, M. Milgate and P. Newman (eds.), *Problems of the Planned Economy*, London: Macmillan, pp. 121–32, and in G. Szell (ed.), *Concise Encyclopaedia of Participation and Co-Management*, Berlin: Walter de Gruyter, 1992, pp. 469–79.
31 'Contemporary Social Systems and the Trends in Systemic Reforms Worldwide', in S. Gomulka *et al.*, *Economic Reforms in the Socialist World*, Macmillan: London, 1989.
32 'Social Ownership', in R. Russell and V. Rus (eds.), *International Handbook of Participation in Organizations*, vol. II, Oxford: Oxford University Press, 1991, pp. 165–69.
33 'The Market Transformation of State Enterprises', in M. Knell, and Ch. Rider (eds.), *Appraisal of the Market Mechanism*, Aldershot: Elgar, 1992, pp. 140–53.
34 'La proprieté publique en Croatie', in R. Iveković (ed.), *La Croatie depuis l'effondrement de la Yugoslavie*, Paris: L'Harmettan, 1994, pp. 101–4.
35 'Full Democracy – Socialism of the 21st Century', in B. Marković (ed.), *Social Democracy in Europe Today*, Belgrade: Institute of International Politics and Economics, 1996, pp. 71–6.
36 'On the Theory of Labour-Managed Firms', in D. Prychitko and J. Vanek (eds.), *Producer Cooperatives and Labour-Managed Systems*, Aldershot: Elgar, 1996, pp. 55–72.
37 'Privatization vs. De-etatization', in Ž. Bogetić (ed.), *The Cost of War in Former Yugoslavia*, Paris & Beograd: Peace and Crises Management Foundation, 1996, pp. 280–87.
38 'Joint Production in a Two-Sector Model', in A. Simonovits and A. Steenge (eds), *Prices, Growth and Cycles*, London: Macmillan, 1997, pp. 255–69.
39 'The Results of the Backward Transition in the Republic of Croatia', in *Enterprise in Transition: 2nd International Conference Proceedings*, Split & Vienna: Faculty of Economics & DAAAM International, 1997, pp. 81–6.
40 'Nationalistic Break-up of Multiethnic States', in R. Iveković. and N. Pagon (eds), *Otherhood and Nation*, Ljubljana: Institutum Studiorum Humanitatis, 1998, pp. 213–28.

III Articles in foreign journals (either original or translated from Croatian) grouped by topic

(a) Economic theory

1 'The Depreciation Multiplier and a Generalized Theory of Fixed Capital Costs', *Manchester School*, (1958), pp. 136–59.
2 'The Optimum Rate of Investment', *Economic Journal*, (1958), pp. 747–67.
3 'The Optimum Rate of Saving: A Note', *Economic Journal*, (1958), pp. 747–67.
4 'Drei Definitionen des Sozailprodukte', *Konjunktur politik*, (1960), pp. 27–40.
5 'The Optimum Rate of Investment Reconsidered', *Economic Journal*, (1965), pp. 572–76. Also in Hungarian in *Agazdasági növekedés feltekeki*, Budapest, 1967, pp. 216–38.

6. 'Prilog zasnivanju teorije jugoslavenskog poduzeća' (A Contribution to the Theory of Yugoslav Enterprise), *Economic Analysis*, (1967), pp. 7–28. Also in Czech in *Ekonomický časopis*, (1968), pp. 789–808.
7. 'Note on Wages and Employment in a Labour Surplus Economy', *Manchester School*, (1968), pp. 63–8.
8. 'Die produktive Arbeit in der socialistischen Gesellchaft', *Osteuropa Wirtschaft*, (1968), pp. 98–107.
9. 'The Rule of Accumulation in a Planned Economy', *Kyklos*, (1968), pp. 239–68. Also in Slovakian in K. Arrow, G. Bombarh *et al.*, *Investicie, rovnovaha, optimalny rast*, Bratislava: Pravda, 1970, pp. 369–95.
10. 'Certain Similarities between Inertial Systems in Physics and Steadily Growing Systems in Economics', *Economic Analysis*, (1973), pp. 47–58.
11. 'Fixed Capital Costs, Depreciation Multiplier and the Rate of Interest', *European Economic Review*, (1973), pp. 163–80.
12. 'Labour-Time Prices of Production and the Transformation Problem in a Socialist Economy', *Kyklos*, (1973), pp. 762–86.
13. 'Real Fixed Capital Cost under Steady Growth', *European Economic Review*, (1973), pp. 85–103.
14. 'Labour-Time Prices of Production under Accumulation', *Economic Analysis*, (1974), pp. 183–201.
15. 'Socialismens politiska ekonomi', *Frihetlig Socialistisk Tidskrift*, (1974), pp. 183–201.
16. 'Fundamentals of a Theory of Distribution in Self-Governing Socialism', *Economic Analysis*, (1976), pp. 24–42.
17. 'Autogestion: efficacité et theorie néo-classique', *Revue économique*, (1979), pp. 361–9.
18. 'Social Property', *Economic Analysis*, (1977), pp. 95–98. Also in German in *Wirtshaft und Gesselchaft*, (1979), pp. 437–41.
19. 'Farewell to Illyrian Firm', *Economic Analysis and Workers' Management*, (1986), pp. 23–9.
20. 'The Theory of Rent', *Economic Analysis and Workers' Management*, (1986), pp. 109–18.
21. 'The Theory of the Labour-Managed Firm Revisited', *Journal of Comparative Economics*, (1986), pp. 9–25.
22. 'Sraffa Systematized and Marx Vindicated', *Economic Analysis and Workers' Management*, (1987), pp. 289–98.
23. 'The Pure Labour Theory of Prices and Interest, *European Economic Review*, (1989), pp. 1183–203.
24. 'What is a Socialist Market Economy?', *Acta Oeconomica*, (1989), pp. 233–5.
25. 'Prolegomena for a New Theory of Value', *Economic Analysis and Workers' Management*, (1990), pp. 1–17.
26. 'A Note on J. E. Woods' Determination of Rent', *Oxford Economic Papers*, (1992), pp. 502–6.
27. 'Market Socialism: A Few Comments', *Dissent*, (1993), pp. 246–8.

(b) Growth, development and planning

1. 'A Restatement of a Simple Planning Model with Some Examples from Yugoslav Economy', *Sankhya, The Indian Journal of Statistics*, series B, (1960), pp. 29–48.

2 'Methodological Problems in Long-term Economic Development Programming', *Industrialization and Productivity, UN Bulletin*, 5(1962), pp. 37–51. Also in *Eastern European Economics*, (1964), pp. 20–30.
3 'Some Aspects of National Economic Planning', *Les annales de l'économie collective*, (1963), pp. 288–98.
4 'An Integrated System of Social Accounts for an Economy of the Yugoslav Type', *Review of Income and Wealth*, (1968), pp. 19–36.
5 'A Model of Maximal Economic Growth', *Kyklos*, (1972), pp. 215–28.
6 'The Relation between Rate of Growth and Level of Development', *Journal of Development Studies*, 3–4 (1974), pp. 382–94.
7 'Short-Run Instability and Long-Run Trends in the Yugoslav Economy's Development', *Eastern European Economics*, (1975), pp. 3–31.

(c) Self-management

1 'Workers' Management in Yugoslavia: A Comment' (with V. Rašković), *Journal of Political Economy*, (1959), pp. 194–8.
2 'Autogestion, centralismo y planificacion', *Arauco*, (1965), pp. 47–54 and 59–65.
3 'On the Theory of the Labour-Managed Firm', *The Florida State University Slavic Papers*, (1970), pp. 7–11.
4 'An Institutional Model of a Self-Managed Socialist Economy', *Eastern European Economics*, (1972), pp. 369–92. Also in Spanish in CEPLAN: *Estudios de planificaciòn*, 22 (1972).
5 'Appunti critici sulla teoria dell' impresa autogestita', *Est–Ovest*, (1974), pp. 39–46.
6 'Workers' Management', *Economic Analysis*, (1976), pp. 197–216.
7 'Paths of Transition to Workers' Management in Developed Capitalist Countries', *Economic Analysis*, (1977), pp. 214–36.
8 'Establishing Self-Governing Socialism in a Less Developed Country', *Economic Analysis*, 1–2 (1978), pp. 135–53. Also in *World Development* (1981), pp. 951–64.
9 'Principes d'une théorie de la repartition en socialisme autogeré', *Les cahiers du seminaire Ch. Gide*, Tome XIII (1979), pp. 60–85.
10 'Searching for a Strategy of Transition', *Economic Analysis and Workers' Management*, (1980), pp. 311–23.
11 'Observations on Actual Social-Economic Problems of Peru', *Economic Analysis and Workers' Management*, (1982), pp. 559–68.
12 'El establicimiento del socialismo autogestionario en un pais desarollado', *Revista iberoamericana de Autogestión y Acción communal*, (1983–4), pp. 117–40.
13 'Industrial Partnership: Utopia or Necessity?', *Economic Analysis and Workers' Management*, (1986), pp. 251–6.
14 'Labour-Management and Neoclassical Economics', *Economic Analysis and Workers' Management*, (1991), pp. 307–10.

(d) Economic policy, economic system and transition

1 'Development Fund as an Institution for Conducting Fiscal Policy', *Economic Analysis*, (1972), pp. 247–51.

2 'The Postwar Evolution of the Yugoslav Agricultural Organization: Interaction of Ideology, Practice and Results', *Eastern European Economics*, (1973–74), pp. 1–106. Also in German in *Jahrbuch der Wirtschaft Osteneropeas*, (1974), pp. 363–93.
3 'Anti-Inflationary Taxation', *The Economic Times Annual*, Bombay (1974), pp. 155–60.
4 'The World Economy from the Socialist Viewpoint', *Economic Analysis and Workers' Management*, (1983), pp. 1–26. Also in English, French and Spanish in *International Social Science Journal*, 3 (1983).
5 'The Economic System and Stabilization', *Eastern European Economics*, (1984), pp. 66–105. Also in Chinese in *Jingjixue yicong*, (1985), pp. 8–11.
6 'Efficiency of the Public Sector', *Economic Analysis and Workers' Management* (1985), pp. 195–204.
7 'Eine hausgemachte Krise', *Ost-west Informationen*, (1991), pp. 9–18.
8 'Nationalization, Privatization or Socialization; the Emergence of the Social Corporation', *Economic Analysis and Workers' Management*, (1991), pp. 1–10.
9 'The Privatization or Something Else, *Communist Economies and Economic Transformation*, (1991), pp. 367–74.
10 'The Economic Integration of Eastern Europe', *Economic Analysis and Workers' Management*, (1992), pp. 1–39.
11 'On the Transition of Post-Communist Economies to a Market Economy', *Acta Oeconomica*, (1992), pp. 290–94.
12 'The Vagaries of the Yugoslav Economy', *Economic Analysis and Workers' Management*, (1992), pp. 255–78. Also in Spanish in *Cuadernos del este*, 5 (1992), pp. 9–26, in French in *Peuples méditerranéens*, 1992, pp. 7–34.
13 'Requiem for the Yugoslav Economy', *Dissent*, (1993), pp. 333–9.
14 'Privatization vs De-etatization', *Emergo*, (1996), pp. 119–23.
15 'Towards the Balkan Union', *Ekonomski pregled*, (1997), pp. 1013–27. Also in Italian and English in *Acque & Terre*, (1998), pp. 20–3 and 57–9.

(e) Sociology, political science, philosophy

1 'Nationalism and Nationality', *International Journal of Politics*, (1972), pp. 14–46.
2 'Welfare of the Common Man in Various Countries', *World Development*, (1974), pp. 29–39.
3 'Alienation and Reification', *Economic Analysis*, 1–2 (1975), pp. 5–24.
4 'Ethical Foundations of Self-Government', *Economic and Industrial Democracy*, 1 (1980), pp. 1–20.
5 'Two Widespread Ideological Deviations in Contemporary Yugoslav Society', *Eastern European Economics*, 1 (1984), pp. 45–57.
6 'Work and Power', *Economic Analysis and Workers' Management*, (1984), pp. 365–70.
7 'The Curse and the Blessings of Direct Democracy', *Zbornik Pravnog fakulteta*, Zagreb, (1987), pp. 537–46.
8 'The Socio-Economics of Workers' Management' (with U. Himmelstrand), *International Social Science Journal*, (1987), pp. 353–64. Also in French in *Révue international des sciences sociales*, (1987), pp. 393–406.
9 'Le minoranze nazionali in Yugoslavia', *La battana*, (1989), pp. 74–83.

1
Ideas and Ideals: Horvat's Contributions to Twentieth-Century Economic and Social Theory

Howard M. Wachtel

1.1 Introduction

Among Branko Horvat's many contributions to twentieth century life and thought, none stands out more than his quest for a new theory of society that integrates ideas and ideals. The ideas derive from economic and political theory; the ideals from a twentieth century fusion of democracy and socialism.

With this project Horvat aligns himself with the great eighteenth century originators of the enlightenment who sought a rational discourse on society that would allow individuals to achieve their full potential within a construct of scientific reasoning. It was a grand project that delivered on some of its promises but not on others, advances in medical sciences alongside Soviet and Chinese Gulags. This led some twentieth century intellectuals to reconsider the enlightenment itself, following on post-World War II revelations about the holocaust and the consequences of science's penetration of the power of the atom.

In economics, the enlightenment method and goals had its origins first in France with the Physiocrats and then subsequently in Great Britain, starting with the work of Adam Smith and his debt to the Scottish Enlightenment during the last third of the eighteenth century. But as the nineteenth century evolved, and capital accumulation contributed both to economic growth and inequities in outcomes, political economists began to turn their attention to the larger economic structures of society, their impacts on the success and failure of economics. Those who sought to extend the progressive aspects of the enlightenment to the twentieth century constructed and examined alternatives to capitalism, with obvious debts to Marx and the utopian socialists who preceded them. The work of Horvat that I want to assess is nested in this intellectual milieu: the search for ideas and ideals in economic thought that extend the enlightenment into economic formations.

1.2 The four cells of economic theory

If nineteenth century economic thought centered on economic growth and the class consequences of capital accumulation, the twentieth's has revolved around the conflict between economic efficiency and economic justice. Using these four abiding issues in economic theory – capital accumulation and growth, class consequences, economic efficiency, and individual economic justice – one can construct a four-cell, two-by-two, matrix implying that one contributor or another offers ideas that address mainly half of the matrix's trade-offs, or locates their ideas squarely in one as opposed to the other three. Adam Smith, for example, starts the discourse squarely in the growth cell; David Ricardo adds class consequences; Karl Marx is squarely in the capital accumulation and class cells, Alfred Marshall in the efficiency cell, and so on. A few great economic philosophers – Keynes most notably – have been able to locate their work at the intersection of this two-by-two matrix, the place near the center where all four cells come together. Keynes's work, for example, is predominantly about two of the cells: capital accumulation and growth and individual economic justice. For someone to cover all four cells, imagine a circle drawn with the exact point of intersection of the four cells as its center, with each quadrant of the circle reaching into a different cell, and you have the visual imagery I want to convey. Not many economist's work stretches across all four cells: Horvat is one.

Branko Horvat's corpus of writing stands out in that it straddles the four cells of the matrix. One can interpret his work at the center of the matrix with a circle reaching into all four cells. His theory of workers' management has both growth and class implications. His theory of society and economics speaks to issues of economic efficiency and individual economic justice. He has confronted the profession of economics with an alternative theory of economy and society, especially its twentieth century obsession with a narrow definition of efficiency that can be at odds with economic justice.

He was not the only challenger. But as we shall see later, he had one of the more synthetic economic and social analyses. Other challenges came from results on the ground and were the most forceful arguments against the *laissez-faire* economic formation – an economic structure that exalts individualism and leaves proportionally more of an economy in the hands of private ownership and individual economic decision-making. Horvat's problem with this is that it exalts individualism over society. He has sought a system that allows both individualism and the liberties it entails but not at the cost of society.

1.3 *Laissez-faire* and beyond

During this last quarter of the twentieth century, the search for an alternative to capitalism appears to be over. Previous efforts have foundered. A consensus around *laissez-faire* economics and individualism is stronger than at any time in its two-hundred year history. Nothing new or promising appears on the horizon. This is very different from the first quarter of the twentieth century when the several variants of socialism were on the cutting edge of the modern and held out the promise of a better society. The confrontation with an aggressive capitalist formation of the late nineteenth century took first the form of theoretical debates and later actual formations on the ground.

Command economies of the Soviet sort were the first to confront *laissez-faire*. When the Soviet Union showed such enormous growth in the midst of the Great Depression that a stream of western intellectuals – from Sydney Webb to Aldous Huxley – made pilgrimages to see how it worked, a serious alternative to *laissez-faire* appeared to emerge. After World War II and reconstruction, first the model of European social democracy and then the Asian miracle further deflated the claims of *laissez-faire*. To the delight of *laissez-faire* devotees and to the chagrin of the contrarians, however, each one of these formerly successful alternatives evaporated in the last quarter of the twentieth century. As an ideology, *laissez-faire* became hegemonic, even though its actual practice fell short of an ideal type.

'Growth versus efficiency', 'efficiency versus distribution', are catchphrases of economics that imply substitutability or trade-offs. For a time, these harsh trade-offs were muted somewhat. The outcome of command economies, for example, produced considerable growth, and some economists conceded fairer distribution as well, but at the expense of efficiency. When the command economies never recovered from the mid-1970s worldwide recession, and continued on a steep downward trajectory, this concession toward growth was dropped. There was a celebratory atmosphere among the adherents to economic efficiency as command economies collapsed. The reason for their inability to continue to grow was directly attributed to the lack of economic efficiency.

A rush to revisionism ensued. Economists who formerly had accepted a trade-off between growth and efficiency, now coupled them and placed efficiency at the absolute core of the debate. Without efficiency nothing would work in an economy. Even the vaunted growth potential of command economies was now reconsidered and found to be wrong. Inefficiency can be camouflaged for a while and growth can emerge, but it is an ephemeral growth eventually to be erased, leaving an economy with such negative rates of growth that the outcome ultimately takes a society back towards a level from whence it started.

Not only command economies succumbed to this analysis: third-world economies, whose capital accumulation process was heavily state-driven, were the next to fall under this general treatment. First in Latin America, then in Africa, and finally in Asia the diagnosis of faltering or negative growth was attributed to the absence of economic efficiency which eventually overcame positive growth outcomes. Behind the facade of growth without efficiency was an economy poised for disaster. Starting in the mid-1970s, a new economic concept – structural adjustment – was invented first by the IMF and then adopted by the World Bank in the 1980s. Some 50 economies were put under nominal receivership. Economic efficiency policies shredded state-driven systems of capital accumulation (Wachtel, 1977).

This consensus in economics of the last quarter of the twentieth century was next taken to western Europe. Here was a region where it appeared that the best practice outcome of growth, equity, capital accumulation, and efficiency had been achieved in the post-war period by following policies most closely associated with Keynes. This was not so. By the mid-1990s, in the midst of what commentators dubbed 'Euro-Sclerosis', the efficiency mantra found a new application. It was the same chant adapted for a different linguistic base. The absence of flexibility in labour markets together with excessive regulatory systems, too large a state sector in capital accumulation, and an inflated guarantee of economic and social security produced economic inefficiencies and stagnation. The remedy, not unlike that for command economies and third-world state-directed economies was de-regulation, labour market flexibility, and privatization.

An ideology and phrase accompanied these developments: Francis Fukuyama's 'end of history' (Fukuyama, 1992). By this, he meant the great economic and social struggles of the past two centuries were resolved. Class conflict within societies and national conflicts among governments over economic ideology had been settled by the hegemony of the market. The fittest survived and they were those societies that had adopted economic efficiency. The uni-dimensional sight lines of tunnel vision allowed these societies to reach the light at the end of that long dark aperture when other societies never found their way out and became mired in the darkness.

A downward trajectory overtook all of the world's economies in the mid-1970s when, led by OPEC, all commodity prices soared. Inflation and unemployment – the stagflation that was not supposed to exist in the Phillips Curve trade-off between unemployment and inflation – shredded the social democratic model. The United States recovered after a decade, as did Europe; Asia was never affected. But these were only transitory exceptions. Eventually Asia and Europe suffered their own forms of decline. The collapse of the command and third-world economies were merely harbingers of what was to come for Asia and Europe, according to this analysis.

When the last regions of the economic globe that had escaped this diagnosis succumbed, the triumph of *laissez-faire* ideology was complete. The late-1990s crises in Asia forced a reconsideration of Asian exceptionalism. Europe's problems in the first half of the 1990s merely added another chapter in, what was by now, a unified narrative. Revisionists attributed the collapse of these economies to the same source – too large a state-directed economy that produced growth for a time but eventually faltered because of inefficiencies. The absence of, what Joseph Schumpeter called, 'creative destruction', built up such an underbrush of inefficiencies and cronyism, and propped up enterprises with bad loans that the miracle came to a crushing collapse. If history had not ended, certainly the effort to create an alternative to *laissez-faire* had.

1.4 Associationist socialism

This rather somber outcome defines the *fin de siècle* intellectual universe of political economy. After more than four decades of intellectual struggle, Horvat would have hoped for a wider set of choices as we approach a new millennium. How should we examine and assess Branko Horvat's contributions for nearly half of this century in terms of the present conundrum? Was his and others' simply a quixotic quest that never had a chance? Another pursuit of an illusory objective? To understand this problematic, we first have to look at Horvat's efforts to both create a political reason for worker participation as the organizing scheme for his society and look at its economic efficiency properties.

By the start of World War II, alternative economic models had been narrowed to those of either the Soviet command economy or European social democracy types. The former had its roots in Leninist pragmatic adaptations of Marx's 'scientific socialism' after the Bolshevik revolution in the newly named Soviet Union. The latter was based in the 'evolutionary socialist' thought of such European parliamentary based democrats as Edward Bernstein and Sidney and Beatrice Webb. In the one, the means of production became appropriated by the state; in the other, they remained substantially in private hands while the state appropriated the regulatory and distributional means to re-allocate a share of the proceeds from capital accumulation.

The irony of the naming of the post-Bolshevik society as 'soviet' did not escape the young Horvat and his Yugoslav compatriots as they embarked upon the project of a third way, between the anti-democratic consequences of the command economy and the limited transformation of society wrought by the capitalist economy of social democracy. Their task – and Horvat became its primary theoretician – was to propose a way to extend the democratic project beyond social democracy; adapt the economic efficiency of capitalism to a market-socialist formation; achieve, organically, a more just distribution of the proceeds of capital accumulation, all the while remaining faithful to the fundamental tenets of socialism.[1]

The answer was in one principle, locating ownership with society – not the state or the private – which came to be called *social ownership* and economic management in workers' councils. In the political realm, the parliament remained as it was under European social democracy – a regulator, adjudicator of economic conflict, investor in the public goods societies need – while the decentralized workers' council became the arena in which all working members of society exercised the influence denied them in both the command and capitalist economies. 'Economic organizations', argued Horvat, 'are transformed into self-governing associations and capitalism is replaced by socialism.' (Horvat, 1969: 23).[2] And the central organizing proposition of this system was social ownership – 'this is the source of its unity', writes Horvat (1969: 92), who goes on to use Joseph Schumpeter's characterization of this arrangement as 'associationist socialism.'[3]

Horvat has a deep and abiding belief in the ability of employees to carry out the necessary functions of the enterprise be they managerial, entrepreneurial or allocational. Technical decisions, he contends, can be separated from other policy problems and properly assigned to professionals. These premises need to be qualified, in my view. Horvat and

I have carried on a friendly three-decade discourse on this. It is my view that control of information is control of policy. Knowledge, distinct from information, also has its particularities that underwrite information differentials. To the extent that the distribution of knowledge and information is unequal, the distribution of influence over policy decisions will be unequal. This form of inequality, moreover, derives neither from any sinister plot nor from any social system construct. Shop-floor workers know more about handling shop floor problems, for example, than do managers and should be allowed much more discretion in this realm, while marketing managers presumably know more about getting the product into the hands of consumers and should be allowed more discretion in that realm. It does not violate the principle of worker participation to allow for spheres of influence, thereby clarifying and simplifying what would otherwise be a most cumbersome project if everyone was supposed to decide upon everything, as some designers of associationist socialism would have it. If everyone tries to decide upon everything, either very little will be decided as processes become bogged down in meetings, or top managers will decide everything by default.

Horvat, on the other hand, contends that the 'exercise of managerial functions is not the task of any special class of individuals, but of the collectivity of members of economic organizations', as is social evaluation and risk-taking. 'Supervision', he continues, 'is a two-directional process in which every member of the collective takes part. The remaining function, coordination, is purely technical and as such is left to technical experts...' (1969: 97). In this succinct description of self-governing workers' council, Horvat presents his organizational conception of the enterprise within a system of associationist socialism.

1.5 The worker-managed firm

Horvat's sharpest departure from conventional economics derives from his theory of self-management. Self-management and social ownership present theoretical challenges to the standard micro- and macro- analyses of the capitalist firm. At the level of macro economics, the worker-managed enterprise is distinguished from the capitalist-managed firm by its responses to economic decline. In the capitalist-managed firm, the reaction is dismissal of employees, after some relatively brief interval of labour hoarding. One can expect that this is not the first or even second option for a worker-managed enterprise. If the self-managed decision-making process works, the expectation is that labour will be hoarded longer, sequestered while the council waits out the economic downturn. This does not necessarily mean that labour is idle. As in Germany until their depression in the 1990s, the firm can use the surplus labour time to invest in human capital upgrading so that its labour force is better positioned to respond to the eventual economic upturn. In the revival, however, a labour-managed enterprise will have a tendency to meet renewed economic activity with investment in new technologies, instead of hiring more labour, when contrasted with a capitalist-managed firm. This apparent counter-intuitive anomaly will be taken up later.

The consequences for the self-managed firm and for policy therefore are, first, that less pressure is placed on macro policy adjustments from the central bank and from fiscal policy. Fewer unemployed produce less political clamour for attention via fiscal and monetary policy. This is a mixed blessing, however, because too much responsibility may be placed on enterprises that are not in a position to absorb the shock of labour redundancy. Firms that have to absorb this shock may have little cushion to do so, and a tendency can develop for central banks to bail out firms by continuing to support employment with injudicious loans. Curiously, it may be better for markets to work their will and displace labour in order to gain the attention of macro policy makers. I return to this point more generally later in this essay when I take up the potential problems in a worker-managed system.

Economists in the United States devoted most of their attention to the differing micro implications of a capitalist and worker-managed system, even though the macro distinctions may be as interesting. In the late 1950s Benjamin Ward instigated the debate with his article on the firm in Illyria.[4] Ward asserts that the worker-managed firm will seek to maximize the average income per worker in the enterprise, the contractual wage plus bonuses. With this optimizing function, he shows that the firm will react to a price increase in the market by lowering output, thereby producing a downward sloping supply curve. The essential explanation for this is that the worker-manager, as stake holder to a claim on the enterprise's surplus, will confiscate higher earnings by voting for higher returns per employee. They will be averse to hiring more employees to expand output, because that would dilute each of the insider's share of profits. In this reasoning higher short-run profits from higher prices are seen as a one-time windfall by the worker-managed enterprise. If the worker-managed enterprise has a *target* profit perspective, instead of some optimization of absolute profits, it can attain those profits with lower output levels when the rate of profit per unit of output is higher due to higher prices. As stake holders, workers as managers lower output in these circumstances, because in the short-term the option of expanding capital is precluded by definition. The consequence of this economic behaviour in a Walrasian equilibrium model is instability, as both demand and supply curves are downward sloping.

There are two problems with Ward's model. First, it is static and does not have a function for reinvestment out of surpluses. In a multi-period model Ward's results are not upheld.[5] Secondly, does he have the right optimizing function? Horvat argues that he does not. The worker-managed enterprise, Horvat argues, 'plans to increase per person income by a specified amount in the planning period, and maximizes the remainder of net income with respect to the firm as a whole and not with respect to the number of the currently employed workers' (Horvat, 1967: 28). With this modification of Ward's optimizing premise, the downward sloping product supply curve disappears, which Horvat demonstrates by working through the implications of a product price increase.

Horvat's stout defense of the micro foundations of the Yugoslav worker-managed firm has never acquired the currency it should have. Western economists continued to view the micro implications of labour management as an oddity with its built-in instabilities. Several articles appeared around the time of Horvat's argument and about a decade after Ward's original firm in Illyria, all reinforcing the results of Ward.[6] A substantial part of the reasons for Horvat's retort being dismissed is that it only became available in English some years later. But even after its publication in English, economists continued to ignore the argument.

The sole controlling element in all of these issues – the downward sloping supply curve, excessive labour hoarding, and inability to expand employment – is the optimizing function. This matter could be readily resolved by examination of the empirical evidence. Prior to the articles in the *American Economic Review*, Jan Vanek had published a comprehensive empirical study of the Yugoslav firm for the International Labor Office. He found support for Horvat's optimizing function, and none for Ward's.[7]

1.6 Labour market implications

More troubling than Walrasian disequilibrium emanating from a downward sloping product supply curve, are the implications for the labour market in an economy organized around workers' management. The problems arise from two sources: first, the tendency, already mentioned, for enterprises to hoard labour during a recession because the worker as manager is reluctant to displace fellow employees. Secondly, there is the problem of choice of technology, whether the optimum capital–labour combinations will be deployed by the enterprise.[8]

One would expect worker-managed enterprises to be more resistant to laying off employees during a recession compared to a capitalist-managed firm protecting the interests of its share holders, as discussed previously. This need not be a problem, depending upon the time frame and what is done with surplus labour time. In the short run, it is certainly a prudent economic decision for enterprises to hoard labour and not immediately displace employees who may have substantial amounts of embodied human capital investment. This human capital can be augmented by further investments in skills-upgrading during a cyclical phase when there is redundant labour time. It would, in fact, be an inefficient economic decision for a firm to lay off employees in the early phase of a recession, thereby squandering an investment. It is as if a manager were to take a sledge hammer to a machine and destroy it the instant it is not being fully utilized. Economics is curiously inconsistent here. In the case of a machine, no economist would advocate its destruction and the implosion of an investment. With individuals and human capital, however, economists propose labour redundancy and extol the virtues of labour market flexibility and structural adjustment, and mitigating what they consider to be the false sentimentality of trade union or public policies that protect labour during economic recessions. With a machine, keep it during the early stages of recession because of the investment in it. For the individual employee, lay-off is the rule in standard economics, notwithstanding the fact that this amounts to squandering an investment.

In the short-run early phase of recession, there is substantial economic logic to hoarding labour in the enterprise. There is, however, a distinction between short-term cyclical recession and deeper declines into depression or general structural imbalances that call for laying off employees. Confronted with this reality, the worker-managed firm will no doubt cling to its employees longer, resist voting to make redundant individuals who have stood next to each other on the factory floor, and seek the necessary financing to keep afloat the enterprise's labour force. If this is coupled with an ideological commitment to the system of self-management, so tenacious that it argues down rational arguments for economic adjustment, then a systemic problem exists.

Banks, backed by the central bank, will funnel money to enterprises, providing the working capital needed to meet payrolls. Labour redundancy is suppressed but not corrected. At the same time, there is no pressure on the enterprise to invest in new technology, either from the state or from markets which will not favour new investments during recession. In short, where is the Schumpeterian creative destruction, that necessary evil of labour redundancy, bankruptcy, and reinvigoration? Without clearing the dead underbrush, the stage is set for a real conflagration when ignited by some exogenous spark.

This is precisely what happened throughout east-central Europe and the Soviet Union between 1975 and 1985 – a general economic lethargy that was sustained by ideology and bad policies. This decade saw economic stagnation overwhelm industrial economies, with the exception of Asia. Europe and the United States recovered in the mid-1980s; the Soviet Union and east-central Europe did not and continued downwards at an accelerated pace. Yugoslavia did not escape this trap. One can argue that Yugoslavia's economic problems became confounded in the furies of nationalism. This is only partially true. Serious economic problems of a systemic character infected Yugoslavia, years before the rise of nationalism. Indeed, a case can be made that nationalistic passions followed on and were stimulated by economic conflicts over diminishing resources as a consequence of stagnation.

Part of the systemic reason is the structural problem a worker-managed system confronts during a long and sustained economic depression, as that which inflicted economies of east-central Europe from 1975 onwards. After a short-term phase when labour hoarding was rational, the worker-managed system was not able to find a way to shed redundant labour in order to set the stage for economic renewal. Instead, economic problems were suppressed, sustained by bank loans that provided the necessary working capital to enterprises. But along with the working capital came massive debt that was not justified by turnover. The postponed day of reckoning became ever worse and the adjustments more arduous. In this milieu, renewed nationalism found a place for incubation and its ferocity grew, along with the magnitude of the economic adjustment that was postponed.

1.7 Technology and investment

The choice of technology, according to the theoretical work of western economists, was also distorted in a self-managed economy. Ironically, starting with Benjamin Ward, the conclusion reached by these studies was that worker-managed firms would have a bias toward capital-intensity and the choice of technology would be too capital-intensive (Ward, 1958). If the worker-managed firm has influence over labour hiring, and maximizes income per employee, the logical result is for those insiders to restrict employment in order to receive higher income per capita. Hence, the labour-managed firm will seek out more capital-intensive modes of production.

The flip side of this coin is that a worker-managed system should generate high levels of investment and technological innovation in order to drive labour productivity higher. How else will the insider employees be able to sustain or increase their income shares but by higher labour productivity that occurs from a relentless incentive to substitute capital for labour with new technologies? Indeed, the first 40 years of Yugoslavia's labour-managed system performed precisely this way: high rates of investment, technological innovation, and sustained growth in labour productivity.

Paradoxically, if a comparable optimizer is posited for a capitalist managed system – namely maximizing income-per-owner, shareholder – a symmetric outcome occurs. Such a firm will tend to have too labour-intensive a mode of production as managers seek to restrain the growth of capital stock in order to spread returns among owners over a limited denominator, capital stock. Such a model is not used and the optimizing function is some measure of absolute returns – profit levels being the most common. However, who is to say that a capitalist-managed firm would not have a maximizing function such as profits per shareholder?

The argument over the form of the maximizing function in a worker-managed enterprise suffers from an absence of symmetry. If worker-managed firms maximize income per employee, why would not capitalist-managed firms maximize income per shareholder? After all, an employee is nothing more than a stakeholder in a worker-managed enterprise, not unlike the shareholder in a capitalist-managed firm. It can be shown that the choice of production methods will be too labour intensive in such a capitalist-managed firm that maximizes income per shareholder just as the production process is too capital intensive in the worker-managed firm that maximizes income per employee.[9] Neither stands up very well to empirical scrutiny.

1.8 The Yugoslav worker-managed system

This brief journey through Yugoslavia's economic history allows a reassessment of the theory of the worker-managed enterprise and its applications. It also permits us to examine Horvat's contribution to twentieth century economic and social thought. The problem with self-managed economies is not the supposed economic irrationalities thrown at it by western economists. It was something quite different.

Yugoslavia's problem with its experience as a worker-managed system invites this question: is the system of workers management a one-generational institutional construct? Does it have a serious dilemma in reproducing itself inter-generationally? An answer to this question is found in a capitalist-managed system. Here the brilliant insight of Joseph Schumpeter provides the answer. The creative destruction of the downside of the business cycle cleans out dead wood, allows for a new foundation for growth, and organically restores profitability – that engine of activity that fixes broken economies. Schumpeter turns what Marx and other socialists saw as the Achilles heel of capitalism – the business cycle – into its most forceful argument. Without state intervention, capitalist economies not only right themselves but do so from an enhanced position of strength. With the unproductive firms passing from the scene, only the most productive survive. They, along with new entrants, set the stage for growth through new investment with nascent enhanced technologies pulled off the shelf. This explains how in the midst of the Great Depression in the United States during the 1930s, massive innovations were put in place – the new forces of sustained growth implanted simultaneously with the picture of economic despair. By 1939, all of this could be displayed at the New York World's Fair – television, the city of the future, washing machines, data processors, and so on. If this process is aborted, suppressed by systems and ideologies that do not permit creative destruction to take place, then the day of reckoning is only postponed.

I contend this is precisely what happened after 1975 – a critical juncture for both capitalist and non-capitalist forms of organization. The former went through a wrenching adjustment process, the latter did not. The collapse of non-capitalist economies in the mid-1980s both brought on the great transformation in the former Soviet Union and east-central Europe and unleashed the furies of nationalism that engulfed the former Yugoslavia.

This is a lesson that needs to be learned and absorbed, lest future experiments founder as well. A worker-managed system, and any non-capitalist system, must figure out how to reproduce Schumpeter's organic form of creative destruction in order to reproduce itself inter-generationally. This is necessary in order for economies to cleanse themselves of accumulated staleness, much like the human body has automatic mechanisms for continually shedding its waste. Failing this the human body dies. For an economy the same process is at work.

1.9 In lieu of conclusions

Finally, what of Horvat's contributions in light of what many of his critics would cite as a failure of theoretical and applied success? First, it is fair to say that he never had the ear of authorities in the former Yugoslavia, and their mistakes should not be attributed to Horvat. Could he, secondly, have anticipated what I consider to be the single most salient theoretical lapse – namely the absence of a Schumpeterian form of creative destruction appropriate to a non-capitalist system? Perhaps, but this is where experience informs the next generation of theorists.

As to Horvat's life work, it is sufficient to celebrate the scope and scale of his contributions to twentieth century intellectual life and not allow ourselves to taint this by attributing to him the failures of Yugoslavia's experiment.

Notes

1 Horvat was always careful to distinguish his version of market-socialism from Oskar Lange's which started with state ownership and blended it with the market (Lange and Taylor, 1964).
2 The roots of the idea for these self-governing associations are found in what Joseph Schumpeter called 'Associationist Socialists' of the nineteenth century – Robert Owen, Charles Fourier and Louis Blanc. The 1871 Paris Commune and French Revolutionary Syndicalists provided limited experiments with associationist socialism. British twentieth century Guild Socialists, most notably G. D. H. Cole, offered the most complete theoretical blueprint for this variant. The Mondragon system in the Basque region of Spain is the most far-reaching western adaptation in the post-World War II period (Horvat, 1969: 27–32; Howard M. Wachtel, 1973: ch. 2; and Thomas and Logan, 1982).
3 Joseph A. Schumpeter (1954: 454–62).
4 Benjamin Ward (1958) and Benjamin N. Ward (1967, chaps. 8–10).
5 Wachtel (1973, ch. 3).
6 Evsey Domar (1966) and Walter Y. Oi and Elizabeth M. Clayton (1968).
7 International Labor Office (1962). The *AER* articles are cited in footnote 6.
8 I analyzed these labour market issues in my 1973 book on Yugoslavia (Wachtel, 1973).
9 The irony of this outcome does not escape Horvat who called this a 'nice and humorous result' (Horvat, 1971: 105).

References

Domar, E. (1966) 'The Soviet Collective Farm as a Producer Cooperative', *American Economic Review*, 56: 734–57.

Fukuyama, F. (1992) *The End of History and the Last Man*, New York: The Free Press.

Horvat, B. (1967) 'Prilog zasnivanju teorije jugoslavenskog poduzeća,' (A Contribution to the Theory of the Yugoslav Firm), *Ekonomska analiza*, 1–2: 7–28.

Horvat, B. (1969) *An Essay on Yugoslav Society*, White Plains, N.Y.: International Arts and Sciences Press.

Horvat, B. (1971) 'Yugoslav Economic Policy in the Post-War Period: Problems, Ideas, Institutional Developments,' *American Economic Review Supplement*, 61(June).

International Labor Office (1962) *Workers' Management in Yugoslavia*, Geneva: International Labor Office.

Lange, O. and Taylor, F. M. (1964) *On the Economic Theory of Socialism*, New York: McGraw-Hill.

Oi, W. Y. and Clayton, E. M. (1968) 'A Peasant's View of a Soviet Collective Farm', *American Economic Review*, 58 (March): 37–59.

Schumpeter, J. A. (1954) *History of Economic Analysis*, London: George Allen & Unwin.

Thomas, H. and Logan, C. (1982) *Mondragon. An Economic Analysis*, London: George Allen & Unwin.

Wachtel, H. M. (1973) *Workers' Management and Workers' Wages in Yugoslavia*, Ithaca: Cornell University Press.

Wachtel, H. M. (1977) *The New Gnomes: Multinational Banks in the Third World*, Amsterdam: Transnational Institute.

Ward, B. (1958) 'The Firm in Illyria, Market Syndicalism,' *American Economic Review*, 58 (September): 566–89.

Ward, B. N. (1967) *The Socialist Economy. A Study of Organizational Alternatives*, New York: Random House.

2
Individual Initiative, Entry and Economic Democracy*

Jaroslav Vanek

2.1 Introduction

The origins of this paper go back to the reforms of President Velasco in Peru over a quarter of a century ago, when both Professor Horvat and myself were invited to advise the Peruvian government on the subject of economic democracy. One of us was coming from the Marxian tradition, the other from the tradition of the social doctrine of the Catholic Church.

The Peruvian attempt at reform and its failure, with its obstacles and myriad flaws of design and implementation, would be lengthy and difficult to describe. But there is one significant problem which arose for me then for the first time and which can be dealt with now with the hindsight of 25 years, whose solution is intimately linked to the search for an optimal socio-economic system. The analysis also permits a certain surprising *rapprochement* between what we often refer to as the Austrian school of economics and economic democracy.

The problem in Peru 25 years ago was this: the semi-primitive economy of that country then was based, besides a handful of large agrarian and mining estates (mostly foreign owned or related), predominantly on relatively small owner-operated firms with none or a small number of hired employees. Where there were no hired employees – basically on family firms – there was no problem, as they represented the ideal form of self-management and economic democracy. But the problem in our rather doctrinal approach to economic democracy was how to

---

*Most of this material is reprinted, with the Egon Sohmen Foundation's permission, from section II of J. Vanek's Egon-Sohmen Lecture, 'Welfare State: Bandaid or Full Cure?', Egon Sohmen Foundation, University of Economics and Business Administration, Vienna, 15 October, 1996 (printed in Germany 1997).

deal with the firms with some hired labour, and especially, how to deal with situations of growth from a small craft-type enterprise to a larger one with perhaps several dozen workers, which should have been the backbone of Peruvian economic development.

The answer, which I then offered in order to preserve a consistent and coherent doctrine and recommendation for a democratic economy, was a certain kind of grandfather clause. Under this formula the original founder of the firm would retain his/her leading position for life, could retain – naturally – the value-ownership of his assets in the firm with income and claim to principal, but without full control, the latter being based on participation in work and not on participation in ownership. Obviously the solution was not fully 'cooked', and may have even contributed to the demise of the reforms which thus remained not fully defined and open to criticism.

Writing in 1997 and dealing with the theory of optimality of social systems based on quality and nature of involvement, it is easier to see, at least for this writer, that in dealing with the problem at hand, clearly, one must recognize a special 'nature' of human involvement. This involvement is fundamental, whether in theology or discussion of family life, or entrepreneurship or technological inventive activity: it is what we want to identify as the *parental* involvement. Let me begin by outlining the theory of optimality, or what I like to refer to as the unified theory of social systems, and then use it in the context of our present subject.

2.2 Theoretical framework: a unified theory of social systems

The happiness or peace of mind of individual people depends on many individual conditions and predispositions. Some of these conditions and predispositions all members of society have in common, because they derive from the overall government, freedoms, constitutional rights and so on, ruling that society. There are overall rights which add up to happy, or more or less happy, societies and others which add up to overall social misery.

The state of Hitler's Germany or Somosa's Nicaragua are illustrations of the state of misery, while conditions of a Swiss canton or perhaps of the Dutch nation come close to the socially happy state. Without any doubt, the most significant group of such social conditions and predispositions is related to the degree to which members of nations or societies can participate in the determination of and decisions bearing on matters affecting them. In the state of misery, we find the extreme case of a dictator who not only does not allow members of society such determination or decisions, but may also arbitrarily imprison or even destroy members of society. On the other side of the spectrum we find the case of a democratic society respecting basic human rights.

But there are so many possible aspects, forms, intensities, social domains and so on, such a tremendous dimensionality, of this 'space' of social conditions, that it is difficult to make any more precise conclusions about which states are to be preferred – and who, if anyone, should make such conclusions or judgments, and how. The differentiation between Hitler's Germany and a Swiss canton may be clear, but there are trillions of intermediate as well as more extreme situations that are hard to evaluate.

The purpose of this analysis is to offer some degree of greater order in these matters and perhaps indicate forms of optimality, not as 'optimal prescriptions' but rather as indications of the breadth or 'fullness' of the dimensionality at hand and of procedures and methods of finding, for any given nation or society, its own optimum.

The full discussion of this subject, too extensive to be undertaken here, falls under three distinct headings: (1) the structure – or static general rules; (2) the social dynamics, procedure and process of finding solutions; and (3) the actual method or technique through which a society composed of many members arrives at solutions and decisions. The first of the three is the most important when it comes to the determination of optimal states of society.

It is this first subject heading that we will discuss here. Because it has been presented several times in both published[1] and unpublished papers of mine, I will restrict myself here to a compact summary statement, often relying on common sense, intuition or analogy, with the intention of presenting to the reader a certain whole which can be evaluated and accepted or rejected.

All the 'static' states of society can be thought of as an all-inclusive set represented by an oval or ellipse, where the optimum is somewhere at the center, and the least desirable states such as Hitler's or Somosa's are at or near the outer edge, as indicated in the sketch of Figure 2.1. What is relevant and what determines the degree of optimality or misery is the relationship between two indexes, or quanta – I and P – the degree of *involvement* and *participation* in a given society or social group and participation by members of the society or group in determination and decisions concerning the group respectively. The case of the two mentioned and many other dictatorial states is that

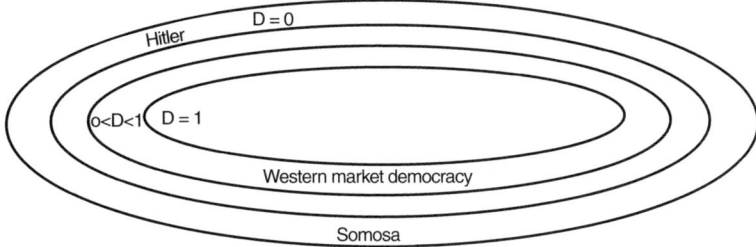

Figure 2.1 First law of optimal participation

there is no correspondence between those involved (that is the nation) and the decision-making process (assumed by the dictator). Thus we can write symbolically:

$$I < ==\text{not}==> P$$

or, more precisely:

$$I < == 0 == > P$$

where the number zero reflects the degree of participation index $D=0$; D could even be given negative values if the dictator, besides determining all the circumstances of the society himself, arbitrarily infringes on the habeas corpus of individual citizens in various ugly ways.

The index D may be thought of as equal to one for maximal or total degree of participation, as determined by the state of society or community, usually written into its constitutional law or statutes. For example, even in the 'ideal' Swiss canton some decades ago, the constitution permitted only men to vote; thus D might be thought of as equal approximately to 1/2.

But there is another degree index which must be introduced into our discussion – refer to it as d – not given by usurpers of power or democratic constitutions but by physical or other circumstances. For example, for the community of residents of New York City (with d varying between minimum of 0 and maximum of 1 or one hundred per cent) the involvement in the affairs of Peking is somewhere near zero ($d=0$), in the affairs of the New Jersey community over the George Washington bridge, say 0.03 and in the affairs of their own city 1.00. It is interesting to note that this type of geographical 'distance' influence on involvement has a parallel in the so-called gravity models in location theory and practice of transport frequency prediction. The involvement of a half-time worker in his place of work is $d = 1/2$, that is one half the involvement of a regular full time worker. As in these examples, the principal meaning of the index of involvement 'd' is primarily as a relative number with respect to the maximum possible involvement of an individual; that is, $d=1$ for a full member of a community, such as nation, state, labour force of a factory and so on; but d can also measure the number of shares of an owner relative to the total outstanding number, or the number of (voting) shares of one stockholder relative to another.

With these notions and definitions in mind, we can state what we refer to as the *first law of optimal social participation*: For optimum, D should always be equal to one (this is based on human dignity and equality) and participation in decisions should (at least approximately) be governed by the index 'd', that is according to the intensity of involvement. This is natural to those living in democratic societies. New Yorkers vote in New York, and not in Peking or New Jersey, but they affect somewhat, through national political participation, the affairs of New Jersey, even though the estimate of 0.03 is quite tenuous and almost arbitrary.

Perhaps the best illustration of an optimal solution, or application of the first law, is participation of consumers operating in perfectly competitive markets. Here, involvement of buyers in two or more products is measured by the desire/consumption of certain quantities of the products, and participation in control over such products is indeed expressed by the expenditures devoted to the products respectively. If I consume twice as much potatoes as my neighbour, I participate in the control of that product by an intensity ratio of 2 to 1. But if the markets are not perfectly competitive, and we both, say, spend the same on potatoes but I buy twice as much as my neighbour (at half price), then the solution is not optimal.

Nor is it optimal if one of the products is subject to a strong negative externality (for example, production polluting the air or water), while the other is not. The intensity of involvement of the 'd' type now is not measured by relative expenditures, because the community is negatively affected by the first product's production – and that residual intensity must be taken care of, for optimum, in some other manner (as is done in some cases in modern democratic market societies). But we will have to return to this subject elsewhere. Here let it only be noted that the first law of optimal participation is indeed respected in some situations in democratic market societies.

There is another well-known example of participation which would at first sight appear as optimal, with $D=1$ and the intensities of involvement 'd' respected. It has to do with common stock ownership and voting in capitalist corporations. But there is a fundamental problem which illustrates the need for, and helps us to define what we call, the *second fundamental law of optimal participation*. In the opinion of this writer – to be judged by the reader as we go along – this second law is of tremendous importance, and if applied, promises a major step in the direction of a more just and happy society and the elimination of a lot of human misery.

Obviously, in the practice of large capitalist corporations the postulates of the first law are not fully respected, with large stockholders typically having disproportionately strong power, and vice versa for the small stockholders. But it is not this flaw that we speak about here. What concerns us is that there is a category of people, the workers, who, while significantly involved, do not participate at all in the decisions of the corporations, save sometimes indirectly, via labour unions. Thus, on our terms, D is significantly below unity and the degree/intensity of involvement 'd' is not respected in determining participation in decisions. This is a highly imperfect, suboptimal, solution indeed.

Some would suggest that the solution should be sought in various forms of co-determination, such as that practiced in the German economy. While probably a step in the right direction, this is not an optimal solution and may even imply a dead-end street. Co-determination in general terms postulates that capital and labour produce jointly. Thus it should be treated along the lines of the first law with the 'd' intensities somehow determined numerically, perhaps as proportions of value added by the various factors and their suppliers.

The suboptimality of co-determination can be argued on both practical and theoretical levels. The economic performance of such solutions is good but certainly not the best:[2] in theory, because the primary objectives of capital is profit maximization, and of labour, maximization of income or wages. The situation is likely to become unstable, depending on who holds the majority, and the incentives structure especially can be quite flawed. But we do not have to spend much time on this subject, because our principal purpose is to move our analysis towards the determination of true optimal solutions.

The key to the road of optimality is, in addition to intensity of involvement, the consideration of the *nature* or *quality* of involvement. We have here at least three major historical analogies or antecedents. (1) The nature and quality of involvement of the owner in his slaves is inferior/subordinated to the involvement of habeas corpus of the slaves themselves. We have abolished slavery, and no one today would question this comparative judgment – on the contrary most of us would attach to it a certain moral or philosophical notion of justice.

(2) Similarly, decolonization was based on the now unquestioned and unquestionable notion that the members of a certain nation (former colony) are differently and far more deeply involved in their society than some colonial *external* power, or even an external owner, such as, the king of Belgium in the case of Belgian Congo.

Finally (3) in the domain of political democracy and self-determination, we have the qualitative 'jump' from poll taxes or right to vote, conditioned by land ownership or wealth, to pure personal rights of all members of society, with equal vote for all, or $D=1$ rather than $D<1$ of the former situations.

In these and all other situations (to which we will turn later) the qualification of *quality* or *nature* of involvement becomes somehow understandable or 'natural' upon critical reflection. Also, the critical reflection usually leads to a conclusion as to how the quality/nature of involvement should impact the form or nature of participation for full optimality. *The second law of optimal participation* can thus be stated as: To attain optimum, participation by those involved in a given domain should also depend on the nature and quality of that involvement.

Whereas the first law can be thought of as uni-dimensional, as measured or reflected by intensity (d or D) – very often a dimensionality reducible to dollars or material values – the second one brings us to a world which is multi-dimensional, recognizing, in addition to intensity, the dimensions of justice, love, faith, human life and many others. The world based on both the first and second law of participation is definitely a better and happier one.

Among the many solutions offered by the two laws, we also find the analytical justification for the claim contained in the title of this paper. To this analysis I now turn in the remaining section.

It may be useful to complete the diagram-set shown for the first law in Figure 2.1 above. Recalling that increasing the degree of optimality (or social desirability) corresponds to movement from the periphery towards the center of the elliptical set, it can be claimed that the fulfilling of the second law corresponds to a quantum leap in desirability, coinciding with the very centre of the total set. However, because we progress here from the unidimensionality of intensity to the multi-dimensionality of nature/quality of involvement which must determine true optimum, we must move to a higher dimension. Limited by

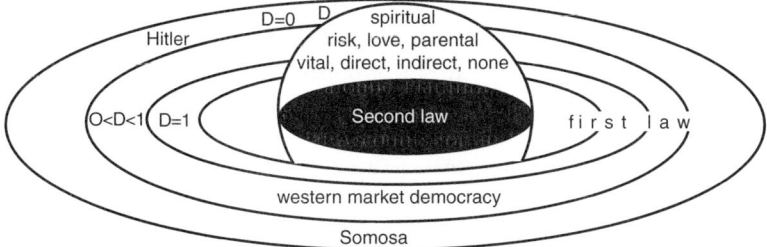

Figure 2.2 Second law of optimal participation

a lack of ability to perceive objects of more than three dimensions, we must content ourselves with the three dimensional. Having drawn such a set with a three-dimensional sphere at its centre we obtain an image resembling the planet Saturn, shown in Figure 2.2.

2.3 Applying the laws of optimal system to 'parental entrepreneurship'

As indicated in the three-dimensional sphere of the Saturn-diagram in Figure 2.2, one of the significant types or natures or qualities of involvement is the parental involvement. It pertains to the creative act of human beings, be it in the domain of procreation of children, any inventive activity, or our present subject, entrepreneurial creation of new firms, organizations, technologies and so forth.

That parental involvement must be recognized as one of the fundamental types of involvement, quite high on the pole of natures of involvement, higher than direct involvement if it also includes direct involvement. For example, a parent who is also present in the life of the family can and must participate in the decisions of the family with greater weight than another member of the household who is not also a parent.

More concretely and introspectively, how could one expect the creator of a firm, possibly the designer or inventor of its product, to surrender the management and exploitation to the democratic quorum of the enterprise of which he is a working (and founding) member? The primacy of direct involvement *is* over other involved individuals and in particular the absentee capital owners; but if the founder, who is probably at least part owner and worker present in the life of the firm, participates in the production process *he* must be given a recognition of his parental involvement in some specific priority manner. The specific nature of this activity need not concern us here: we merely want to point out this special situation. Once the 'parental' member of the community disappears from it, by death, retirement and so on, then of course the optimality precepts of direct involvement and equality of involvement of the working members obtain.

It can be said – perhaps again referring to the family situation – that the parental act really continues with the parent well beyond the initial conception (which in the case of an enterprise may be just the first moment of a creative idea), well into the actual working of the enterprise, in fact until the founder leaves the enterprise. This is somehow a matter of the spirit rather than that of ownership or just mere presence in the productive process.

I find this interpretation and solution of the 'Velasco-reform' problem not only correct but also intriguing from another, also historical, point of view. It concerns the so-called Austrian school of Karl Menger, Böhm-Bawerk, Schumpeter, Hayek, Von Mises and others. For the Anglo-Saxon neoclassical mainstream economist, the school is quite marginal, neglected by or unknown to the majority. Given his graduate economics education at MIT forty years ago, this roughly pertains also to the present writer. But looking back over my economist's career from the point of view of my unified theory of social systems, and more concretely from that of the present subject originating in the Velasco reforms (and perhaps because both of my parents were born Austrians), the following comes to mind.

As far as I know, one of the centrepieces of the Austrian School was the key role of the founder-innovator-entrepreneur of the enterprise. But that role was not one of capital formation, accumulation or investment, but rather of the qualities of spirit and of conceiving an idea and successfully carrying it out and continuing with it in an everlasting process of life of the firm. In summary, the question is one of spirit and ideas versus Mammon, capital, accumulation without limit and so on. The former can be associated with our notion of social optimality, the latter with the notion of suboptimal (even if virulent and prevailing) capitalism.

In the Austrian firm of the nineteenth century, the two were united in the person and activity of the Austrian entrepreneur. But then history went on for another hundred years, now ending, and there were two trajectories, one emanating from the entrepreneur *qua* human spirit, the other emanating from the entrepreneur *qua* Mammon-developer capitalist. The first trajectory, while optimal, was rejected and the second, while suboptimal, prevailed. And that is the tumorous state of the end of the twentieth century. Our thesis of parental involvement both explains and rehabilitates the Austrian position and provides the logical missing link and clarification of the correct path for the next century and millennium, if it is not too late.

If the first trajectory had been entered on at the bifurcation somewhere in the early years of our century, at the time when small entrepreneurial firms were transforming into or being replaced by large capitalist corporations, we might have lived to this day in a saner, happier and more optimal world. The critical juncture, in my view, and the tragic moment of history arose when the partly human entrepreneur underwent an inhuman metamorphosis and let his human nature be submerged by his capitalist nature, especially in his descendants of later generations.

I use the term 'partly human' for the old entrepreneur not only because he was also the capital owner or supplier, but because in many cases his nature and character was not quite parental towards those whom he hired into his enterprise. The continuation, and in fact worsening, of the labour contract was a more natural and logical process for those in power, than the allowance to share that power and management rights once the old entrepreneurial firm was nearing extinction. The only sign of the existence of the human paternal entrepreneur today is the occasional case of the entrepreneurial firms being, often for lack of a willing heir in the family, offered to and taken over in a friendly and cooperative spirit by the workers when the old owner retires.

Notes

1 See Vanek, J. (1976); Vanek, J. (1996); Vanek, J. (1997).
2 See Doucouliagos, Chris (1995).

References

Doucouliagos, C. (1995) 'Worker Participation and Productivity in Labor-Managed and Participatory Capitalist Firms: a Meta-Analysis', *Industrial and Labor Relations Review*, 49(1): 58–77.

Vanek, J. (1976) 'From Participation and Dialogue to a World of Justice,' unpublished ms.

Vanek, J. (1996) 'A General Theory of Efficient Participatory Society,' in D. L. Prychitko and J. Vanek (eds), *Producer Cooperatives and Labor-Managed Systems*, Vol. I: 315–28, Aldershot: Edward Elgar.

Vanek, J. (1997) *Welfare State: Bandaid or Full Cure?*, Egon Sohmen Foundation, University of Economics and Business Administration, Vienna, 15 October, 1996, Kiel: Egon-Sohmen-Foundation.

3
Egalitarianism On Its Own
Samuel Bowles and Herbert Gintis

3.1 Is equality *passé*?

Seven decades ago Branko Horvat was born into a world where dramatic economic inequalities were soon to come under confident assault by egalitarian movements of the left. The moral case for egalitarian redistribution was clear, and its practical implementation commanded wide support among workers and the less well off. But radical egalitarianism today is the orphan of a defunct socialism. The unruly and abandoned child of the liberal enlightenment had been taken in by socialism in the mid-nineteenth century. Protected and overshadowed by its new foster parent, radical egalitarianism was relieved of the burden of arguing its own case. As socialism's foster child, equality would be the by-product of an unprecedented post-capitalist order, not something to be defended morally and promoted politically on its own terms in the world as it is.

It thus fell to reformists, be they labourist, social democratic, Eurocommunist or New Deal, to make capitalism livable for workers and the less well off, a task they accomplished with remarkable success in the advanced economies. But in the process, the egalitarian project was purged of its Utopian yearnings for a world of equal freedom and dignity, and narrowed to the pursuit of a more equal distribution of goods. Over the years, even this project has encountered increasingly effective resistance and experienced major political reversals.

Is egalitarianism passé? We think not. But recasting the egalitarian project will require a radical reconsideration of both goals and the means for achieving them. An apt beginning for this reconsideration is the Atlantic republicanism of the late 18th century, a tradition born of the tension between egalitarianism and emergent liberal democratic thought.[1]

Thomas Jefferson's draft of the Virginia Constitution of 1776 included a radical provision for freeborn male suffrage with the rather minimal property qualification of 25 acres. In the same document we find Jefferson advocating that 'Every person of ill age neither owning or having owned 50 acres of land shall be entitled to an appropriation of 50 acres' (Jefferson, 1950: 349). The personal autonomy on which a democratic society must be based required, in Jefferson's eyes, an end to economic dependence and hence, secure access to the means of one's livelihood.[2]

Jefferson's vision of a yeoman democracy based on a commercial agrarian economy now seems quaint, for the autonomous property-owning farmer has been replaced by the collective work and dispersed property of modern industry. Writing in *Democracy in America* just two generations later, Alexis de Tocqueville (1933/69) observed that in the great industrial centres 'the workman is generally dependent on the master...' and he warned his readers:

> I am of the opinion...that the manufacturing aristocracy which is growing up under our eyes is one of the harshest that ever existed in the world...the friends of democracy should keep their eyes anxiously fixed in this direction; for if ever a permanent inequality of conditions and aristocracy again penetrates into the world, it may be predicted that this is the gate by which they will enter.
>
> (II, 170–1)

As Tocqueville feared, with the waning of the bucolic foundations of yeoman democracy and the emergence of a modern capitalist economy, the Jeffersonian marriage of autonomy and equality would prove increasingly elusive. Tocqueville's warning of the fragility of Jefferson's egalitarianism under modern conditions bore implications for political accountability in a democratic order as well:

> It is indeed difficult to conceive how men who have entirely given up the habit of self-government should succeed in making a proper choice of those by whom they are to be governed; and no one will ever believe that a liberal, wise, and energetic government can spring from the suffrages of a subservient people.
>
> (II, 339)

Karl Marx echoed the agrarian republican conviction that secure access to one's livelihood is a precondition of freedom, but like Tocqueville recognized the anachronistic nature of the Jeffersonian solution in a world of increasingly collective production. Democratic socialists subsequently elaborated models of common property ownership as the basis of a democratic and egalitarian society. Yet the common ownership of property, whether in nationalized industry or local environmental commons, often undermines the effectiveness of markets in assuring economic accountability, and thus exacerbates the difficulty of reconciling personal autonomy with effective economic governance.

In *Recasting Egalitarianism* (Bowles and Gintis, 1998), we have sought to revive and update the Jeffersonian vision, providing a foundation for its egalitarianism in the realities of modern economic life and addressing the related problem of the accountability of power. Our 'neo-Jeffersonian' paradigm is based on three constitutional desiderata governing the nature and assignment of property rights and other rights of governance.

First, asset-based policies of redistribution should seek to implement a sustainable assignment of private property rights that make economic actors both effective decision makers and the owners of the results of their actions.

Secondly, insurance-based policies of redistribution should seek to indemnify individuals against risks they cannot avoid and over which they have no control, including accidents of birth, while maintaining individual responsibility for the consequences of one's own actions.[3]

Thirdly, state, market, and community should be complementary, not competing, governance structures. Government policies should seek, not to supplant markets and communities, but to ensure their accountability and enhance their capacity to support equitable and efficient outcomes. Conversely, market and community should be organized to promote the accountability of government to the people.

These desiderata reflect our understanding of how individuals interact with the rules of the game structuring economic and other social interactions. Our understanding is far from universally shared among those who count themselves as egalitarians. Because commonly held views on the left are at variance with those motivating our proposals, it may be useful to spell out our position on four points of contention.

First, we see no point in advocating particular social outcomes unless we can specify the structurally determined individual incentives and sanctions that allow the implementation of these outcomes and support their sustainability in the long run. This includes, of course, having compelling reasons to believe that those entrusted with *applying* the incentives and sanctions have the incentive to do so. Egalitarian projects often founder on the failure to take account of the incentive structures facing the relevant actors. Instead, such projects often assume 'oversocialized' decision-makers who fully internalize the objectives motivating the policy in question.

Secondly, egalitarian policies must not only be sustainable in their implementation, they must also be politically and economically sustainable in the long run. By this we mean that they are capable of securing the support of effective governing coalitions and that they cannot be undone through the private contracting of individuals and groups.

Thirdly, many egalitarians overstate the benefits of simply redividing the pie. The gains from what we have termed 'hard redistribution' are limited for the obvious reason that redistributing the wealth of the rich to the less well off would accomplish relatively little redistribution: unearned income (meaning income from non-human assets) constitutes less than a third of all income in most advanced capitalist economies, and since the wealthy tend to invest a large fraction of their income, consumption from unearned income is considerably less than a third of all consumption.

If economic interactions had the character of zero-sum games, then hard redistribution would be the only option; but most interactions are neither pure conflicts (situations in which one's gains entail another's losses) nor pure coordination problems (situations in which if anyone gains, everyone does). The 'prisoner's dilemma' is an archetypal example of this joint conflict and coordination structure of interaction. Our proposals are based on the conviction that there exist egalitarian policies that allow mutual gains, through what we have termed 'efficiency enhancing redistributions'.

Fourthly, while we advocate new roles for the government in regulatory and insurance activities, we have no predisposition for a large role for government production. We find little reason for the state to engage extensively in productive activities, and we stress the many unavoidable obstacles to citizen accountability over governmental actions. The assumption of oversocialized decision-makers is nowhere more evident and damaging than in the presumption that state managers and functionaries will faithfully carry out what an egalitarian citizenry would have them do.

In this brief reflection, we will address the question of the objectives of egalitarian redistribution and then take up the question of means. Along the way, we will respond to a few of the critical comments on our initial essay.

3.2 Ends: what is wrong with inequality?

Programs to assure a modicum of economic security for the poor and guarantee equality of opportunity for all have faltered in recent years. Other egalitarian initiatives have come under attack and suffered defections from erstwhile supporters. Unemployment rates have risen in some countries and real wages have fallen in others. Redistributive programs have been cut and dramatic increases in measured inequality of income have taken place in a number of countries. For the most part, people have responded with resignation or approval rather than resistance.

Among the reasons for this reversal, we think, is a growing ambiguity in public sentiment concerning the requirements of justice and scepticism concerning the possibility of achieving a more just distribution of society's rewards. Even Americans, no doubt one of the most conservative of the world's bodies politic, remain deeply committed to equality of opportunity as a goal. But Americans, and others, are profoundly divided on how to define this objective, and bewildered by contradictory claims on how any of the competing conceptions of equality of opportunity might be advanced through social policy. An orphaned egalitarianism, detached from its erstwhile base in popular movements for institutional change, has sought to defend itself on moral and empirical grounds that many, even among the less well off, find weak and uncompelling. Four sources of the demoralization of the egalitarian project are notable.

The first concerns objectives. When applied to national aggregates, both 'equality' and 'income' are depersonalized abstractions unlikely to evoke visceral reactions or to move people to act politically. The standard measures of inequality, the Gini ratio, for example, are abstractions which are only with difficulty related to everyday concerns of fairness and compassion. Knowing that the Gini ratio for male workers is 0.42 evokes shrugs, which is not the case for the fact that a white person whose income is below $7500 is three times as likely to be the victim of rape, sexual assault or other violent crime as another earning over $50 000.[4] Moreover, except among the very poor, income is surprisingly weakly related to one's reported sense of well-being.[5]

Secondly, the concept of fairness, in the everyday sense of a level playing field, no longer enjoys a consensus as to its implications. As a result, the concept fails to provide much guidance in promoting egalitarian efforts. Even so basic a concept as equality of educational opportunity eludes definition, with proposals ranging from securing the absence of overt discrimination based on race, gender or family class origins, to the far more ambitious goal of eliminating race, gender, and class differences in educational outcomes.

Thirdly and relatedly, publics appear to focus attention on the process of redistribution rather than on the state of inequality that distributive programs are intended to correct. It may be, as Daniel Kahneman (1993) has suggested, that people tend to evaluate events rather than states in making judgments: people are more affected by *getting* a new shirt or *losing* one than by *having* one or *not having* one. Or it may be that loss aversion is such a powerful predisposition that egalitarian programs are thwarted by a strong *status quo* bias in people's evaluation. Whatever the cause, redistributive processes are closely scrutinized while seemingly (to us) unjust levels of inequality are unblushingly accepted. Moreover, some redistributive programs fail commonly held tests of fairness. Examples include violations of equal treatment and protecting people from their own mistakes, often at great cost to others.

The fourth contributor to the unravelling of the egalitarian project concerns the belief that public policy cannot affect the degree of inequality in a cost-effective manner. Many hold the view that our current levels of inequality, however reprehensible, are simply immune to public policy intervention whether in the form of employment training, tariff protection of goods produced by low-wage labour, or expanded educational opportunity. Thus, for example, the much touted hypothesis that cognitive abilities are partially inherited is falsely thought to imply that the knowledge capacities of people are immune to societal influences such as enriched education. Many who believe that deficiencies of 'cultural capital' impede the economic advancement of the poor, argue that the scope for public policy in the expansion of economic opportunity is severely limited. Many go beyond the view that the government cannot affect inequality to embrace the conservative position that government action is the *source* of poverty and inequality. In a 1991 US poll, over two thirds agree strongly or somewhat with the statement that 'one of the main reasons for poverty is bad government policy' (Wright, 1994: 34).

How might this analysis of the current trials of egalitarianism inform our own project? To some extent, if we are right, egalitarianism has suffered political reversals because it has substituted an abstract and morally ambiguous objective, such as greater equality in the distribution of income, for egalitarian objectives at once more fundamental and more compelling. What offends the public's moral sensibilities is not so much inequality of income *per se*, but severe deprivations, unfairness and social indignities that so often accompany income inequality.

First, people object to severe deprivation, including people's lack of access to an adequate diet, health care, and personal and economic security, particularly when the rectification of these lacks would not be unduly costly to others.

Secondly, unfair treatment, including discrimination by race, gender, religion and sexual preference, as well as some forms of privilege transmitted from generation to generation, excite widespread condemnation.

Thirdly, socially contrived inequality that deprives people of dignity and the capacity to pursue full lives is generally seen as reprehensible.

Displacing the target of egalitarianism from income to more fundamental determinants of dignity and well-being does not reduce the importance of economics in the pursuit of a more just society. But it does make clear that forms of egalitarianism which provide a basis for personal autonomy and effective voice in shaping one's life trajectory should be given priority. We believe that the asset-based strategy we have outlined does just this.

A second implication of the above is that the necessity to contain costs of pursuing egalitarian strategies is not simply an unfortunate constraint imposed by the veto power of the well-to-do. Costs imposed on others affect the political viability of egalitarian programs in a democratic society because, for wholly defensible reasons, people's concerns are not limited to the well-being of the least well off. Egalitarian policy must therefore be based on the willingness of non-wealthy citizens to support policies that redistribute in favour of the less well off among themselves.

The poor showing of egalitarian projects in recent years has convinced many that it is naive to expect support to be forthcoming from a selfish and indifferent electorate. This pessimism is fundamentally misdirected, however. It misunderstands the reasons for opposition to egalitarian programs, and it underestimates the ability of egalitarians to design redistributive programs capable of evoking deeply-rooted human commitments to justice. Unlike many who suspect that the basis for an egalitarian movement collapsed with the demise of socialism, we discover a solid foundation for cooperation and sharing at the root of human motivation.

3.3 *Homo reciprocans*: the motivational basis of sustainable redistribution

The modern welfare state is but a single example of a ubiquitous social form. Sharing institutions, ranging from families, extended gift giving, tithing and other religion-based charity, potlatches, to egalitarian division rules for the catch of the hunt, have cropped up in human history with such regularity and under such diverse circumstances that one is tempted to place them among Talcott Parsons' (1964) *evolutionary universals*: social institutions that confer such extensive benefits upon their users that they regularly appear and reappear in the course of history in otherwise diverse societies. The evolutionary viability of sharing institutions and of the motivations which support them counsels against those who have written off egalitarianism as an idea whose time has come and gone.

Consider one of these institutions, the practice that the Peruvian highlanders call *sunay* whereby herders give a llama to a fellow herdsman in need. Economists and biologists might doubt that this practice would be evolutionarily viable, as it appears to confer no benefit on the giver while imposing substantial costs. Yet sunay and the associated practice *kuyaq* of confirming ritual status of family membership on needy individuals persisted over centuries. Seeking to solve the mystery of this evolutionarily improbable form of generosity, Kent Flannery, Joyce Marcus and Robert Reynolds (1989) studied the demography of the llama herds and then simulated the evolution of the herds under various sharing rules including the lack of sharing of any kind. They found that:

> ...the advantages of widespread generosity in sunay outweigh the advantages of cheating or ignoring those who are not one's kin.... the custom of sunay, once adopted, might have been strongly selected for at the group level. In our models, herd systems that practice it have larger and far more stable herds after 100 years than systems without it.... universal adherence to sunay – even if it includes giving good breeding stock to non-kin – can make it possible for one's children to pass on more animals to one's grandchildren. It does that by ensuring that there will be lots of other herds around from which the children and grandchildren can get sunay when they need it.
>
> (202)

Sunay, aided by the fictive kin generated by kuyaq, is practiced on an extended scale: 'in the context of a ritual, [kuyaq] converts non-kin into kin and makes possible the universal extension of sunay' (203). Flannery *et al*. conclude that unlike other species, humans

> can use culture to create fictive kin towards whom they behave altruistically,...and there may be situations in which such ex-tensions

of kinship would be selected for. Note that we do not argue that such extensions result from shrewd decisions based on practical reason; rather, we suggest that, once made, they may be selected for – which is not the same thing.

(203)

Thus the motivations supporting sharing rules need be neither explicitly altruistic nor instrumentally self interested.[6] Moreover, over very long periods of time, cultural or genetic group selection may have supported the emergence and proliferation of other-regarding, individual traits, sharply at variance with the dismal predispositions of *Homo economicus*. We will see that a wide range of motivations apparently influences people's stance towards redistribution in modern societies.

There are two distinct reasons why the non-wealthy might support egalitarian redistribution. The first is that many egalitarian programs are forms of social insurance that will be supported for prudential reasons, even by those who may anticipate paying in more than their expected claims over a lifetime. Included among these are unemployment and health insurance and, more broadly, the various social programs that soften the blows during the rocky periods that many people experience in the course of their lives.

The insurance motive supporting egalitarian programs is consistent with conventional notions of self interest, once account is taken of risk aversion. The second reason for support of egalitarian programs, by contrast, is not fundamentally self regarding: egalitarianism is often based on a commitment to what we will term 'reciprocal fairness'.[7] As we will see presently, people are considerably more generous than the model in economics text-books allows, and they are equally unselfish in seeking to punish, often at great cost to themselves, those who have done harm to them and others. Programs designed to tap these other-regarding motives may succeed where others that offend underlying motivational structures have been abandoned.

Both historical and contemporary experimental evidence support this position. In his magisterial *Injustice: The Social Bases of Obedience and Revolt*, Barrington Moore (1978) sought to discern if there might be common motivational bases, 'general conceptions of unfair and unjust behavior' (21), for the moral outrage fueling struggles for justice that have recurred throughout human history. 'There are grounds', he concludes from his wide-ranging investigation,

> for suspecting that the welter of moral codes may conceal a certain unity of original form...a general ground plan, a conception of

what social relationships ought to be. It is a conception that by no means excludes hierarchy and authority, where exceptional qualities and defects can be the source of enormous admiration and awe. At the same time, it is one where services and favors, trust and affection, in the course of mutual exchanges, are ideally expected to find some rough balancing out.

(509)

Moore termed the general ground plan he uncovered '... the concept of reciprocity – or better, mutual obligation, a term that does not imply equality of burdens or obligations...' (506).

Recent experimental research has affirmed the centrality of the reciprocity motive. An impressive body of evidence, much of it deployed in the first instance to validate the model of the selfish purveyor of market rationality, *Homo economicus*, in fact has served to bury this model. In its place this body of evidence suggests a new persona, whom we may call *Homo reciprocans*. *Homo reciprocans* comes to new social situations with a propensity to cooperate and share, responds to cooperative behaviour by maintaining or increasing his level of cooperation, and responds to selfish, free-riding behavior on the part of others by retaliating against the offenders, even at a cost to himself, and even when he could not reasonably expect future personal gains from such retaliation. *Homo reciprocans* is neither the unconditional altruist of socialist theory, nor the hedonistic sociopath of neoclassical economics. Rather, he is a conditional cooperator whose strong instincts for sharing can be elicited under the proper circumstances, towards achieving socially egalitarian goals.

A convenient starting point in tracing the birth of *Homo reciprocans* is the study of the iterated 'prisoner's dilemma' undertaken two decades ago by Robert Axelrod at the University of Michigan.[8] Axelrod asked a number of behavioural scientists (game theorists, economists, political scientists, sociologists, and psychologists) to submit computer programs giving complete strategies for playing the iterated prisoner's dilemma. Each program was pitted against every other program, as well as itself and a program that randomly chose to cooperate and defect. The winner among the fourteen strategies submitted was the simplest, called 'tit-for-tat' (submitted by game theorist Anatol Rappoport). Tit-for-tat cooperates on the first round, and then does whatever its partner did on the previous round.

Following up on this result, Axelrod held a second tournament in which a larger number of participants, including the original contributors, were told of the success of tit-for-tat and asked to submit another program for playing the iterated prisoner's dilemma. Knowing that tit-for-tat was the strategy to beat did not help the players: once again Rappoport submitted tit-for-tat, and once again, it won.

Speculating on the strong showing of tit-for-tat, Axelrod noted that this strategy for cooperation has three attributes that are essential for successful cooperation. The first is that tit-for-tat is *nice*: it begins by cooperating, and it is never the first to defect. Second, tit-for-tat is *punishing*: it retaliates relentlessly against defection. Finally, tit-for-tat is *forgiving*: as soon as a defecting partner returns to cooperating, tit-for-tat returns to cooperating.

The reader may wonder whether a battle of computer games created by behavioural scientists has a counterpart in dynamic social processes. To explore this issue, we simulated a society composed of two hundred individuals. Each was assumed to follow a 'rule of thumb' represented by a particular strategy in playing an iterated prisoner's dilemma against a randomly chosen partner.[9] Our objective was to determine which, if any, of these rules of thumb would come to predominate in competition with a wide variety of alternative strategies played over thousands of generations.

In each round of the game, we randomly matched individuals and allowed them to play the prisoner's dilemma a varying number of times with each other. We determined the number of repetitions with a given partner by setting a probability of two per cent that the encounter would end with each play, so partners played an average of 50 repetitions with each other before the round terminated. We endowed our individuals with a memory of the three previous plays, so an individual strategy consisted of a particular response, cooperate or defect, for each of the eight possible patterns of cooperation and defection of the player's partner in the past three plays of the game. We also included in an individual strategy a predisposition to cooperate or defect upon an initial meeting of a new partner, so that in all there were over 2000 possible strategies, of which fewer than ten had the characteristics of tit-for-tat (nice, punishing, and forgiving). Finally, we randomly assigned a rule of thumb strategy to each player at the start of the simulation.

Our simulation is designed to represent the process of differential replication by either cultural learning or genetic copying. After each hundred rounds, with a certain probability, low-scoring individuals replaced their rules of thumb with those of high-scoring individuals. We also added a small probability that newly-acquired strategies had random mutations, so that new strategies were continuously injected into the game. The results are exhibited in Figure 3.1. In this figure, the solid

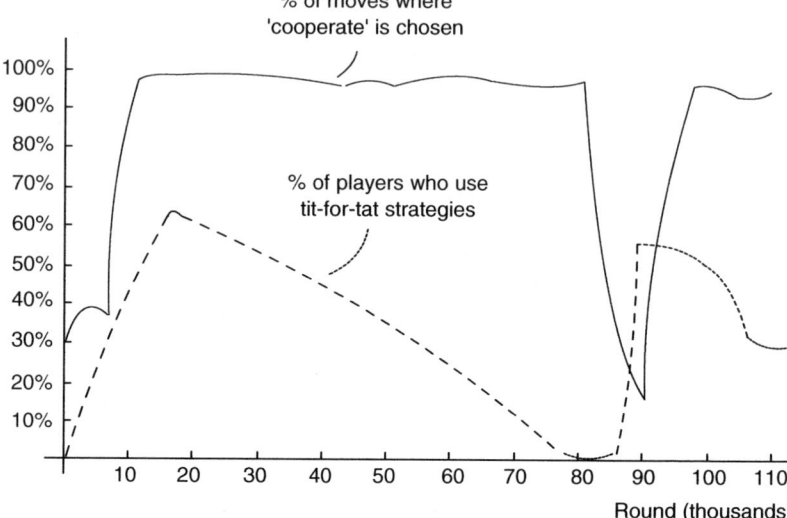

Figure 3.1 The evolution of cooperation in a dynamic setting

line is the fraction of all plays by all individuals using their given rules of thumb, play the 'cooperate' move. The dashed line is the fraction of members of the population currently holding rules of thumb corresponding to the generic tit-for-tat behaviours, namely nice, punishing, forgiving. In line with the Axelrod experiment, we find that after about 15 000 rounds, the rate of cooperation has risen from 30 per cent at the start to nearly 100 per cent, and the fraction of tit-for-tat strategies has risen from zero to about 65 per cent. Since the level of cooperation is so high at this point, however, players rarely meet defectors, and hence the propensity to punish defectors is rarely exercised. As a result, random mutations undermine the propensity to retaliate, until by round 75 000, there are virtually no tit-for-tat'ers left, and the dominant strategy type cooperate unconditionally. At this point, a mutant defector can 'invade' the population of cooperators and do extremely well. This accounts for the precipitous decline in cooperation at round 85 000, to a low of about 18 per cent. At this point the benefits of tit-for-tat are restored, and there is a fairly rapid return to cooperation, and the growth of tit-for-tat to almost its earlier peak level. Once cooperation becomes complete, however, the process of deterioration of tit-for-tat resumes.

This 'artificial life' experiment suggests that there may be a cyclical pattern of rise and fall in the frequency of tit-for-tat strategies. In periods in which levels of defection are high, tit-for-tat spontaneously emerges as an individually successful strategy that leads to a very high level of cooperation. In a highly cooperative society, however, the attractive features of tit-for-tat disappear, and there is a movement towards unconditional cooperation (altruism) that in turn invites high levels of defection and non-cooperative behaviour.

What does this have to do with people? There have been many experiments with human subjects involving the iterated prisoner's dilemma. If Axelrod's tournaments showed that nice guys finish first, the experiments reveal that there are lots of nice guys, even among the economics majors who show up for experimental games. Among the most revealing of these experiments are those that use the 'public goods game', designed to illuminate such problems as the voluntary payment of taxes and the restriction of one's use of an endangered environmental resource. The following is a common variant. Ten subjects are told that $1.00 will be deposited in each of their 'private accounts' as a reward for participating in each round of the experiment. For every dollar they move from their 'private account' to a 'public account', the experimenter will deposit 1/2 dollar in the private accounts of *each* of the subjects. This process will be repeated ten times, and at the end, the subjects can take home whatever they have in their private accounts.

In this public goods game, if all ten subjects are perfectly cooperative, each will put this $1.00 in the public account, and having received $10 in the public account, the experimenter will put $5.00 in the private account of *each* subject on each round, for a total of $50.00 per subject after ten rounds. But if a subject is perfectly selfish, he will keep all of his money in his private account, so if the other nine subjects remain perfectly cooperative, he will end up with $55.00 at the end of the game, and the other players will end up with $45.00 each. If all players are perfectly selfish, each will end up with $10.00 at the end of the game. It is thus clear that this is indeed an iterated prisoner's dilemma, since whatever anyone else does on a particular round, a player's highest payoff comes from contributing nothing to the public account, but if all do this, all receive less than they would had all cooperated.

Public goods experiments of this type have been run literally hundreds of times, under varying conditions, since the pioneering work of the sociologist G. Marwell, the psychologist R. Dawes, the political scientist J. Orbell, and the economists R. Isaac and J. Walker in the late 1970s and early 1980s.[10] We may summarize this research as follows. Only a fraction of subjects conform to the *Homo economicus* model, contributing nothing to the public account. In fact, in the early stages of the game, people generally make contributions that average about halfway between the perfectly cooperative and the perfectly selfish levels. In the later stages of the game, contributions decay until at the end, they are close to the *Homo economicus* level.

Proponents of the *Homo economicus* model initially suggested that the reason for decay of public contribution is that participants really do not understand the game at first, and as they begin to learn it, they begin to realize the superiority of the free-riding strategy. However, there is considerable evidence that this interpretation is incorrect. For instance, Andreoni (1988) finds that when the whole process is repeated with the same subjects, the initial levels of cooperation are restored, but once again cooperation decays as the game progresses. Andreoni (1995) suggests a *Homo reciprocans* explanation for the decay of cooperation: public-spirited contributors want to retaliate against free-riders and the only way available to them in the game is by not contributing themselves.

Support for this *Homo reciprocans* interpretation has been supplied by Fehr and Gächter (1996). The experimenters here allow cooperators to retaliate directly against free-riders, at a cost to themselves. In this context, *Homo economicus* will always free-ride, and will never punish other free-riders, because punishing is itself a public good of little personal benefit to the punisher. In fact, however, the authors find that people do retaliate, and expecting this to happen, potential free-riders do not free-ride. The result is that cooperation begins as expected at about one half the total and over successive rounds *rises* to virtually complete cooperation.[11]

This research into public goods sharing shows an uncanny parallelism with Axelrod's computerized tournaments. Much like the tit-for-tat strategy, *Homo reciprocans* is nice, punishing and forgiving. What is not clear from these experiments is that reciprocity involves a well-developed notion of *fairness*.

The notion of fairness underlying reciprocity is brought out in a series of experiments involving what have come to be known as *ultimatum games* and *dictator games*. In the ultimatum game (Güth, Schmittberger and Schwarz, 1982), the experimenter chooses two subjects and tells the first: 'I am going to provisionally allocate $10.00 to you. You, the proposer, can offer any amount of this, from one cent to the whole $10.00, to the other player, the respondent. If the respondent accepts your offer, he gets that amount and you get whatever is left over. If the respondent rejects your offer, I take back the $10.00 and you each get nothing.' If both proposer and respondent were *Homo economicus* in this game, the proposer would offer the respondent one cent, and the respondent would accept, the proposer walking away with $19.99. In fact, as dozens of replications of this experiment have documented, under varying conditions and with varying amounts of money, proposers commonly offer the respondent very substantial amounts, and respondents frequently reject offers that are below one-third of the total.[12] Similar results have occurred in experiments with stakes as high as three months' earnings.[13]

When asked why they offer more than one cent, proposers commonly say that they are afraid that respondents will consider low offers unfair and reject them as a way to punish proposers' unfairness. When respondents reject offers, they give virtually the same reasons for their actions. The proposers' actions might be explained by selfish motives but the respondents' cannot, and, possibly anticipating the desire of the respondent to punish offers considered to be unfair, the proposer makes a substantial offer. The experimental evidence gives additional support to this interpretation. Thus Roth *et al.* (1991) conducted ultimatum games in four different countries (United States, Yugoslavia, Japan, and Israel), and found that while the level of offers differed in different countries, the probability of an offer being rejected did not. This indicates that both proposers and respondents share the same notion of what is considered 'fair' in that society. In fact, evidence from dictator games indicates that proposers also may act out of fairness motives. In the dictator game, the proposer offers a split of the money and the respondent has no choice but to accept. While proposers could keep all the money themselves, they typically offer respondents a considerable share of the total (Forsythe *et al.*, 1994; Hoffman, McCabe and Smith, 1996b).

A remarkable aspect of these experiments – and one very germane to our concern with redistributive policy – is the degree to which behaviours are affected by the experimentally contrived social relationship between players. Communication among participants prior to the game, or experimental conditions that reduce the subjective 'social distance' among participants, lead to higher and more sustained levels of generosity and cooperation.[14] For example, subjects facing a prisoner's dilemma pay-off structure tended nonetheless to cooperate rather than defect when they were matched with fraternity brothers, but to defect when they were informed that their partner was a police officer (Kollock, 1997). Eckel and Grossman (1997) found that proposers in a dictator game gave more when told that the respondent was the Red Cross, rather than another experimental subject. Finally, when the right to be proposer in the ultimatum game is 'earned', by being a 'winner' in a general knowledge quiz, proposers offered less, and respondents accepted lower offers (Hoffman *et al.* 1994). It appears that minor manipulations of the social context of interactions may support significant behavioural differences.

In all of the experiments, a significant fraction of subjects (about a quarter, typically) conform to the self-interested preferences of *Homo economicus*, and it is often the self-serving behaviour of this minority that, when it goes unpunished, unravels initial generosity and cooperation.

These experiments also indicate that reciprocity is linked to a concept of fairness across all the societies studied, but that the content of fairness is somewhat flexible and subject to varying cultural forces. The following generalizations appear to be compatible with the experimental evidence. This model of *Homo reciprocans* supports our optimism concerning the possibility of egalitarian redistribution. Moreover, it may begin to explain the rising tide of opposition to welfare state policies in the advanced market economies in the past decades. Specifically, in light of the experimental regularities outlined above, we suspect the following to be true as well: redistributive policies that reward people independent of whether and how much they contribute to society are considered unfair and are not supported, even if the intended recipients are otherwise worthy of support, and even if the incidence of non-contribution in the target population is rather low. This would explain the opposition to many welfare measures for the poor, particularly since such measures are thought to have facilitated various social pathologies. At the same time it explains the continuing support for Social Security and Medicare in the United States, since the public perception is that the recipients are 'deserving' and the policies are incentive compatible. The public goods experiments are also consistent with the notion that tax resistance by the non-wealthy may stem from their perception that the well-to-do are not paying their fair share.

The implication of this analysis concerning our proposal for asset-based redistribution is straightforward. First, asset-based egalitarian redistribution, on the grounds that it can be efficiency enhancing, and by relocating control of productive resources to direct producers, increases the scope for policies involving egalitarian wealth redistribution. Second, because asset-based redistribution makes the recipients residual claimants on the consequences of their actions, their rewards are more likely to be considered fair, and hence approved of by *Homo reciprocans*, thus justifying the social policies leading to these rewards.

3.4 Conclusion: recasting egalitarianism

In other work (Bowles and Gintis, 1996) we have stressed the importance of developing *economically efficient* egalitarian policies. In the current essay we have stressed the need to design egalitarian policies that affirm and evoke widely held *moral sentiments*.

There is an obvious criticism of this new direction in our argument. 'Morality is socially determined', we hear the reader musing, 'so why not transform morality to fit the needs of egalitarian policy rather than the other way round?' Have not radical egalitarians, from nineteenth century abolitionists to contemporary feminists and civil libertarians, made consciousness raising a central part of their political practice? Why bow to the puny morality instilled by a society that thrives on greed, when we can look for a model of moral sentiments to the Enlightenment idea of the 'perfectibility of Man' and the socialist ideal of 'from each according to his ability, to each according to his need'? Why, in short, be trapped by the present in designing a future?

Our answer is that we have no choice. Abolitionists, feminists, civil libertarians, and advocates of the welfare state alike have been successful in appealing to the more elevated human motives precisely when they have shown that domination and inequality violate fundamental notions of reciprocal fairness and may be overcome, or at least attenuated, by policies and institutions consistent with these motives. Countless other egalitarian initiatives have failed.

The human mind is not a blank slate that is equally disposed to accept whatever moral rules are presented to it as valid, right and just. Rather, human beings are predisposed to accept some moral rules, others can be imposed upon them with some difficulty, and still others cannot be imposed in any stable manner at all. Barrington Moore, Jr., in his comparative study of revolution and revolt, expresses this idea in the following words: '... awareness of social injustice would be impossible if human beings could be made to accept any and all rules. Evidently there are some constraints on the making of moral rules and therefore on the possible forms of moral outrage' (1978: 5).

What accounts for our moral predispositions? The answer, uncontroversially, is some combination of genes and culture. Neither is immutable but, likewise, neither is amenable to reconstruction in an arbitrary and ahistorical manner. The cultural and the genetic structures that frame our lives and affect our propensity to accept or reject particular moral principles are products of social and biological evolution. Moral principles succeed, not because they conform to a particular philosophical, political, or religious logic, but because they have aided those individuals who have used them and those groups in which they have been prevalent. The individuals and social groups that have deployed these moral principles have flourished, while others that have not have perished or been assimilated.

The question as to whether genes or culture is more responsible for the inertial character of moral sentiments is not the issue, since genes and culture are evidently jointly responsible, and it is the nature of their interaction that is of importance for social change. Again, quoting Barrington Moore:

> To the extent that there are any recurring or constant features in moral outrage, they would have to derive from the interaction between more or less constant aspects of human nature and equally recurring imperatives that stem from the fact that human beings live with each other, that is, in human society.
>
> (1978: 5)

This is not to say that cultural change is always conservative and slow-moving, for we know that this is not the case. Rather it is to say that cultural change, like technical change, is subject to enduring laws and material constraints. The evidence is that among these regularities is the ease with which people assume the behaviour of *Homo reciprocans* and the difficulty of devising egalitarian principles that violate norms of reciprocity. If we are correct, an egalitarian society can be built on the basis of these norms.

Notes

1 On goals, see Roemer (1993) and Parijs (1995).
2 One hardly need add that Jefferson's egalitarian impulse did not extend to women or to his or anyone else's slaves.
3 See Roemer (1996, Chapters 5–8), for an elaboration of an egalitarian ethic based on personal responsibility. In some cases this goal may not be completely attainable. For instance, if an 'accident of birth' includes having irresponsible and uncaring parents, then indemnifying this accident rewards, and hence implicitly encourages, irresponsible parenting.
4 See Levy and Murnane (1992) for the Gini coefficient statistics and U.S. Bureau of the Census (1993) for victimization rates.
5 Lane (1991: 524–47) surveys the evidence. In one study of the United States (Oswald, 1994), being unemployed (statistically holding income constant) has a larger negative impact on subjective well-being than having one's

income halved, being divorced, separated or widowed. This is true for both men and women.
6 We have considerable confidence in the conclusions of Flannery et al. (1989), in part because their study was replicated in a similar but distinct population. D. A. Weinstein, H. H. Shugart and C. C. Brandt (1983) studied the Quechua indians of the Peruvian highlands, concluding: 'A population without substructures for resource sharing is shown to be unstable in such an unpredictable environment.... Under such potential conditions of intense selection, complex sharing institutions should develop and be maintained' (201, 222).
7 The term is Ernst Fehr's. See Fehr and Tyran (1996).
8 See Axelrod and Hamilton (1981) and Axelrod (1984) for details and theoretical development. The iterated prisoner's dilemma is simply repeated play of the well known game with 'winners' being those with high cumulative scores over however many rounds are played.
9 The details of this simulation are available from the authors.
10 For a summary of this research and an extensive bibliography, see Ledyard (1995).
11 These results are reported in Fehr, Gächter and Kirchsteiger (1997). For a similar outcome in an employer/employee simulation in which 'employers' can pay higher than market-clearing wages in hopes that 'workers' will reciprocate by supplying high level of effort, see Fehr and Gächter (1996).
12 For examples and analyses of ultimatum games, see Forsythe, Horowitz, Savin and Sefton (1994); Hoffman, McCabe, Shachat and Smith (1994); Hoffman, McCabe and Smith (1996a); Roth, Prasnikar, Okuno-Fujiwara and Zamir (1991).
13 See Cameron (1995) on experiments in Indonesia and Fehr and Tougareva (1995) on experiments in Russia.
14 For the communication result, see Isaac and Walker (1988), and for the social distance result, see Kollock (1997).

References

Andreoni, J. (1988) 'Why Free Ride? Strategies and Learning in Public Good Experiments', *Journal of Public Economics*, 37: 291–304.
Andreoni, J. (1995) 'Cooperation in Public Goods Experiments: Kindness or Confusion', *American Economic Review*, 85(4): 891–904.
Axelrod, R. (1984) *The Evolution of Cooperation*, New York: Basic Books.
Axelrod, R. and Hamilton, W. D. (1981) 'The Evolution of Cooperation', *Science*, 211: 1390–6.
Bowles, S. and Gintis, H. (1996) 'Efficient Redistribution: New Rules for Markets, States, and Communities', *Politics & Society*, 24(4): 307–42.
Bowles, S. and Gintis, H. (1998) *Recasting Egalitarianism: New Rules for Markets, States, and Communities*, London: Verso.
Cameron, L. (1995) 'Raising the Stakes in the Ultimatum Game: Experimental Evidence from Indonesia', Discussion Paper #345, Department of Economics, Princeton University.

Eckel, C. and Grossman, P. (1997) 'Chivalry and Solidarity in Ultimatum Games', Working Paper #E92-23, Virginia Polytechnic Institute.

Fehr, E. and Gächter, S. (1996) 'Cooperation and Punishment', Working Paper, Institute for Empirical Economic Research, University of Zürich.

Fehr, E., Gächter, S. and Kirchsteiger, G. (1997), 'Reciprocity as a Contract Enforcement Device', *Econometrica*, 65(4): 833–960.

Fehr, E. and Tougareva, E. (1995) 'Do Competitive Markets with High Stakes Remove Reciprocal Fairness? Experimental Evidence from Russia', Working Paper, Institute for Empirical Economic Research, University of Zürich.

Fehr, E. and Tyrant, J.-R. (1996), 'Institutions and Reciprocal Fairness', *Nordic Journal of Political Economy*.

Flannery, K., Marcus, J. and Reynolds, R. (1989) *The Flocks of the Wamani: A Study of Llama Herders on the Puntas of Ayacucho, Peru*, San Diego: Academic Press.

Forsythe, R., Horowitz, J., Savin, N. E. and Sefton, M. (1994) 'Replicability, Fairness and Pay in Experiments with Simple Bargaining Games', *Games and Economic Behavior*, 6(3): 347–69.

Güth, W., Schmittberger R. and Schwarz, B. (1982) 'An Experimental Analysis of Ultimatum Bargaining', *Journal of Economic Behavior and Organization*, 3: 367–88.

Hoffman, E., McCabe, K. and Smith, V. L. (1996a) 'Social Distance and Other-Regarding Behavior in Dictator Games', *American Economic Review*, 86(3): 653–60.

Hoffman, E., McCabe, K. and Smith, V. L. (1996b) 'Behavioral Foundations of Reciprocity: Experimental Economics and Evolutionary Psychology', April (unpublished).

Hoffman, E., McCabe, K., Shachat, K. and Smith, V. L. (1994) 'Preferences, Property Rights, and Anonymity in Bargaining Games', *Games and Economic Behavior*, 7: 346–80.

Isaac, R. M. and Walker, J. M. (1988) 'Group Size Effects in Public Goods Provision: The Voluntary Contribution Mechanism', *Quarterly Journal of Economics*, 103: 179–200.

Jefferson, T. (1950) *The Papers of Thomas Jefferson, Volume I: 1760–1776*, edited by Julian P. Boyd, Princeton, NJ: Princeton University Press.

Kahneman, D. (1993) *The Cognitive Psychology of Consequences and Moral Intuition*, Princeton, NJ: Princeton University Press.

Kollock, P. (1997) 'Transforming Social Dilemmas: Group Identity and Cooperation', in Peter Danielson (ed.) *Modeling Rational and Moral Agents* Oxford: Oxford University Press.

Lane, R. (1991) *The Market Experience*, Cambridge: Cambridge University Press.

Ledyard, J. O. (1995) 'Public Goods: A Survey of Experimental Research', in J. H. Kagel and A. E. Roth (eds.) *The Handbook of Experimental Economics*, Princeton, NJ: Princeton University Press, pp. 111–94.

Levy, F. and Murnane, R. (1992) 'U.S. Earnings Levels and Earnings Inequality: A Review of Recent Trends and Proposed Explanations', *Journal of Economic Literature*, 30(3): 1333–81.

Moore, Jr. B. (1978) *Injustice: The Social Bases of Obedience and Revolt*, White Plains: M. E. Sharpe.

Oswald, A. (1994) 'Four Pieces of the Unemployment Puzzle', Working Paper, London School of Economics.

Parijs, P. Van (1995) *Real Freedom for All: What (if Anything) can Justify Capitalism?*, Cambridge: Cambridge University Press.

Parsons, T. (1964) 'Evolutionary Universals in Society', *American Sociological Review*, 29(3).

Roemer, J. (1993) *A Future for Socialism*, Cambridge: Harvard University Press.

Roemer, J.(1996) *Theories of Distributive Justice*, Cambridge: Harvard University Press.

Roth, A. E., Prašnikar, V., Okuno-Fujiwara, M. and Zamir, S. (1991) 'Bargaining and Market Behavior in Jerusalem, Ljubljana, Pittsburgh, and Tokyo: An Experimental Study', *American Economic Review*, 81(5): 1068–95.

Tocqueville, A. de (1933/69) *Democracy in America*, Garden City, N.Y.: Doubleday and Company.

US Bureau of the Census (1993) *National Crime Survey*, Washington: Government Printing Office.

Weinstein, D. A., Shugart, H. H. and Brandt, C. C. (1983), 'Energy Flow and the Persistence of a Human Population: A Simulation Analysis', *Human Ecology*, 11(2): 201–23.

Wright, E. O. (1994) *Interrogating Inequality*, London: Verso.

4
Determinants of Cross-Country Income Inequality: An 'Augmented' Kuznets Hypothesis*

Branko Milanović

4.1 Introduction

This paper presents an alternative hypothesis as to why income inequality differs between countries. The only currently existing hypothesis was formulated by Kuznets (1955). Kuznets' hypothesis is briefly reviewed in Section 4.2. It provides an indispensable background to our 'augmented' Kuznets' hypothesis which is formulated in Section 4.3. The empirical assessment of our hypothesis is presented in Section 4.4. The hypothesis is tested on a cross-sectional sample of 80 countries including all OECD countries, all European (former) socialist countries, and 50 African, Asian, and Latin American countries. The data are from the 1980s. Section 4.5 spells out the main conclusions and implications of our hypothesis.

4.2 The background: the Kuznets relationship

When it comes to factors that explain differences in income-size distribution between countries, there exists only one broad hypothesis, proposed almost 40 years ago by Simon Kuznets (1955). It became famous as the 'Kuznets inverted U curve'. The hypothesis states that at very low levels of income, income inequality must also be low, as practically

---

*I would like to thank Yvonne Ying and Vesna Petrović for excellent research assistance. I would also like to thank, for very useful comments, Anthony Atkinson, Andrea Brandolini, Annette Brown, Alan Gelb, Bill Easterly, Ravi Kanbur, Martin Ravallion, Klaus Schmidt-Hebbel, Gur Ofer, Milan Vodopivec and Mike Walton, participants of a World Bank seminar and International Economic Association Congress in Tunis in December 1995 where the paper was presented, and the two anonymous reviewers. The views expressed are solely my own; I am also solely responsible for any remaining mistakes.

everybody lives at, or close to, subsistence level. There is no room for increased inequality because with the small size of overall output, increased inequality would push many people below the subsistence level. As the process of growth begins, income inequality increases. People migrate from the traditional agricultural sector where incomes are low to the modern industrial sector where both the (expected) wage is higher and wage differentiation is greater. Kuznets' model is also consistent with the Lewis-type pattern of growth. At the early stage of development, both physical and human capital are scarce and unequally distributed (that is, heavily concentrated among the few), and owners of human and physical capital are able to command high returns. As the two types of capital accumulate and become more diffused among the population, the rate of return on the physical capital declines while wage differentials between skilled and unskilled labour diminish. Income distribution becomes more equal. The process was summarized by Kuznets (1966: 217) as follows:

> It seems plausible to assume that in the process of growth, the earlier periods are characterized by a balance of counteracting forces that may have widened the inequality in the size distribution of total income for a while because of the rapid growth of the non-A [non-agricultural] sector and wider inequality within it. It is even more plausible to argue that the recent narrowing in income inequality observed in the developed countries was due to a combination of the narrowing inter-sectoral inequalities in product per worker, the decline in the share of property incomes in total incomes of households, and the institutional changes that reflect decisions concerning social security and full employment.[1]

Kuznets' empirical relationship has been extensively studied in both the cross-country and inter-temporal contexts. It remains the subject of controversy.[2] The controversy has centered on: (1) the very existence of the relationship (it was argued that the Kuznets relationship critically depends on the Latin American countries which are at an intermediate stage of development, and for reasons peculiar to them, exhibit high inequality);[3] (2) its validity for different countries and regions;[4] and (3) its validity for different epochs. Kaelble and Thomas (1991: 32) have recently thus summarized the empirical results of the Kuznets hypothesis:

> Income levels explain only a small part of the variance of the inequality measures. This suggests that national characteristics (whether in

50 *Determinants of Income Inequality*

terms of economic structure, political institutions, socio-cultural heritage, or whatever) play an important part in determining exactly what level of inequality is to be found at any particular level of modernization.

No comprehensive alternative hypothesis regarding determinants of income inequality has so far been suggested, however.

It is worth pointing out, in light of the alternative hypothesis proposed here, that the Kuznets hypothesis puts at centre stage the role of economic factors, that is, the supply of, and demand for, various factors of production.[5] The forces of economic development determine the shape of income distribution. Societies do not choose the income distribution that they would like to have. The process is led by inexorable economic forces, and deviations from the income distribution that a country must have at a certain level of development are small and non-systematic.

4.3 A new hypothesis

Here I propose an 'augmented' Kuznets' hypothesis. I argue that income-size distribution is determined (1) by a factor that is in the short-run, from the point of view of policy makers or society as a whole, 'given'; and (2) by social (or public policy) choice. The given factor is the level of development measured by income (GDP) per capita. The public policy factors are (1) the percentage of workers employed in the state and para-statal sectors; and (2) the extent of government transfers, measured as a share of a country's GDP. These two factors are the products of political decisions, both current and past (for example, a country might have a large state sector because of a strong past influence of socialist parties). In the empirical section that follows, I will address two key questions: (1) Are social choice factors statistically significant 'explanators' of cross-country income inequality; and (2) if so, how large is their influence?

Our hypothesis says that, once income is 'accounted for', there is still sizeable discretion regarding income inequality. Income distribution is viewed also as the product of *social choices* mediated through elections, lobbying of various social groups, societal preferences or historical developments. Thus, some countries may have a greater proportion of state-sector workers because socialist or Communist parties were historically stronger; or the population may have a high preference for eradicating poverty and redistributing income through transfers; or the middle classes which decisively determine the size of transfers in developed democracies may have had experience of downward mobility and may regard transfers as an insurance proposition (lest they become poor) as argued by Lindert (1989 and 1991). In any case, variables such as the size of the state sector and the size of transfers will be determined through the interaction of social forces or, put more broadly, by the political economy of the country.

Consider now the influence of the two 'social choice' elements in greater detail. The large size of the state sector will tend to reduce inequality because of a more compressed wage distribution existing in the state compared to the private sector. More bureaucratic structures, in which earnings are largely determined by seniority and academic credentials, are believed to reward those at the top relatively less and to pay those at the bottom relatively more. This is confirmed by empirical studies. Bishop, Formby, and Thistle (1991: 430) find that wage distribution in the US government sector is consistently more egalitarian than in manufacturing, services or agriculture (all of which are entirely private). Meron (1991) obtains the same result for France. Blank (1993: 29–30) writes:

> Public sector workers [in the US and the UK] face more compressed wage distribution than do private sector workers. For almost every occupation in every year in both countries, both the 10th per centile and the 90th per centile of wages in the public sector are closer to the mean public sector wages than are 10th per centile and 90th per centile of wages in the private sector.

Further confirmation of the levelling tendencies present in state-owned enterprises is provided by the former socialist countries, where the majority of workers (outside agriculture) were employed in the state sector. Wage distribution in socialism tends to be more equal than in capitalism. Thus Phelps-Brown (1988: 303) writes that lower inequality in Soviet-type economies 'arises mainly from a slower rise of income above the median, that is, broadly: the more skilled manual occupations and still more the higher clerical, the professional and administrative, are paid less than in the West relatively to the bulk of manual workers'.[6]

There is yet another reason why a high level of state involvement in the organization of an economy may lead to lower inequality. The point was made by Hirschman (1973: 558):

> [if] decision-making is perceived to be largely decentralized, individual advances are attributed to chance, or possibly merit (or demerit).

When decision making is known to be centralized, such advances will be attributed to favoritism. ... [Centralized systems] will strain to be more egalitarian not just because they want to, but also because they have to: centralization of decision making largely deprives them of tolerance for inequality that is available to more decentralized systems.

I am not aware of previous attempts to link explicitly, at the economy-wide level, the share of the state-sector employment to income-size inequality. Some indirect attempts were made – for example, through the introduction of the dummy variable for socialist countries. In some studies (for example, Kaelble and Thomas, 1991, or Ahluwalia, 1976) the socialist dummy variable was found to be significant (lowering inequality) while in others its effect was negligible (Dye and Ziegler, 1988). Here, however, I propose to use a continuous variable that spans almost the entire theoretical spectrum from 100 per cent of state employment (USSR and Czechoslovakia before the change of the regime), to almost 0 per cent (for example, 3 per cent for Madagascar and Senegal).

The extent of government transfers will also tend to reduce inequality. The relationship, however, is not unambiguous, because the reduction in inequality achieved by a given amount of government transfers will vary. The reduction of inequality will depend on the extent to which transfers are focused on the poor. If most transfers are captured by those who pay taxes out of which the transfers are financed, the reduction in inequality may be small (the theory of the middle class capture of benefits, as argued by Le Grand, 1982, and Sawyer, 1982). However, on balance, the larger the transfers are, the greater will be the reduction in inequality, even if the marginal impact of transfers may be diminishing.

4.4 Testing the new hypothesis

4.4.1 The data

The sample consists of 22 OECD countries, 8 socialist European countries including the former Soviet Union, 16 African, 17 Asian, and 17 Latin American countries. For these 80 countries I have been able to collect the necessary information, compatible in both the definition of the variables and the time-period (early to mid-1980s). These 80 countries account for 97 per cent of world GDP and 90 per cent of world population. Some data-related issues are discussed in Annex. A full list of the countries, the data used, and their sources are given in Annex Tables 1–4 and are available from the author on request. The explanatory variables are the following: INCOME = the country's purchasing power 1988 GDP per capita (in thousands of 1988 international dollars); STATE = the percentage of economically active population who work in the state sector (inclusive of government administration); and TRANS = the percentage share of cash and in-kind social transfers (pensions, maternity and family allowances, temporary sick pay, unemployment compensations, education, and health) in the country's GDP. The dependent variable is the Gini coefficient of disposable income (GINI)[7] expressed for convenience in percentages: Gini coefficient of 30 (instead of 0.3).[8]

Two points need to be clarified. An apparent inconsistency may be detected between the inclusion of in-kind transfers like education and health in the TRANS variable, and disposable income inequality (which *excludes* public in-kind transfers) in the GINI variable. The rationale for this is that transfers in kind over the period with which we are concerned here reflect their long-term importance in the country's GDP, and that the same or similar level of *past* spendings on health and education affect the recorded inequality in the mid-1980's. In other words, while current health and education spending may not have much to do with current inequality, a higher level of such past spending will tend to depress current inequality (for example, more widely spread public education may reduce wage differences). However, one might wonder if that is indeed the case and prefer a more narrow definition of transfers where TRANS includes only current cash transfers: I shall use such a formulation too.[9]

Secondly, the analysis is conducted in per capita terms rather than in terms of equivalent consumption units. There are several reasons for this. There are practical ones, because most of the income distribution data for non-OECD countries are expressed in per capita terms. There are also more substantive reasons for using the per capita measure. First, if we require that GINI be reported in equivalent units, should we not require the same for GDP? Second, and the more compelling reason, is that the very idea of equivalency units is country-dependent (or rather, price-structure dependent). If rents, for example, are subsidized, then economies of scale are much less important than if they are not; if education is private, the cost of children is much higher than if education is public and free.[10] In consequence, the use of per capita measures has both practical and substantive advantages.

54 *Determinants of Income Inequality*

Table 4.1 Summary statistics for the five regions

Region	GINI	STATE	TRANS	INCOME	Number of countries
OECD	31.2	21.2	22.6	12501	22
E. Europe	24.8	90.0	17.2	6234	8
Africa	52.3	11.3	5.7	1778	16
Asia	41.0	12.6	6.8	4851	17
L. America	49.2	19.3	7.6	4156	17

All the statistics are unweighted averages.
Definition of the variables:

GINI: Gini coefficient of disposable income for OECD and socialist economies; Gini coefficient of gross income for Africa, Asia and Latin America. Gini coefficients are expressed in per cent.

STATE: Share of state-sector workers (general government and state-owned enterprises) in total labour force.

TRANS: Share of cash and in-kind social transfers in GDP, in per cent.

INCOME: Purchasing power GDP in international dollars for 1988.

4.4.2 Empirical analysis

Table 4.1 gives summary statistics for the five regions. The most important conclusions are the following.

- In terms of income inequality, the five regions have distinctly different averages: inequality is highest in Africa (Gini of 52), closely followed by Latin America (49), then Asia (41), OECD countries (31), while the European socialist economies are the most equal (25).
- Eastern Europe and the former Soviet Union have a much larger share of state-sector employment than does any other region (90 per cent); the African and Asian samples have the lowest share (11 to 12 per cent of the labour force).
- The size of social transfers is much greater in OECD and socialist countries than elsewhere.

Figures 4.1a–4.1c display the relationship between GINI and the three explanatory variables. We test first equation (1.0). The income variable is quadratic, since we test for the existence of an inverted U-shaped relationship. β_3 and β_4 are expected to have negative signs.[11] The observations in all the regressions are arranged in

$$\text{GINI} = \beta_0 + \beta_1 \ln(\text{INCOME}) + \beta_2 [\ln(\text{INCOME})]^2 + \beta_3 \text{ STATE} + \beta_4 \text{TRANS}$$
(1.0)

ascending order according to INCOME; each country has an equal weight.

All the coefficients (see Table 4.2) have the predicted sign and are statistically significant at 1 per cent level.[12] The intercept is not statistically significantly different from zero. This means that, for a sufficiently low per capita income (at the limit for INCOME=0) and in the absence of state sector employment and transfers, the Gini coefficient would be close to zero: that is, no inequality would exist. The adjusted coefficient of determination is 0.70.[13] The interpretation of the results is as follows. Each ten percentage point increase in the share of state-sector workers reduces inequality, on average, by 2.2 Gini points; each increase in social transfers by 10 GDP percentage points lowers inequality by 4.15 Gini points. The relationship between income level and inequality is quadratic: at first, inequality rises with income and then declines. The turning point is reached for $2100 per capita (at 1988 international prices) which is broadly the level of income of the Philippines, Swaziland, or Sri Lanka.[14]

There is a heteroskedasticity problem with equation (1.0). It was observed in the literature (see Lindert and Williamson, 1985: 344; Lecaillon *et al.*, 1984: 40) that the dispersion of the Gini is greater at low than at high income levels. One can therefore expect some heteroskedasticity because standard errors would systematically decline with increase in income level. Indeed, this is exactly the case, as shown in Figure 4.2, where residuals from equation (1.0) are plotted against income levels. Regression (1) is the same as (1.0) except that I correct for heteroskedasticity by running OLS with White's heteroskedastic-consistent standard errors.[15] Values of the coefficients do not change. Significance of STATE or TRANS is also unaffected but the two income terms become statistically significant at 5 per cent level rather than at 1 per cent as in regression 1.0. Since the same problem exists in all equations, all regressions will henceforth be run with the correction for heteroskedasticity. I shall explore next whether these results are sufficiently robust to a different specification of *each* of the variables used here. I shall start with the dependent variable, a measure of inequality.[16] As explained in the Annex, I have collected the income Gini coefficients for 80 countries for the period of the 1980s with a specific purpose to use it for this study (I call it, for simplicity, even if somewhat self-servingly, the Milanović data set).[17] Since inequality measures are notoriously fickle, one can wonder if the same results would obtain with inequality measures coming from a different source. To do this, I use the Deininger and Squire (1996) 'high-quality' data set

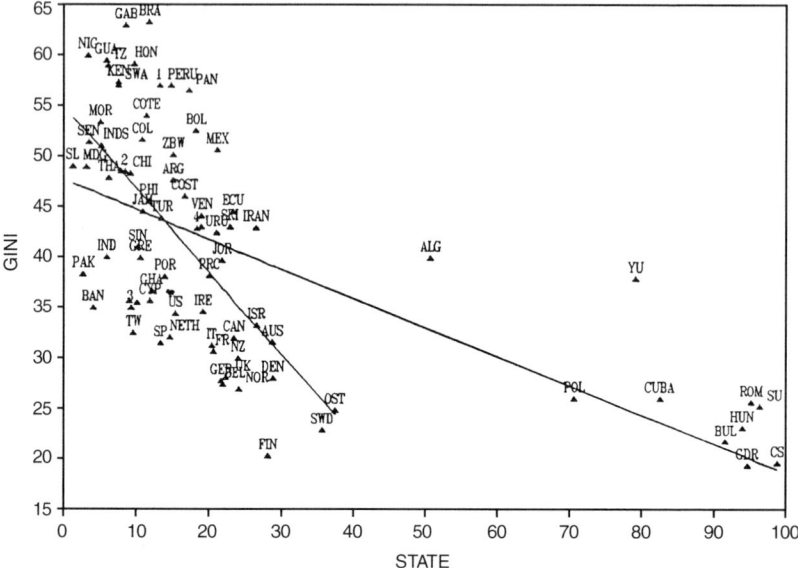

Figure 4.1a Relationship between GINI and STATE
Note: Steeper regression excludes socialist countries.

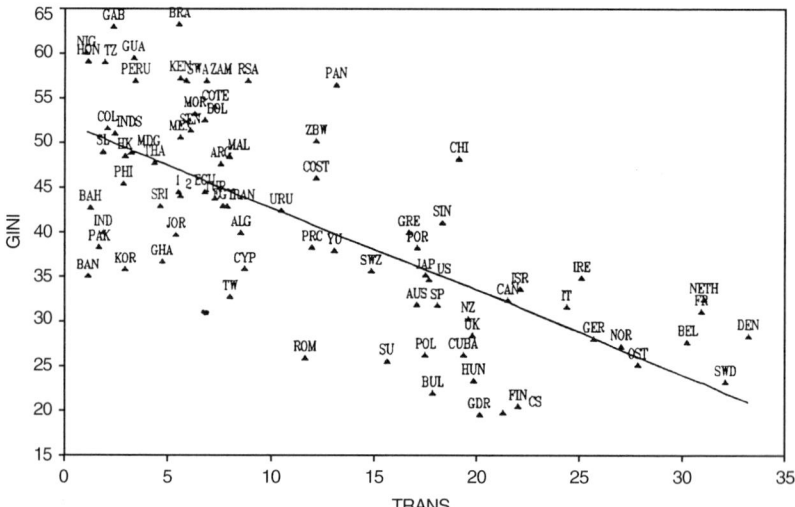

Figure 4.1b Relationship between GINI and TRANS

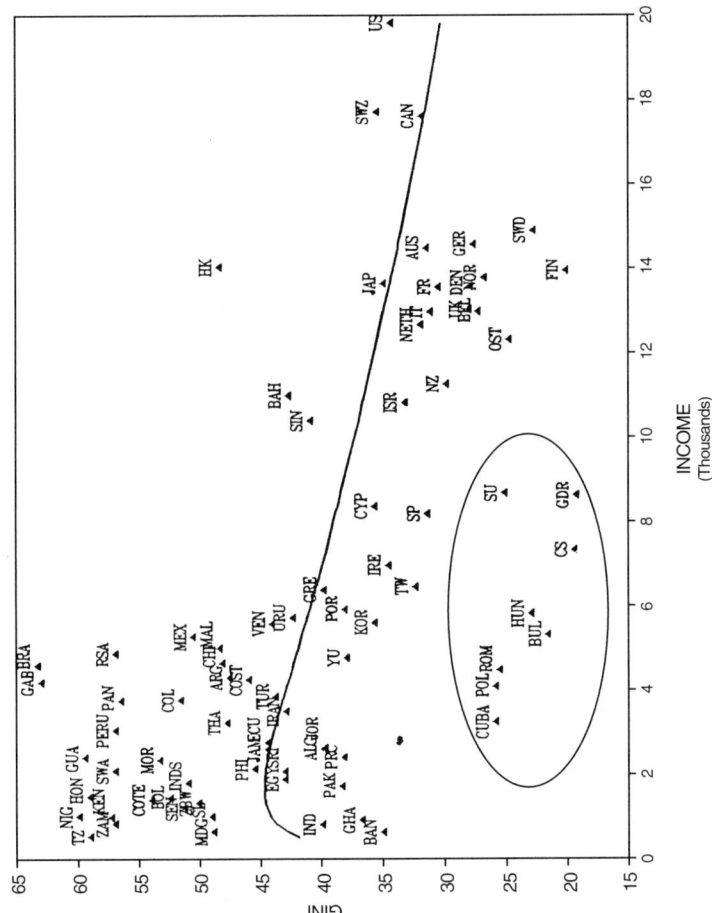

Figure 4.1c Relationship between GINI and INCOME
Socialist countries shown in the circle.
Regression is: GINI = Constant + $B_0 \ln(\text{INCOME}) + B_1 \ln(\text{INCOME})^2$.

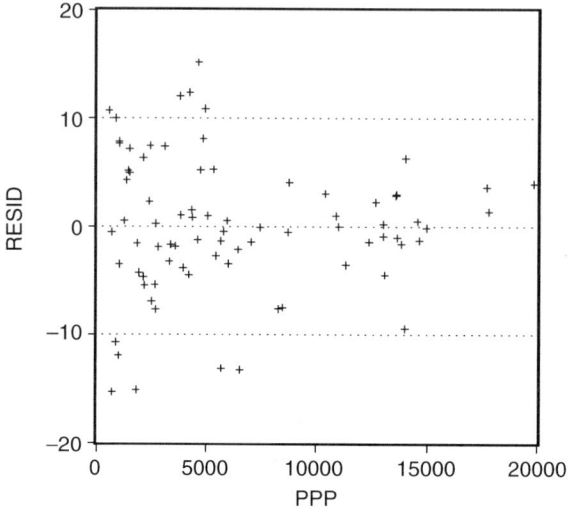

Figure 4.2 Residuals from equation 1.0 as a function of INCOME
PPP = GDP per capita in 1988 dollars of equal purchasing power parity.
RESID = residuals from equation 1.0.

which had become available since the first draft of this study was completed. The Deininger–Squire data set is an unbalanced panel of inequality measures for 101 countries covering the period from the 1950s onward. Unfortunately for my purpose, it combines both income and expenditure inequality measures: for a number of countries, only the distribution of expenditures is available.[18] For each of the 80 countries in my sample, I have selected from the Deininger–Squire data base, the Gini coefficient and the quintile ratio[19] based on income (or if unavailable, expenditures) from the mid-1980s. The sample size declines to 70 due to the fact that 10 countries from my data set are not included in the Deininger–Squire set. Equation 1 is then rerun first, over the Gini coefficients from the Deininger–Squire data set (equation 1A), and then over the quintile ratios from the same set (equation 1B). The signs of all the coefficients are the same as predicted and as in equation 1. All coefficients except the one for TRANS remain statistically highly significant, and their values (except for TRANS) change very little (compare, for example, equations 1 and 1A in Table 4.2).[20] The $\bar{R}^2$ decreases from 0.7 to 0.42, and the constant term becomes significant at 5 per cent level. The results seem robust to the use of an alternative data base, and I return to the discussion of other results using the Milanović data set.[21]

Are our results, and in particular the role of STATE, perhaps driven by the presence of socialist countries and their high share of state-sector employment? Regression (2) is the same as regression (1) except that all socialist countries (7 from Eastern Europe, the Soviet Union, Algeria, China, and Cuba) are dropped. The values of the coefficients change but slightly: the coefficient of STATE becomes, in absolute terms, greater, rising from -0.22 to -0.29 (see also Figure 4.1a where the regression line becomes steeper when socialist countries are omitted) and the coefficient of TRANS becomes smaller (in absolute terms). Both income coefficients increase and their statistical significance rises. The $\bar{R}^2$ decreases from 0.7 to 0.63. Overall, the inclusion or exclusion of socialist countries makes little difference.

The steeper relationship between STATE and GINI when socialist countries are omitted requires an explanation. It implies that decreases in inequality recorded by socialist countries are small compared with the huge size of the state sector in their economies. Indeed, even from the summary Table 4.1, it can be seen that while the difference in GINI between East European countries and, say, OECD countries is only some 6 Gini points, employment in the state sector is more than four times greater in Eastern Europe. Therefore, when socialist countries are dropped from the sample, a given increase in state-sector share produces larger decreases in GINI.

Another issue is whether our STATE variable really adds something to the common practice of using a dummy variable for socialist countries in income distribution studies. We argued above that STATE is more general because it covers the whole spectrum of values from 0 to 100, and thus differentiates also between various capitalist (or even socialist) countries. In regression (3), I introduce both STATE and a socialist dummy variable (otherwise the regression is the same as 1). The regression coefficients are practically unchanged. Only the coefficient of STATE decreases somewhat (from -0.22 to -0.185) but remains highly significant. The dummy variable is statistically insignificant. We can reject the hypothesis that the dummy variable is statistically significant in presence of STATE.

Would our results be affected by a somewhat different, narrower, definition of TRANS? In equation 4, I use the TRANS variable which is defined as the share of social cash transfers (pensions, family allowance, unemployment benefits, social assistance) in GDP.[22] The values of the coefficients and the significance levels are almost the same as in regression 1. The $\bar{R}^2$ increases to 0.74.

Finally, do our results depend on the countries' population structure? It is sometimes argued that the share of transfers in GDP depends largely on the population age structure: 'older' countries will tend (everything else being the same) to spend more because of higher pension and health expenditures needed for the other people.[23] In equation 5, I use the 'old' TRANS which includes both transfers in kind and cash to express it per equivalent adult, where the weight attached to the people under the age of 14 is 1/2.[24] The significance of the income variables now decreases somewhat, but the equation practically remains the same as regression 1 (except for the change in the value of β_4 due to the scaling of TRANS).[25]

4.4.3 Is Asia different?

From Figure 4.3a, which displays residuals from regression (1), it emerges that in the case of Asian countries, the actual level of inequality is often smaller than predicted. Out of six countries whose actual inequality is 10 Gini points (about one-and-half standard deviations) and more below the predicted inequality, five are Asian (Bangladesh, India, Pakistan, South Korea and Taiwan).[26] Also, out of 17 Asian countries, in only four is the actual inequality higher than the predicted inequality. However, in African and Latin American economies, inequality seems to deviate upward from the predicted values.

Several possible explanations for the contrast between Asia and other continents can be adduced. For example, more equal distribution of physical and human capital in Asian countries may result in lower market (pre-government involvement) inequality. Then, even if transfers are small, inequality in disposable income (that is, after transfers and taxes) will be less than in the countries in which the underlying market distribution of income is skewed. Take, for example, Taiwan and Uruguay, both probably the most highly educated and among the most developed countries in their respective regions. The per capita GDPs of these countries are very close ($6500 for Taiwan and $5800 for Uruguay). Uruguay's share of state-sector workers is twice as high as Taiwan's (21 vs. 10 per cent), and social transfers are greater (10.5 per cent of GDP vs. 8.1 per cent). Yet Taiwan's Gini coefficient is 32 and Uruguay's is 42. But the average number of years of education completed by the population over 25 years of age is 9.2 years for Taiwan and 7.8 years for Uruguay. The high importance of education in Taiwan is also reflected in the structure of social transfers: while total social transfers, in terms of GDP, are smaller in Taiwan, public education expenditures are three times as high: 4.6 per cent of GDP in

Taiwan vs. 1.5 per cent in Uruguay. Another indicator of the high dispersal of assets in Taiwan is the proportion of stock-owning population, which at 27 per cent is twice as large as in most West European countries and about the same as in the United States.

One possible explanation of the lower (than predicted) inequality in Asia may then lie in a more equal distribution of physical and human capital. The former is extremely difficult to approximate; the latter can be approximated by the spread and depth of education. I introduce (equation 6) the average number of school years completed by the population 25 years of age or older (EDUC).[27] However, because of strong collinearity between education and income, no new insight is obtained. These two variables can be used practically as substitutes. The introduction of education renders both INCOME terms statistically insignificant. Moreover, EDUC does not reduce the downward deviation of GINI observed in Asian countries (not shown here). Education, therefore, does not provide an independent explanation (that is, an explanation that is different from what is implied by income) for the lower inequality in Asia.[28]

We are left with the alternative of introducing a dummy variable for Asian countries (equation 7). This improves the fit and eliminates the systematic negative residuals for the Asian countries (Figure 4.3b). All the coefficients, including those of both INCOME terms, are statistically significant at less than 1 per cent level. The dummy variable has the expected negative sign and is highly significant: Asian countries have, all other elements being the same, an income inequality that is some 8.2 Gini points less than that of non-Asian countries. This, of course, is not an entirely satisfactory conclusion because we are unable to explain what real factors lie behind the observed lower inequality in Asia.

4.4.4 What explains the differences in inequality?

On the basis of these results we can find the causes for the difference in the levels of inequality between the five groups of countries. OECD countries are used as a yardstick and the difference in GINI between them and the other groups is explained by the differences in social choice variables (state-sector employment and transfers), 'given' variable (income level), and an Asia dummy. I use regression 7 for the calculations. The results are displayed in Table 4.3. In the case of Latin America, Asia and Africa, the main reasons for greater inequality, in comparison with OECD countries, are lower transfers (which explain between 8.4 and 9.4 additional Gini points) and lower income (which explains between 6.2 and 7.3 additional Gini points). These two

Table 4.2 The regressions: dependent variable GINI (except in equation 1B: quintile ratio)

Regressions	No. of countries	Constant	STATE	TRANS	INCOME	INCOME^2	DUMMY	EDUC	$\bar{R}^2(F)$	SE (DW)
1.0	80	−97.08 (0.11)	–	–	39.80** (0.009)	–	–	–	0.70 (46.4)	6.449 (1.99)
1 (White correction)	80	−97.08 (0.21)	0.223** (0.000)	0.416** (0.002)	–	2.608** (0.006)	–	–	0.70 (46.4)	6.449 (1.99)
1A (Deininger Squire data)	70	−146.7* (0.04)	0.223** (0.000)	0.416** (0.000)	39.80* (0.035)	−2.608* (0.020)	–	–	0.41 (13.1)	7.994 (1.81)
1B (quintile ratio)	70	−126.2* (0.01)	0.214** (0.000)	−0.292 (0.070)	48.16** (0.006)	2.941** (0.006)	–	–	0.23 (6.0)	5.431 (1.8)
2 (without socialist)	69	−113.2 (0.16)	0.010** (0.000)	−0.116 (0.240)	34.07** (0.009)	2.059** (0.01)	–	–	0.63 (27.9)	6.779 (2.02)
3 (socialist dummy)	80	−100.3 (0.20)	0.288** (0.004)	0.343** (0.002)	44.13* (0.024)	−2.888* (0.013)	–	–	0.69 (36.9)	6.479 (1.98)
4 (only cash transfers)	72	−128.0 (0.13)	0.185** (0.000)	0.423** (0.000)	40.66* (0.032)	−2.671* (0.018)	−2.949 (0.413)	–	0.74 (51.7)	6.03 (1.98)
			0.235** (0.000)	0.470** (0.000)	46.39* (0.02)	−2.957* (0.01)	–	–		

5 (age composition)	76	−74.4 (0.33)	– 0.230** (0.000)	– 3.875** (0.000)	33.37 (0.07)	−2.172* (0.05)	– –	– –	0.71 (47.0)	6.306 (2.18)
6 (with education)	80	−79.71 (0.309)	– 0.206** (0.000)	– 0.336** (0.001)	34.06 (0.072)	−2.092 (0.064)	– –	1.144** (0.013)	0.71 (40.6)	6.259 (2.06)
7 (Asia dummy)	80	−115.1 (0.076)	– 0.244** (0.000)	– 0.558** (0.000)	44.47** (0.005)	– 2.849** (0.003)	8.199** (0.000)	– –	0.77 (53.8)	5.625 (1.93)

In equation 2, non-socialist countries only. Values in parenthesis are the complements of the level of confidence with which the null hypothesis is rejected. Two (one) asterisks indicate that coefficient is significantly different from zero at less than 1 (5) percent level. Variable INCOME is in purchasing power per capita GDP. Variable INCOME² is INCOME squared. In regression 3, DUMMY variable takes value 1 for socialist countries, zero for others. In regrsssion 7, DUMMY variable takes value 1 for Asian countries, zero otherwise.

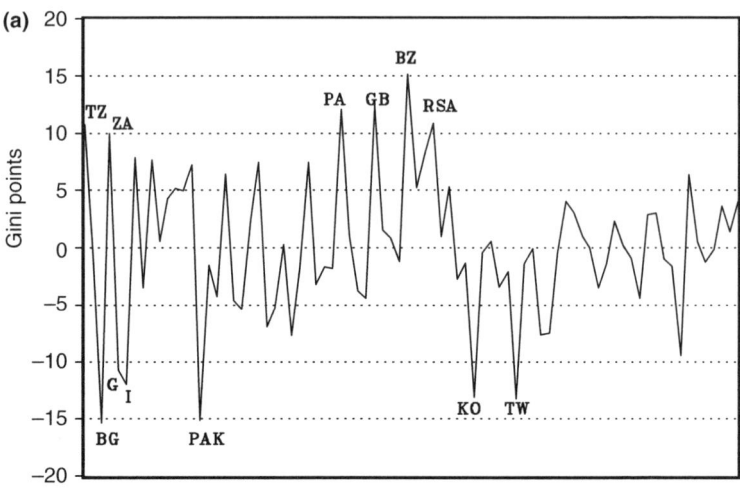

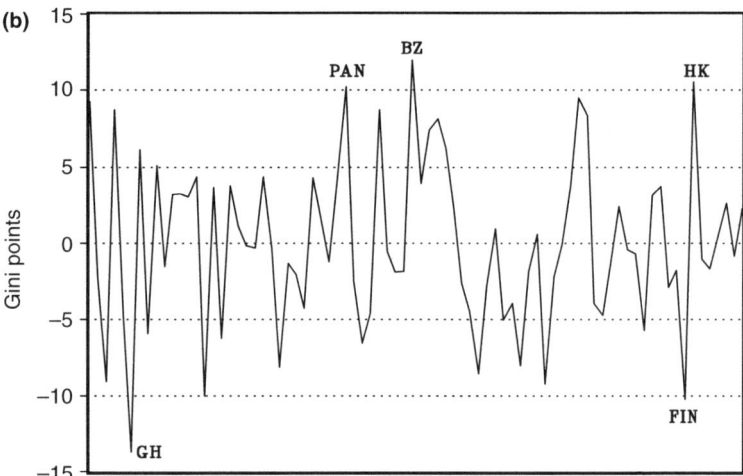

Figure 4.3   The Residuals.... (a) from equation (1); (b) from equation (7)

elements alone would make inequality in Africa, Asia, and Latin America some 15 to 16 Gini points greater than in OECD countries. It is interesting to observe that, despite other differences, Africa and Latin America display very similar patterns in the explanation of inequality. Asia, however, is different because the Asia dummy variable lowers

Table 4.3 Factors explaining the difference in inequality compared to OECD countries (in Gini points)

Due to:	Socialist	Africa	Asia	LAC
(1) State sector	−16.8	+2.4	+2.1	+0.5
(2) Size of transfers	+3.0	+9.4	+8.8	+8.4
(3) The Asia dummy			−8.2	
Social choice (1) to (3)	−13.8	+11.6	+2.7	+8.9
Income level	+5.1	+7.3	+6.2	+6.8
Unexplained	+2.3	+2.2	+0.9	+2.3
Actual difference	−6.4	+21.1	+9.8	+18.0

Calculated from the coefficients in regression 7 in Table 4.2 and summary data in Table 4.1. Negative sign indicates that a given element reduces inequality in the region in comparison with inequality in OECD countries.

inequality, from the levels predicted by the three general variables, by about 8 Gini points. Because of lower state-sector employment, the Gini coefficient in Africa and Asia would be greater by between 2 and 2 1/2 points, and by only 1/2 Gini points in Latin America.

In the case of Eastern Europe, by far the most important factor explaining lower inequality than the OECD countries' is the greater share of state-sector workers: this lowers the Gini coefficient by 16.8 points on average. All other elements point to a greater inequality in Eastern Europe than in OECD countries, but their impact is not sufficient to offset the impact of the large state sector. The debate about the lower income inequality in socialist economies (Ahluwalia 1976, Morrison 1984) can now be placed within a larger context of factors which explain income inequality in general. Socialist economies display lower inequality owing to the key feature of their system: the high share of state-sector employment.

If the Asian dummy is, *faute de mieux*, interpreted as some kind of specifically Asian social choice variable, then the difference between the social choice elements in OECD countries and Asia is very small (see row 5 in Table 4.3, where the OECD-Asia difference is only 2.4 Gini points, much less than compared to any other area). However, this is only a speculation because the Asian dummy might also reflect something very different (say, family values, large inter-household transfers, or an economic and not at all social variable that we were unable to pin down).

In conclusion, how do we account for higher inequality in less developed countries and the lower inequality in Eastern Europe, compared

66 Determinants of Income Inequality

to OECD countries? For Africa and Latin America, inequality is higher because of lower social transfers and lower income; for Asia, inequality is higher only because of lower income; and for Eastern Europe, inequality is lower because of the high share of the state sector.

4.4.5 How important are social factors?

Our next question is: What is the importance of social factors compared with 'given' factors? This is an important question because it is only after we empirically know the relative importance of social factors that we can make a judgment about the extent to which the standard version of the Kuznets hypothesis needs to be modified. If social choice variables reduce income inequality by only a few Gini points, then the general validity of the standard version cannot be seriously questioned. Societies can, at the margin, tamper with income distribution, but it is overwhelmingly determined by the factors that they cannot influence in the short-run, and in particular by their level of income. However, if social choice variables lower income inequality significantly, then the standard version of the Kuznets hypothesis needs to be

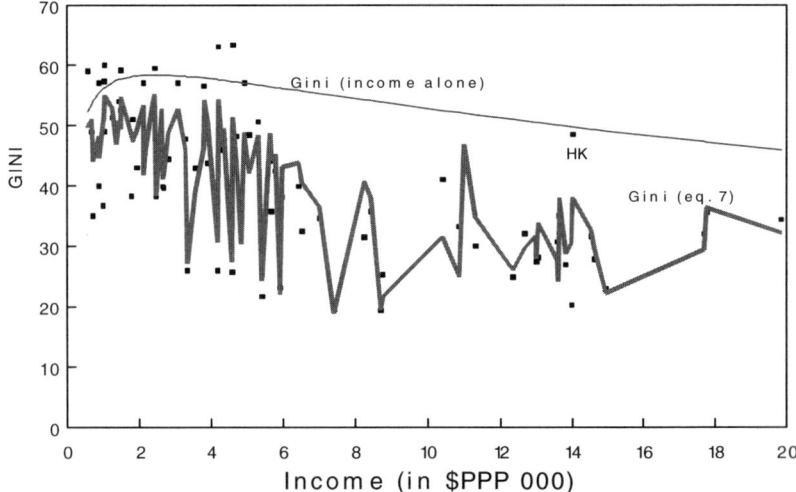

Figure 4.4 Predicted and actual GINIs

'Gini (income alone)' is the Gini coefficient calculated by using the coefficients from regression 7 for INCOME, and setting TRANS and STATE at zero. 'Gini (eq. 7)' is the Gini coefficient calculated from the full formulation of equation 7. Points represent the actual GINIs.

substantially altered. The line labeled 'Gini (income alone)' in Figure 4.4 shows the calculated Gini coefficients that would obtain if income alone determined inequality. An upward and short bulge in inequality is followed by a prolonged and slow decrease in inequality as income levels rise. The Figure also shows that, if income alone mattered, the differences in inequality between rich and poor countries would be relatively small. While the standard deviation of the actual GINI in our sample is 11.7, the standard deviation of the thus calculated GINI is only 3.4 (see Table 4.4). The distance between the 'Gini (income alone)' line and the line obtained from our regression (6) is due, save for the statistical discrepancy, to the role of social choice variables. The distance widens around $5000 per capita. For all countries with higher incomes (except for Hong Kong; see point HK in Figure 4.4), the divergence, and hence the role of social factors, is substantial. One can therefore propose two turning points of inequality: the first would occur at the level of approximately $2100 where, as noted before, the standard Kuznets curve linking income and GINI begins to turn downward. The second occurs at around $5000 when social choice variables become significantly more important than before and reinforce the downward trend in inequality. The difference between the unweighted Gini based on 'income alone' and the actual Gini in the whole sample amounts to 14.3 Gini points (Table 4.4). This is, therefore, the joint effect of social transfers and

Table 4.4 The role of social choice variables

Level of income in $ PPP (number of countries)	(1) GINI 'income alone'	(2) Actual GINI	Effect of social choice: (2)–(1)	Due to: STATE	Due to: TRANS
Under 1500 (14)	56.0	50.7	−5.3	−2.0	−2.4
1500–3000 (13)	58.4	46.0	−12.4	−3.9	−3.1
3000–4500 (11)	57.9	46.2	−11.7	−6.3	−4.9
4500–6000 (14)	56.8	41.2	−15.6	−8.7	−6.5
6000–10,000 (7)	54.7	29.8	−24.9	−12.0	−9.4
Over 10,000 (21)	50.0	31.4	−18.6	−5.3	−12.2
Total (80)	55.0	40.7	−14.3	−5.8	−6.8
Standard deviation	3.4	11.7			

GINI 'income alone': Calculated from regression (7) by setting STATE and TRANS = 0.
Effect of STATE and TRANS: Calculated from regression (7) by multiplying the corresponding coefficients with the actual values of STATE and TRANS. All of the difference in column (3) is not explained by STATE and TRANS. Some of it is explained by the Asia dummy and some unexplained because of the discrepancy between the values predicted by the regression and the actual GINIs.
All values are unweighted averages.

68 *Determinants of Income Inequality*

state-sector employment: a reduction of the Gini coefficient from 55 to 41. How important is this effect? How big is it in practical terms? It is equivalent to transforming Bolivia or Côte d'Ivoire (both with actual Ginis of about 55) into Sri Lanka or Uruguay (Ginis of 41). The 14.3 Gini point reduction is almost evenly shared between the effect of state-sector employment and social transfers: state employment reduces inequality, on average, by 5.8, and social transfers by 6.8 points.

The effect of the social choice variables is not independent of the level of income. At low levels of income – less than $1500 at purchasing parity – the Gini that depends on income alone and actual Gini differ by very little: by about 5 Gini points, with STATE and TRANS being of about the same importance in reducing inequality (see the last columns in Table 4.4).[29] Between $1500 and $4500, social choice variables reduce inequality by some 12 Gini points. The state sector now becomes more important than transfers. After $4500, the importance of social choice variables further increases, reducing the GINI that would obtain, if income alone mattered, by between 15 and 25 Gini points or, in other words, cutting the level of inequality by more than a third. The importance of STATE remains greater than that of TRANS, reaching its peak for the countries with incomes between $6000 and $10 000 where almost all socialist countries are located. Finally, for the richest countries, the reduction in inequality due to social choice variables, equal to 18.6 Gini points, owes much more to transfers than to state-sector employment.

Two conclusions can be drawn. First, variables which represent social choice have an important role in determining the degree of inequality. On average, social choice variables reduce the unweighted Gini coefficient in our sample by 14.3 Gini points (that is, by a quarter). Secondly, the importance of social choice variables increases with level of income. Social choice variables do not matter very much at low levels of income, but as income rises, society's preference for policies that reduce inequality seems to increase. Equality seems to be a superior good. The standard version of the Kuznets hypothesis, with income level alone, is therefore less valid as income increases and non-economic factors – compared with strictly economic factors – become more important in shaping personal income distribution.

4.5 Conclusions and implication of the findings

We have set out to answer two questions. First, do social choice variables – jointly, with the purely economic variables included in the standard formulation of the Kuznets hypothesis – determine income inequality? The answer to this question is 'Yes'. We have found that social choice variables (social transfers and state-sector employment) uniformly, in all formulations of the regressions, have a statistically significant negative impact on inequality.

The second question is, how important is the effect of social choice variables? Here, we have found that, for the sample of 80 countries in the 1980s, the social choice variables reduce inequality by some 14 Gini points. Actual inequality is, on average, only about three-quarters of what it would be if social variables were not operative. But this relation is not uniform with respect to income level. At a low level of income, the role of social choice variables is almost negligible. As income rises, their importance becomes greater. This finding cannot be interpreted by arguing that, at a low level of income, social choice has no role to play because there is nothing to redistribute as everyone is poor. This is patently not true because at low levels of income, inequality is relatively high.[30] Thus, social choice variables could, a priori, play a significant role even at low income levels. Why they do not do so can only be conjectured now. My hypothesis is that society's preferences change in the process of development and that people, as average income rises, tend to place greater emphasis on equality. The preference for social equality is therefore income-elastic. But, whatever the cause for the increasing role of the social choice variables, the implication of our results is that the validity of the standard formulation of the Kuznets hypothesis diminishes as society develops. The level of inequality that a society charts in its development diverges increasingly downward from the level predicted by the standard hypothesis. The discrepancy is therefore systematic. This is so because inequality in richer societies does not decrease because of economic factors, but also because societies *choose* less inequality.

We also find that Asian countries, once all these elements are taken into account, tend to have a lower than predicted inequality. The difference amounts to some 8 Gini points. Further research may be needed to find out just what accounts for the lower inequality. One hypothesis has been that the distribution of physical and human capital may be more equal in Asian countries, for a given level of income, than elsewhere. If this is the case, then, to achieve a given level of disposable income equality, government redistribution via transfers and taxes need not be as extensive in Asia as in other regions with more unequal personal distribution of assets. Equal distribution of assets, if confirmed, may be that missing 'social choice' variable that not only explains lower inequality in Asia (compared to what 'it should be') but provides a potential clue for high growth rates recorded by some Asian countries. Recent literature on the link between economic growth and political economy (for example, Alesina and Rodrik, 1994; Perotti, 1991 and 1992; Persson and Tabellini, 1992) argues that the size of transfers is determined by the political process: in short, by the gain that the median voter expects from redistribution. Thus, the population in countries in which assets are highly unequally distributed and in which, consequently, inequality in original income is high, will have an interest to vote for large social transfers. To the extent that transfers reduce the incentive to accumulate wealth and to work hard, either economic growth will be slow or democracy will be impossible to achieve. The dilemma, familiar from the 19th century Europe, was eloquently summarized by the Spanish statesman Canovas del Castillo: rebutting those who complained about electoral fraud, he wrote: 'To have to choose between the permanent falsification of universal suffrage and its abolition is not to have to choose between universal suffrage and preservation of property' (quoted in Ubieto *et al.*, 1972: 731). But if a country's assets are relatively widely distributed and market-generated inequality is moderate, then large, particularly cash, transfers are not needed. Fast growth becomes compatible with democracy (as the median voter does not have an interest to vote for high taxes) and relatively equal distribution of income.

Annex – some data issues

In large cross-sectional analyses, the data – because of differences in coverage, definitions, and sources – represent a particular problem. It is therefore important to discuss them in some detail. Income distribution data are generally thought to be among the least reliable types of macroeconomic data. The problems that hinder comparability are numerous. The most frequently mentioned are the following: How representative are household surveys, on the basis of which income inequality is estimated? What is the type of income (original, gross, or disposable)? Who are the recipients (households, families or individuals)? How are they ranked (by total household income or by household per capita income or by equivalent household income)? In my Annex Table 3 (not reproduced here),[31] I have indicated exactly the type of income and recipient from which the Gini coefficients are calculated. A general requirement, satisfied for all the countries, was twofold: the data should be derived from household surveys, and the surveys should be nationally representative.

For the OECD countries, I have relied heavily on the Luxembourg Income Study (LIS) where a special effort was made to generate consistent data across the countries. For most of the OECD countries, the Gini coefficients are calculated for disposable (after both transfers and personal taxes) per capita income. The recipients are individuals. This means that each individual in a household is assigned the same household per capita income. The same principle was applied to Eastern Europe and the former Soviet Union, where most of direct taxation is in the form of payroll taxes so that gross and net income are practically the same. Most of East European data were directly calculated from the published household surveys where income is defined as money income (net of payroll taxation) plus consumption in kind.[32] For the Latin American and Caribbean (LAC) countries, the majority of the data come from a single source (Psacharopoulos *et al.*, 1992) which itself is based on household surveys of a very similar design as those used for OECD countries and Eastern Europe (distribution of individuals by their household per capita income). However, income is almost always gross (that is, inclusive of transfers but not of personal taxes) rather than disposable income: since personal taxation is minimal in LAC countries, the two measures do not differ by much. Full comparability was more difficult to ensure for Africa and Asia. The problem here is less the income concept – gross and disposable income are practically the same – but rather the reliability of the surveys. I have used published results which I have tried to render as consistent as possible, often by using the data from the same source (for example, a single comparative paper). The problems, however, remain: it is mostly households, rather than individuals, that are treated as recipient units. This generally gives a higher Gini (see Coulter, Cowell and Jenkins, 1992). Specificities of individual country surveys are associated with 'fixed country effects', that is, a consistent over- or underestimation of countries' Ginis. In an attempt to eliminate these effects, Ravallion (1995) proposes to take the first difference of poverty or inequality measures. I am unable to do that because a series of the Ginis, similar to the one used here, would have to be constructed for the period of the 1960s or 1970s, and this would have severely reduced the size of the sample. Finally, regarding the time-period: for all but 10 countries, the Gini coefficients are from the 1980s (including 1979). I believe that the data represent the most consistent set of the Gini coefficients existing at present.

Among the explanatory variables, social transfers as a percentage of GDP, and GDP per capita in equivalent purchasing power are relatively easily available. OECD and ILO data (*The Cost of Social Security 1984–86* and *1985–87*) are the source for cash and in-kind social expenditures for most of the countries; these data were complemented by various World Bank, IMF and individual countries' publications (more in Annex Table 2, but see note 32). For practically all the countries, the data refer to the year 1985 or the 1980s average. The purchasing power equivalent GDP per capita in 1988 or 1985 is obtained for practically all the countries from Summers and Heston (1991). The exceptions are several East European countries that were not included in the Summers–Heston sample. Estimates for these countries are made by the World Bank.

Since both income concepts (disposable and gross income) used for the calculation of the Gini coefficient include transfers, size of transfers will, I argue, directly influence both types of GINI. But, in addition, there may be also indirect effects of social transfers. As documented (see Danziger, Haveman and Plotnick, 1981 for a review of the US experience, or Atkinson, 1987 and Atkinson *et al.*, 1984 for the UK experience), the existence of transfers leads to changes in behaviour of firms and individuals and thus affects their pre-fisc income. For example, existence of unemployment insurance may reduce willingness to work and reduce a person's labour income. If that person is poor and his overall income, equal to income from unemployment allowance, is less than what would be his income from labour (in absence of unemployment insurance), a perverse situation may appear where increased transfers – existence of unemployment insurance – lead to greater inequality. I cannot account for this effect. I must assume that the indirect effect is sufficiently small to be swamped by the direct effect of transfers on income distribution.

The size of the state sector is more difficult to obtain. Again, for the OECD countries, the OECD publications are the best source (even if such publications are not as exhaustive and up-to-date as one would expect). East European countries generally provide, in their statistical yearbooks, very detailed data on the size of the state sector (and the cooperative sector). For the LAC countries, Psacharopoulos *et al.* (1992) has been used extensively because household surveys provide information on the employer (state, private, own-account) of the interviewed individuals. For Africa and Asia, the main sources were the countries' statistical yearbooks. In almost all cases, the denominator (state sector as percentage of what) was the labour force or the economically active population. Both include the officially unemployed and agricultural underemployment; both exclude students, housewives, and so on, that is, people of working age who are not economically active outside their household.[33] Almost all of the data refer to the 1980s (Annex Table 1, see note 31).

Notes

1 Historically, probably the first explicit formulation of the hypothesis of the inverted U-shape of inequality may be that of Tocqueville presented in his 1835 *Memoir on pauperism* shortly after the author completed his famous *Democracy in America*. Tocqueville writes, 'If one looks closely at what has happened to the world since the beginning of society, it is easy to see that equality is prevalent only at the historical poles of civilization. Savages are equal because they are equally weak and ignorant. Very civilized men can all become equal because they all have at their disposal similar means of attaining comfort and happiness. Between these two extremes is found inequality of conditions, wealth, knowledge – the power of the few, the poverty, ignorance, and weakness of all the rest.' (1997, pp. 42–3).
2 Reviews of theory and evidence on the Kuznets curve are numerous. A particularly useful subset would include Lindert and Williamson (1985), Kaelble and Thomas (1991), Williamson (1991a), Polak and Williamson (1993), Paukert (1973), and Lecaillon et al. (1984). Williamson (1991) provides a useful summary of the country studies and tries to determine if there is historical evidence for the Kuznets' curve in Great Britain; Dumke (1991), Soderberg (1991), and Thomas (1991) in the same volume do the same thing respectively for Germany, Sweden, and Australia. Ram (1991) applies the Kuznets hypothesis to the US.
3 See, for example, recent criticism by Atkinson and Micklewright (1992: 35).
4 For the denial of its validity in Asia, see Oshima (1991: 121); for the absence of the Kuznets curve in Japan, see Lindert and Williamson (1985: 354).
5 I use the qualifier 'at centre stage' because Kuznets was indeed aware, as the earlier quotation makes clear, of the role of institutional factors in income distribution.
6 See also Phelps-Brown (1977: 286) and Lydall (1968). Atkinson and Micklewright (1992: 81ff.) show that Czechoslovakia, Hungary and Poland have consistently lower earnings inequality than the UK. The USSR and the UK have about the same level of inequality of earnings; the former is, however, regionally much more heterogeneous. Comparisons are, of course, strewn with many problems. State-sector wages in socialism are almost always on net basis, wages in capitalism are gross. This imparts an upward bias to income inequality in market economies. The opposite bias, however, has to do with the absence of unemployment in socialist countries. This means that even those with low productivity, often unemployed in market economies, will be wage earners in socialist economies.
7 Disposable income is equal to market income (that is income *before* government benefits and taxes) plus government cash transfers minus direct personal taxes. In cases when most direct taxation is through payroll taxes, market income already includes payroll taxes. Market income also includes consumption in kind. I use disposable income as a measure of inequality because it includes government cash transfers (a key requirement given my

hypothesis), and may be thought to reflect actual income inequality between individuals better than other income concepts: for example, gross income does not include direct personal taxes, while final income adjusts, in an often arbitrary fashion, disposable income for consumption of government in-kind benefits (education and health).

8 In some cases, gross income is used when personal income taxes are small, and disposable and gross income are virtually the same.

9 The point was raised by a referee.

10 This explains why equivalence scales vary between the countries and why there cannot be equivalence scales independent of specific country conditions. The 'correct' scale for a country is a function of the country's relative price ratios. Consider the example of housing, assuming, for simplicity, that a family needs to pay only for housing and food. Suppose that food costs are proportional to the number of people, while housing is not. For the same level of housing comfort, a single person in the US might need $800 per month, and a five-member family $2000. This implies that a five-member household should be (for the housing purposes) treated as 2½ adults. Food costs for each household member are, say $300. Then the household of five would require $5 \times \$300 + \$2000 = \$3500$ to be equally well-off as the household of one that has $1100 ($300 for food + $800 for housing). The implicit equivalence scales is 3.18 (3500/1100). Now let housing costs become practically zero, as they were in the former socialist countries. Suppose that the costs are now $8 for a single person and $20 for the family of five. While the economies of scale for the *housing alone* are the same, their overall importance is much less now simply because housing costs no longer matter very much. Thus, a single person would now require $308 and the five-member household $5 \times \$300 + \$20 = \$1520$. The implicit equivalence scale is now 4.93 (1520 divided by 308), and we are practically in the world of per capita comparisons. This is exactly the reason why per capita measurement made quite a lot of sense in the former socialist countries.

11 The expected negative sign of TRANS deserves a further comment. As has been argued, increased social transfers will tend to reduce the inequality of *disposable* or *gross* income. But in some recent studies (for example, Alesina and Rodrik, 1994; Persson and Tabellini, 1992) which are concerned with determinants of social transfers, higher income inequality is shown to lead, in conditions of wide franchise, to high redistribution. It would hence appear that inequality and transfers are positively related. The example underscores the ambiguity with which the term 'income inequality' is used. The positive relationship between income inequality and transfers makes sense only if one has in mind inequality of *market income* (before government benefits and taxes). It is then logical to assume that if market incomes are distributed unequally, people (that is the median voter) will vote for large redistribution because they will thereby gain. But both Alesina and Rodrik (1994) and Persson and Tabellini (1992) use measures of income inequality *after* government cash transfers. Consequently, the cross-country relationship between market income inequality and TRANS may be positive (because taxes are higher in more unequal countries), while the cross-country relationship between TRANS and disposable or gross income inequality may be negative (because transfers paid out of taxes lower inequality). The two

income inequalities – pre- and post-government – are in effect two entirely different variables.
12 I have experimented with a number of other formulations, some of them suggested recently by Anand and Kanbur (1993). The log-squared gives the best results. This was the original formulation used by Ahluwalia (1976).
13 The $\bar{R}^2$ with the two income variables alone (that is the standard Kuznets formulation) is 0.38.
14 This is somewhat higher than the turning point shown in Figure 4.1c (about $1800) where GINI is a function of INCOME alone. Ahluwalia (1976) finds the turning point at $468 per capita at 1970 prices and current exchange rates. On the basis of a somewhat smaller sample, Kaelble and Thomas (1991) find the turning points to range, depending on the measure of inequality used, between $322 and $489. Converting these values to 1988 prices and then applying the ratio between the purchasing power parity exchange rate and the current exchange rate from Summers and Heston (1991), we can express the turning points in 1988 purchasing power GDP per capita (as in our sample). Ahluwalia's value is then equivalent to $3070, and Kaelble and Thomas's range turns out to be $2175 and $3176.
15 See White (1980).
16 This was a point raised by one of the referees.
17 The data set has since been used by Bulir (1998).
18 Deininger and Squire (1996) show that, on average, expenditure-based inequality (Gini) will yield lower inequality than income-based Gini by about 6 points.
19 Defined as the ratio between the top and the bottom quintile.
20 Obviously, the coefficient values in equation 1B cannot be directly compared with those in other equations because the dependent variable is different.
21 Note, however, that with a quintile ratio on the LHS, the TRANS variable is no longer significant and the coefficient of determination is much smaller.
22 The number of countries drops to 72, since for eight countries I could not break the overall transfers into cash and in-kind components.
23 On the offsetting side, however, are social spending on education and family allowances – which is, of course, an argument in keeping with the per capita measurement.
24 The new variable is defined as

$$\frac{\text{TRANS}}{1 - 1/2 \text{ YOUNG}}$$

where YOUNG is the share of the population under 15 years of age (obtained from World Bank's *World Development Report 1990*, Table 26).
25 If the age variable (percentage of the population under 14 years of age) is run alongside the other variables (as defined in regression 1), the age variable itself is significant. The regression becomes:

GINI = $-26.3(0.08) + 37.13(0.03)$ INCOME $- 2.15(0.03)$ INCOME^2
$- 0.187(0.000)$ STATE $- 0.317(0.01)$ TRANSFERS $+ 0.555(0.004)$ AGE,

where the significance levels of the coefficient are shown between brackets. The signs and significance of other coefficients are not affected.

26 The only other one is Ghana.
27 The data come from the United Nations Development Program (1992).
28 Different formulations using INCOME and EDUC were tried; none dispenses with the need for a dummy variable.
29 The 'importance' is measured by how much GINI is reduced owing to changes in STATE and TRANS at various levels of income.
30 At some, possibly mythical, extremely low level of income, everyone would be equally poor. But this is not true at the actual low levels of income which we observe in our sample.
31 Annex Table 3, as well as Annex Tables 1 and 2 (referred to later in the text) can be obtained from the author upon request.
32 Consumer subsidies and *nomenklatura* in-kind benefits are not included in income. Including an estimate of the latter would make inequality greater although not by a substantial amount. Using Matthews's (1978) estimates for the Soviet Union, and his own estimates for Eastern Europe, Morrisson (1984) finds that including the monetized value of the nomenklatura benefits raises the Gini coefficient by 3 to 4 Gini points (see Morrisson, 1984, Table 2). As for consumer subsidies, they are overall income equalizers since they were mostly concentrated on goods with low income elasticity of consumption, like food. Two very careful studies that assessed the impact of consumer subsidies in Poland (World Bank 1989) and Hungary (Kupa and Fajth 1990) find that they reduce income inequality by about 2 Gini points. Similar results were reported for Czechoslovakia (World Bank 1991). The studies cover all consumer subsidies, including those that are neutral or pro-rich, like housing, transportation or electricity subsidies. In conclusion, it seems that the inclusion of consumer subsidies on top of the nomenklatura perks would probably bring the Gini coefficient close to its reported value. A more serious problem with income distribution data from socialist countries exists in the case of the USSR, Bulgaria and Romania. The sampling procedure in these countries was biased because the selection was done, not at the place of residence, but at the work-place. The likelihood of being selected was a function of employment status. There was, in addition, informal pressure to select the 'average' households (both spouses working in the state sector, two children and so on) – a kind of model 'socialist' household. Pensioners, students, housewives, the unemployed, vagrants and so on were systematically undersampled. Although the surveys tries to correct for this by, for example, adding on a quota of pensioners, their numbers were still relatively few. The procedure led to 'averaging out' and thus an underestimate of inequality. However, this bias was much less or did not exist in other socialist countries, whose sampling procedures were comparable to those in the West (see Atkinson and Micklewright 1992, and Garner, Okrasa, Smeeding and Boyle Torrey 1993).
33 The distinction is, of course, somewhat artificial in the case of countries with agricultural underemployment.

References

Ahluwalia, M. S. (1976) 'Inequality, Poverty and Development', *Journal of Development Economics*, no. 3.

Alesina, A. and Rodrik, D. (1994) 'Distributive Politics and Economic Growth' *Quarterly Journal of Economics*, 109: 465–90.
Anand, S. and Kanbur, R. (1993) 'Inequality and Development: A Critique', *Journal of Development Economics*, 41: 19–43.
Atkinson, A. B. (1987) 'Income Maintenance and Social Insurance' in A. J. Auerbach and M. Feldstein (eds), *Handbook of Public Economics*, Amsterdam, New York: North Holland.
Atkinson, A. B. and Micklewright, J. (1992) *Economic Transformation in Eastern Europe and the Distribution of Income*, Cambridge: Cambridge University Press.
Atkinson, A. B. *et al.* (1984) 'Unemployment Benefit, Duration and Incentives in Britain: How Robust is the Evidence', *Journal of Public Economics*, 23: 3–26.
Bishop, J. A., Formby, J. P. and Thistle, P. D. (1991) 'Changes in the US Earnings Distributions in the 1980s', *Applied Economics*, 23: 425–34.
Blank, R. M. (1993) 'Public Sector Growth and Labor Market Flexibility: the United States vs. the United Kingdom', National Bureau of Economic Research Working Paper no. 4339, April.
Bulir, A. (1998) 'Income Inequality: Does Inflation Matter', IMF Working paper no. 98/7, January 1998.
Coulter, F. A. E., Cowell, F. A. and Jenkins, S. P. (1992) 'Equivalence Scale Relativities and the Extent of Inequality and Poverty', *The Economic Journal*, 102: 1067–82.
Danziger, S., Haveman, R. and Plotnick, R. (1981) 'How Income Transfer Programs Affect Work, Savings, and the Income Distribution: A Critical Review', *Journal of Economic Literature*, 19: 975–1028.
Deininger, K. and Squire, L. (1996) 'Measuring Income Inequality: a New Data Base', *The World Bank Economic Review*, 10: 565–91.
Dumke, R. (1991) 'Income Inequality and Industrialization in Germany, 1850–1913: the Kuznets Hypothesis Re-examined', in Y. S. Brenner, H. Kaelble and M. Thomas (eds), *Income Distribution in Historical Perspective*, Cambridge and Paris: Cambridge University Press and Editions de la Maison des Sciences de l'Homme.
Dye, T. R. and H. Ziegler (1988) 'Socialism and Equality in Cross-National Perspective', *PS: Political Science and Politics*, Winter: 45–56.
Garner, T., Okrasa, W., Smeeding, T. and Torrey, B. Boyle (1993) 'Household Surveys of Economic Status in Eastern Europe: An Evaluation', in S. Powers (ed.), *Proceedings from the Conference on Economic Statistics for Economies in Transition: Eastern Europe in the 1990's*, Washington, D.C.: US Bureau of Labor Statistics.
Hirschman, A. O. (1973) 'The Changing Tolerance for Income Inequality in the Course of Economic Development: With a Mathematical Appendix', *Quarterly Journal of Economics*, 87(4): 544–65.
Kaelble, H. and Thomas, M. (1991) 'Introduction', in Y. S. Brenner, H. Kaelble and M. Thomas (eds), *Income Distribution in Historical Perspective*, Cambridge and Paris: Cambridge University Press and Editions de la Maison des Sciences de l'Homme.
Kupa, M. and Fajth, G. (1990) 'Hungarian Social Policy and Distribution of Incomes of Households', mimeo, Budapest.
Kuznets, S. (1955) 'Economic Growth and Income Inequality', *American Economic Review*, 45(March): 1–28.

Kuznets, S. (1966) *Modern Economic Growth: Rate, Structure and Speed*, New Haven: Yale University Press.

Lecaillion, J., Paukert, F., Morrisson, C. and Germidis, D. (1984) *Income Distribution and Economic Development: An Analytical Survey*, Geneva: ILO.

Le Grand, Julian (1982) *The Strategy of Equality: Redistribution and the Social Services*, London: Allen and Unwin.

Lindert, P. H. (1989) 'Modern Fiscal Redistribution: A Preliminary Essay', Agricultural History Center, University of California, Davis, Working Paper Series no. 55, June.

Lindert, P. H. (1991) 'How Welfare Spending Evolves', Agricultural History Center, University of California, Davis, Working Paper Series no. 66, July.

Lindert, P. H. and Williamson, J. G. (1985) 'Growth, Equality, and History', *Explorations in Economic History*, 22: 341–77.

Lydall H. F. (1968) *The Structure of Earnings*, Oxford: Oxford University Press.

Matthews, M. (1978) *Privilege in the Soviet Union*, London: Allen and Unwin.

Meron, M. (1991) 'La dispersion des salaires de l'Etat 1982–1986', *Economie et Statistique*, no. 239 (Janvier).

Morrison, C. (1984) 'Income Distribution in East European and Western Countries', *Journal of Comparative Economics*, 8(2): 121–38.

Oshima, H. T. (1991) 'Kuznets' Curve and Asian Income Distribution', in T. Mozoguchi (ed.), *Making Economies More Efficient and More Equitable: Factors Determining Income Distribution*, Economic Research Series no. 28, The Institute of Economic Research, Hitotsubashi University, Tokyo: Kinokuniya Company Ltd and Oxford University Press.

Paukert, F. (1973) 'Income Distribution at Different Levels of Development: A Survey of Evidence', *International Labor Review*, 108 (2–3): 97–125.

Perotti, R. (1991) 'Income Distribution, Politics and Growth: Theory and Evidence', mimeo, Columbia University.

Perotti, R. (1992) 'Income Distribution, Politics, and Growth', *American Economic Review Papers and Proceedings*, May.

Persson, T. and G. Tabellini (1992) 'Growth, Distribution, and Politics', Theory and Evidence', in A. Cukierman, Z. Hercowitz and L. Leiderman (eds), *Political Economy, Growth and Business Cycles*, Boston, Mass.: MIT Press, pp. 3–22.

Phelps-Brown, H. (1977) *The Inequality of Pay*, Oxford: Oxford University Press.

Phelps-Brown, H. (1988), *Egalitarianism and the Generation of Inequality*, Oxford: Clarendon Press.

Polak, B. and J. G. Williamson (1993) 'Poverty, Policy and Industrialization in the Past', in M. Lipton and J. van der Gaag (eds), *Including the Poor*, Proceedings of a symposium organized by the World Bank and International Food Policy Research, World Bank, World Bank Regional and Sectoral Studies, pp. 219–48.

Pryor, F. L. (1971) 'Economic System and the Size Distribution of Income and Wealth', Indiana University, International Development Research Center.

Pryor, F. L. (1973) *Property and Industrial Organization in Communist and Capitalist Nations*, Bloomington and London: Indiana University Press.

Psacharopoulos et al. (1992) *Poverty and Income Distribution in Latin America: The Story of the 1980s*, Washington, D.C.: World Bank, Latin American and the Caribbean Technical Department, Regional Studies Program, Report no. 27, December.

Ram, R. (1991) 'Kuznets's Inverted U-Hypothesis: Evidence from a Highly Developed Country', *Southern Economic Journal*, 57(April): 1112–23.

Ravallion, M. (1995) 'Growth and Poverty: Evidence for Developing Countries in the 1980s', *Economics Letters*, 48: 411–17.

Sawyer, M. (1982), 'Income Distribution and the Welfare State', in A. Boetho, *The European Economy*, Oxford: Oxford University Press.

Soderberg, J. (1991) 'Wage Differentials in Sweden, 1725–1950', in Y. S. Brenner, H. Kaelble and M. Thomas (eds), *Income Distribution in Historical Perspective*, Cambridge and Paris: Cambridge University Press and Editions de la Maison des Sciences de l'Homme.

Summers, R. and Heston, A. (1991) 'The Penn World Table (Mark 5): An Expanded Set of International Comparisons', *Quarterly Journal of Economics*, 106 (2).

Thomas, M. (1991) 'The Evolution of Inequality in Australia in the Nineteenth Century', in Y. S. Brenner, H. Kaelble and M. Thomas (eds), *Income Distribution in Historical Perspective*, Cambridge and Paris: Cambridge University Press and Editions de la Maison des Sciences de l'Homme.

Tocqueville, A. de (1997 [1835]) *Memoir on Pauperism*, Chicago: Ivan R. Dee, Inc. Publishers.

Ubieto, A., Regla, J., Jover, J. M. and Seco, C. (1972) *Introducción a la Historia de España*, Editorial Teide, Barcelona.

United Nations Development Program (1992) *The Human Development Report*, New York: UNDP.

Williamson, J. (1991) 'British Inequality during the Industrial Revolution: Accounting for the Kuznets Curve', in Y. S. Brenner, H. Kaelble and M. Thomas (eds), *Income Distribution in Historical Perspective*, Cambridge and Paris: Cambridge University Press and Editions de la Maison des Sciences de l'Homme.

Williamson, J. (1991a) *Inequality, Poverty, and History*, Cambridge, Mass.: Basil Blackwell.

White, H. (1980) 'A Heteroskedasticity-Consistent Covariance Matrix and a Direct Test for Heteroskedasticity', *Econometrica*, 48: 817–38.

World Bank (1989) *Poland: Subsidies and Income Distribution*, World Bank Report 7776-POL, Washington: World Bank.

World Bank (1991) *Czechoslovakia: Transition to a Market Economy*, A World Bank Country Study, Washington D.C.

5
Illyrian Theories of Cooperative Rent-Sharing and Their Application in Real Life*

Dinko Dubravčić

5.1 Introduction

In this paper we review some long-standing Illyrian propositions and identify cooperative rent-sharing as their essential component. We compare rent-sharing in producer cooperatives with rent appropriation by organized labour in real life developments in Western economies. We also evaluate the possible application of Illyrian theories to new domains, such as acquisition of capital by joint-stock companies, or immigration policies of modern states.

5.2 The d-maximand and co-operative rent-sharing in Illyrian firms

The introduction of self-management into the enterprises of former Yugoslavia in the early 1950s has offered economic scholars a new field of research. The theoretical reflection of real-life self-management – the labour-managed firm (**LMF**) – was created with the postulate that it maximizes income per worker ($d = I/L$), instead of absolute profit (π), as done by the textbook entrepreneurial firm (**EF**). On that basis, the theory of the firm and some other chapters of economics have been reworked – the Illyrian[1] theories were the result.

The **d**-maximand seemed logically acceptable, even inevitable, for a **LMF**, since it satisfied the aspiration of each member of the cooperative to attain the highest personal income. These aspirations appeared just

---

* An early draft of this paper was presented at the Fifth International Conference on the Economics of Self-Management held in Vienna in 1988 under the title 'Illyrian theories in Quest for Application'. I would like to thank the participants of the conference, especially Jan Svejnar and Branko Horvat, for their valuable comments.

and reasonable, with no visible harm done to other aspirants under normal competitive conditions.

Illyrian scholars agree on one important characteristic of the **LMF**: if **d** does not differ from the wage **w** that workers would obtain, in market equilibrium, in a twin **EF**,[2] both **LMF** and **EF** would have identical optima. However, as Keren and Levhari[3] point out, whereas the **EF** competitive equilibrium is stable, an economy populated by **LMF**s has no forces that tend to lead it toward equilibrium.

Whenever **d** exceeds **w**, and this case is almost the exclusive domain of Illyrian research, all the symptoms of the 'Illyrian disease' become apparent. The most notorious are the negative slope of **LMF**'s supply curve, the insensitiveness to changes in labour price **w** (which obstructs movement of labour from a poor to a rich **LMF**), increased hazards concerning the allocation of resources in monopoly markets,[4] and a capital-intensive expansion path.[5]

Some Illyrian scholars, who were attracted to the subject out of interest for social reform, suggested various remedies for the malfunctioning of the **LMF**, such as modifications of the maximand, special measures taken by a benevolent government, or institutional arrangements that remodeled the **LMF**.

Horvat's proposals to amend the maximand are dated at a very early stage of Illyrian research. In a later contribution,[6] he reasserted his basic premise: the worker-managers in the **LMF** increase employment in discrete intervals and in the short run, while the workforce is fixed, they use a non-ratio maximand, making all abnormalities in **LMF**'s behaviour disappear. Ireland and Law (1978) tried to remove the barrier for labour to move from a poor to a rich **LMF** by transfer payments from a central investment fund to each **LMF**, so that **d**-maximizing becomes identical to profit-maximizing at a given shadow wage rate. A simple systemic remedy would be to allow the division of **LMF**'s members into those with full membership, and those employed on wage terms[7] who would be allowed gradually to filter into the tenured group.

In general, free entry is a panacea recommended for all troubles that befall a **LMF** economy – it obviously causes the difference between **d** and **w** to disappear. But this must, then, be the clue for the Illyrian affliction: we can safely conclude that when **d** is larger than **w**, a rent in the **LMF** exists that all its members share. Free entry must, as expected, destroy this rent.

However, if members succeed in defending the rent, their **LMF** will not employ labour to the point where the wage equals the value of the marginal product of labour, which would satisfy the job-seeking non-members. Instead, LMF will stop employing new members when **d** reaches its maximum, protecting the members' interest. This rent-sharing behaviour, embodied in the seemingly innocuous **d**-maximand, is the cause of the difficulties **LMFs** encounter when expected to approach equilibrium.

Since not all **LMFs** can be in a monopoly position, it appears sensible to think of the rent as an entrepreneurial residual, a term normally associated with profit. We may, then, say that members exert 'entrepreneurial control' over the **LMF**, namely, they appropriate the residual, they bear the risk of the firm's activities since the income per member **d** could amount to less than the wage **w**, and they control the management of the firm.[8]

In addition to the consequences of using a ratio-maximand,[9] the **LMF** will have to solve some problems stemming from the fact that workers control the firm and share the rent. Some assumptions are, therefore, necessary on the relationship of members among themselves and toward the firm.

Since it can hardly be expected that labour is fully homogeneous, the members must agree on the 'unit of labour' as the basis for distributing the rent. They must resolve the relationship of old members who invested part of their earned income (including the rent) and the new ones who, when employed, use the firm's assets to gain their income. They must also regulate the 'firing' procedures, that is the selection of members who will become redundant when, because of external factors, maximizing **d** requires a reduction of employment.

Illyrian scholars did not pay much attention to the process of homogenizing labour: it was generally assumed that members would agree on a system of job evaluation. As for the 'property rights' of the old members, who contributed to the assets of the firm, a market for membership stakes is usually recommended: the outgoing members may sell their share in the firm to newcomers. In the absence of such a market, however, the investment horizon of the members would be restricted to their expectations to stay in the firm. This would reduce the volume of self-financing with resulting under-investment. Vanek (1971) suggested external financing as a remedy, that leads the **LMF** to a behavioural pattern similar to that of a capitalist firm. Understanding that a conventional banking system would not be effective, since limited self-financing would not produce sufficient security for the lender, he admitted that an act of political will was indispensable to providing the features of the capital market that would support a participatory economy or a participatory sector.

5.3 Producer cooperatives in real life – why are they so few?

In their extensive review of the performance of producer co-ops in Western economies,[10] Bonin *et al.* (1993) state that there are no significant negative findings of free-riding and lower productivity that could be the consequence of entrepreneurial control by workers. It seems that 'horizontal monitoring' successfully replaces vertical (hierarchical) monitoring in capitalist firms. There are less managers in producer co-ops and they receive more modest salaries, which possibly indicates that the elimination of the antagonistic environment of capitalist firms makes managerial duties less demanding.

The acceptance of non-members vary among producer co-ops. In Mondragon, non-members are accepted on a temporary basis only, and no member has ever been dismissed. In most other producer co-ops, non-members are admitted and receive the same wage and bonuses as members. Non-members, however, have no say in the essential decisions in the co-op and have a less secure employment status. Although the existence of a negative supply curve is not confirmed in practice, it seems that supply, and especially employment, are less elastic than in comparable capitalist firms. Protection of employment is an important element of the objective function of co-ops and is often even more significant than rent sharing.

In practice, all co-ops demand from their would-be members an admission fee that is well below the amount of funds per capita needed to secure assets for a normal functioning of the co-op. There are few cases where individual stakes can be bought (by newcomers) and sold (by departing members), the plywood co-ops in the northwestern part of the United States being the best known instance.[11] Even there, however, the price of the stake is well below a computed discounted rent, the cause probably being the risk element in the anticipated income as well as liquidity problems of the incoming members.

Empirical findings on plywood co-ops, as well as on other producer co-ops, confirm a lower capital intensity (that is, comparative capital 'starvation' of the co-ops), due to lower investment out of internal funds, and more expensive external financing. The co-ops, obviously, are not accepted as good loan takers by the conventional financial institutions.

When trying to explain the comparatively low share of producer co-ops in economic activities[12] in Western countries, Bonin *et al.* point to the problem of securing funds as the main cause of their sluggish development. They state that 'the explanation of the relative scarcity of producer co-ops lies in the nexus between decision making and financial support...worker controlled (producer co-ops) have difficulty finding internal sources and competing with the capitalist firm for investment funds'.[13]

Although the issue of securing funds is a crucial one for producer co-ops, we would prefer to look for other explanations for their low share in Western economies. An attractive possibility is to look at the relative success of union bargaining compared to workers' management. Moene and Wallerstein (1993) suggest that this could be explained by the fact that creating worker-owned firms requires capital, while organizing unions requires only the effort of union activists. The latter was much more available than the former, especially in the early years of labour movements.

It seems promising to expand on this rather crude thesis. Capital could be replaced by a broader content that also includes entrepreneurship and managerial activities. To form and develop a firm, an entrepreneur or a group of them is indispensable – in due course they will delegate some of their activities to management. When entering market transactions, they must own some capital so as to be able to guarantee the fulfillment of contractual obligations, even if their projections prove wrong.

On the other hand, unions could be thought of as monopolist or perhaps oligopolist sellers of the work-force to firm-owners or entrepreneurs, the subject of bargaining being not only wages but all aspects of working conditions. The unions' power to achieve a good contract for their members depends on the consequences of the threat of strikes that can disrupt production and harm the capitalist-entrepreneur as well as other parts of the economy or consumers.[14] Successful unions can, thus, appropriate a significant part of the industry's rent for their members. They will sometimes be able to grab part of the rent of other industries by forcing their employers to rise prices.

It can, therefore, be claimed that the prevalent institutional form of firms in Western economies with entrepreneurs and management on the one side, and workers represented by unions on the other, has produced for the workers a larger proportion of appropriated rent than could possibly be achieved in producer co-operatives. This seems a plausible explanation for the limited spontaneous development and success of producer co-operatives in market economies.

Whatever the reason for the negligible role of producer co-ops in traditional Western economies, it seems doubtful that the **d** maximand best expresses the objective function of this type of enterprise in real life. The rigid economic goal of rent-sharing contradicts the solidarity of workers that must be the characteristic of producer co-ops. Securing employment (possibly even for members of the local community) and the aversion to risk-taking, will usually be more important. We may conclude that the general circumstances of the members of the co-op prevent explicit entrepreneurial behaviour of rent appropriation and rent-sharing.

We may, therefore, consider other cooperative instances where rent-seeking and rent-sharing is important, but no limitations are imposed by specific conditions of workers as members of producer co-ops.

5.4 The p-maximand of joint-stock companies

The joint-stock company has been a theme of Illyrian studies only on a few occasions.[15] There is, however, a clearly Illyrian aspect of joint-stock companies – namely, the conspicuous object of sharing a rent (profit) by a group of shareholders. The basis of sharing is the quantity of capital supplied by a single shareholder.[16] A ratio maximand of the form $p = \pi/C$, that is, the rate of profit, will then adequately express the objective function of the joint-stock company (the 'capitalist co-op').

Since capital is homogeneous and easily divisible in comparison with labour, it will be easier to arrange sharing of the rent here than in producer co-ops. A positive element would also be the possibility that capital owners can simultaneously be members of various capital co-ops and thereby reduce their exposure to risk while workers in producer co-ops do not have the same facility. Another critical difference is the well developed market for membership in capitalist co-ops – the value of shares, that can be bought and sold at any time, fully reflects the valuation of future rents.[17]

Securing loan capital to joint-stock companies is a parallel to recruiting non-members into the work-force of producer co-ops. This is definitely accepted in the real-life world of capitalist co-ops. Since the shareholders' capital serves as a collateral, creditors will prefer, as we have seen, capital co-ops to producer co-ops as loan takers.

The joint-stock company will have different criteria when considering an increase of its equity capital (that is, accepting new members into the capitalist co-op) on the one hand, and taking new loans (recruiting non-members with a fixed compensation, that is, interest rate) on the other. New equity capital will be sought only if it secures a rate of return at least equal to the existing one: otherwise p, the maximand of the capitalist co-op, would decrease. Loan capital will, however, be accepted whenever the rate of return exceeds the rate of interest so that the new funds contribute to an increase of profit to be shared by the stockholders.[18] Various kinds of 'preferred stocks' represent different levels of seniority in the capitalist co-op; similar instruments are rarely applied in producer co-ops.

Easy marketing of shares and the smooth passage from non-membership to full membership makes the capitalist co-op very different from the producer co-op. Although there are some advantages (uncomplicated sharing arrangements, possibility of risk dispersion or attractiveness to creditors), Illyrian theories do not seem easily applicable.

Nevertheless, there are some points where an Illyrian approach could help us to explain phenomena in the real-life stock companies. One could, for example, argue that the high rate of increase of share prices in the last few decades is the result of Illyrian behaviour of the capitalist co-ops: by restricting the emission of new stock capital, the joint-stock companies act in favour of the 'old members' increasing the value of the existing shares. This obviously corresponds to the restriction of new membership in successful producer co-ops aiming at securing the rent to old members.

5.5 The d-maximand and immigration policies of modern states

The description in Illyrian terms of a model modern state (**MS**) when considering its immigration policies may seem bizarre. It does, however, require little effort to identify similarities between the **LMF** and the **MS** in some aspects of their 'employment policies'.

If the **MS** is a democratic country, its citizens will have substantial control over the government's management of the economy. The gross income per head ratio (**D**) will be their legitimate criterion for the government's success in long-term economic policies. **D** will reflect the amount of total – individual and other – consumption[19] accessible to any of them. Citizens of developed **MS**s, and their democratically controlled governments, have an interest to defend the above average **D** against non-members, that is, immigrants from less developed **MS**s who are prepared to supply labour for a lower, market clearing, gross income per head or 'wage'[20] **W**.

The governments of developed **MS**s will then follow restrictive immigration policies with similar consequences as the restrictive hiring policies of **LMF**s. In economic activities, **MS**s will try to substitute the labour supplying immigrants with other productive inputs. Their expansion paths will, therefore, be capital intensive and they will use comparatively more of other inputs – for example, energy.

When introducing the concept of an inegalitarian producer co-op, Meade (1972) described the process of assimilation of new members. Older members will try to retain, at least for some time, an inegalitarian distribution of decision-making power that will result in a larger share of the rent. One can easily visualize the same happening in model (and real life) **MS**s. Meade also suggested the possibility of making lump-sum payments to co-op members willing to leave, when this increases **d** of the remaining members. Similar payments can be introduced by **MS**s to short term immigrants willing to be repatriated to their countries of origin if this increases **D** of the old nationals.

Illyrian theories have an explanation for the fact that movements of goods prevail over movements of labour among countries. Sacks (1983: 47) analyzes the relations between two **LMF**s, each in a **d** optimum and therefore unwilling to allow labour movements between them. He defines the conditions that increase **d** in both **LMF**s and reduce the difference of their marginal productivities by trading in goods and services.

Some conspicuous similarities concerning selective employment of 'non-members' by producer co-ops and developed states can be noted. Both 'employers' will give special treatment to highly qualified entrants, such as managers in the first case and scientists in the second. They will also try to attract 'employees' that are prepared to do menial work that old members prefer to avoid. We must admit, however, that the complexity of **MS**s in real life will be a major hurdle for their modeling as Illyrian 'citizens co-ops'. In addition to having 'employee-citizens' who expect the **MS** to help them maximize their labour rent, states will consist of 'capitalist-citizens' who expect to be helped in maximizing the rate of return on their capital. In real life, the amount of capital rent will be limited in comparison to the labour rent since the barriers to capital movements among countries are much less significant than those to labour movements. The capitalist-citizen may try to reduce the labour rent by exporting capital to cheap labour countries, or by lobbying for a free flow of immigrants. The government will have to arbitrate, and solutions suggested by Aoki (1980), where managers in firms mediate between owners and workers, may become relevant.

Very large differences of **D**-ratios among countries, as well as long queues of willing migrants in less developed countries, indicate the presence of large amounts of Illyrian rents in developed countries. It may be claimed that this is the most important cause of misallocation of productive factors in the world economy. Model building of the **MS** along Illyrian lines can, however, only marginally improve our understanding of the problem and the possibilities to find solutions.[21]

Empirical research concerning similarities of operation of producer co-ops and citizen co-ops can probably be of some interest only in the field of structures and dynamics of employment/immigration.

5.6 Is there a future for Illyria?

The Illyrian co-op model of economic activity based on a ratio maximand can be functional only if several conditions are met. A group of people must act so as to create and share a significant rent. They must possess a sense of solidarity among themselves and a wish to obtain the results while restricting non-members from taking part in them. Hiring of non-members under other than sharing arrangements will reduce the applicability of the Illyrian model. In real life, neither the producer co-op, the capitalist co-op, nor the citizen co-op meet all the necessary conditions.

The producer co-ops realize rents of little substance and have difficulties in reaching fair sharing arrangements especially concerning income retained for investment. In addition, they cannot efficiently solve the problem of development by external financing. Historically, oligopolistic selling of labour by trade unions has produced better results for workers than forming producer co-ops and sharing their rent.

The application of the Illyrian model to capitalist co-ops is impaired by the ability of members to participate in many firms and change their affiliation easily. The institution of various intermediate levels of membership also reduces the validity of the co-op model.

In the modern state defined as a citizen co-op, the inegalitarian aspect of its members as well as non-economic aspects will crucially complicate the application of Illyrian models.

The expansion of Illyrian theories in the last few decades of this century has been the result of various factors – the appearance of the socially engineered workers' managed firms in former Yugoslavia, the search for a third way of economic and social organization beyond capitalism and communism, the feeling that industrial democracy was ethically correct and, finally, the tendency of economic scholars to follow model experiments to all possible ends. The last element may probably be the most significant determinant of future research.

Illyrian theories may retain some marginal relevance in just one field – the process of hiring new members in various types of co-ops, these being workers, stock-owners, nationals or others. Some similarities may be found there as the consequence of a veiled influence of a co-operative ratio-maximand.

Notes

1. When introducing the d-maximand, Ward (1958) used the term 'Illyrian' to denote the model-character of his construction as well as a possible resemblance to the real-life self-managed enterprises in Yugoslavia (partly covering the territory of ancient Illyria).
2. The term 'twin' applies to a π-maximizing **EF**, that has all the characteristics as well as the economic environment of the **LMF** – the only difference being their maximand.
3. See Keren and Levhari (1992: 656).
4. See, for example, Meade (1974).
5. See Dubravčić (1970).
6. See Horvat (1986).
7. This possibility was discussed by Domar (1966).
8. For a more extensive discussion of the term 'entrepreneurial control' see Dubravčić (1970).
9. At an early phase of the development of Illyrian theories, this author suggested that 'the aberrant behaviour of the producer co-operative, when compared to the orthodox profit maximizing firm... (was) the consequence of two very distinct factors. The first, reflected in the ratio-form of... the 'maximand', is the co-operative character of entrepreneurial control... The second, determining the content of the numerator and denominator in the maximand ratio, denotes the fact that labor is chosen as the vehicle of entrepreneurial control.' See Dubravčić (1970: 298–9).
10. Bonin *et al.* (1993) consider only producer co-ops that naturally develop within market economies, eliminating those which are the result of social engineering such as self-managed firms in former Yugoslavia, kolhozes in the Soviet Union, and possibly even the kibbutz in Israel. They define, as producer co-ops, only those where key entrepreneurial decisions are taken on the basis of one worker, one vote.
11. See, for example, Berman and Berman (1989).
12. Employment in producer co-ops amounts to only 1% of the total in Western economies. There are, however, some branches (for example, construction) where the share is slightly higher.
13. See Bonin *et al.* (1993: 1316).
14. The unlimited use of strikes must, then, be suppressed; this is accomplished in the legislation of all modern states.
15. See, for example, Dubravčić (1970) and Meade (1972).
16. In the Illyrian sense, stockholders are cooperative entrepreneurs, but they take fundamental decisions and appoint management according to the principle of one-share-one-vote and not, as is the practice in producer co-ops, one man – one vote.
17. When considering investment, the capitalist co-op will take into account the full discounted stream of rents that will result from the project. Workers in the producer co-op will not be able to recapture the full effects of investment because of their limited time horizon of being employed in the firm, and an inefficient market for membership stakes.
18. This is well explained by Chamberlain (1962: 61) as quoted in Dubravčić (1970: 302).

19 Including investment as the ground of future consumption.
20 **W** would include the same items of consumption as **D**.
21 Applying Illyrian remedies brings only derisory results. Free entry, that is, the formation of new **MS**s by the 'poor of the world' is a classic utopia. Funds, to establish an incentive scheme so that labour receives an equal shadow price all over the world, will never be gathered by a world government. The concept of 'tenure' is perhaps the easiest to apply, but even here, a generally accepted solution will be difficult to achieve.

References

Aoki M. (1980), 'A Model of the Firm as a Stockholder – Employee Cooperative Game', *American Economic Review*, 70: 600–10.

Berman, K. V. and Berman M. D. (1989) 'An Empirical Test of the Theory of the Labor-Managed Firm', *Journal of Comparative Economics*, 13: 281–300.

Bonin, J. P., Jones, D. C., and Putterman L. (1993) 'Theoretical and Empirical Studies of Producer Cooperatives: Will Ever the Twain Meet?', *Journal of Economic Literature*, 31: 1290–1320.

Chamberlain, N. W. (1962), *The Firm: Microeconomic Action and Planning*, New York: McGraw-Hill.

Domar, E. D. (1966), 'The Soviet Collective Farm as a Producer Co-operative', *American Economic Review*, 56: 734–57.

Dubravčić, D. (1970), 'Labour as an Entrepreneurial Input: An Essay in the Theory of the Producer Co-operative Economy', *Economica*, 37: 297–310.

Horvat, B. (1986), 'Farewell to the Illyrian Firm', *Economic Analysis and Workers' Management*, 20: 23–9.

Ireland, N. J. and Law, P. J. (1978) 'An Enterprise Incentive Fund for Labour Mobility in the Co-operative Economy', *Economica*, 45: 143-51.

Keren, M. and Levhari, D. (1992) 'Some Capital Market Failures in the Socialist Labor-Managed Economy', *Journal of Comparative Economics*, 16: 655–69.

Meade, J. E. (1972) 'The Theory of Labour-Managed Firms and of Profit Sharing', *Economic Journal*, 82 (Supplement): 402–28.

Meade, J. E. (1974) 'Labour-Managed Firms in Conditions of Imperfect Competition', *Economic Journal*, 84: 817–24.

Moene, K. O. and Wallerstein, M. (1993) 'Collective Bargaining Versus Workers' Ownership', *Journal of Comparative Economics*, 17: 628–45.

Sacks, S. R. (1983) *Self-Management and Efficiency: Large Corporations in Yugoslavia*, London: George Allen and Unwin.

Vanek, J. (1971) 'The Basic Theory of Financing of Participatory Firms', Working Paper No. 27, Department of Economics, Cornell University (quoted from J. Vanek (1977), *The Labor-Managed Economy*, Cornell University Press, pp. 186–98).

Ward, B. (1958) 'The Firm in Illyria: Market Syndicalism', *American Economic Review*, 48: 566–89.

6
Employee Participation in Enterprise Control and Returns: Patterns, Gaps and Discontinuities*

Mario Domenico Nuti

6.1 Introduction

This paper reviews and attacks the standard classification of enterprise types by degree of employee participation in enterprise returns and control rights, an approach exemplified by the work of Ben-Ner and Jones (1995). This is conceptualized as a continuous spectrum of combinations of different degrees of the two forms of participation, with continuous though non monotonic effects on productivity.

An alternative approach is developed in which, unlike that of Ben-Ner's and Jones's:

1. Returns may include not only net profits but also the net increase in enterprise capital value.
2. Control is divided between industrial democracy and entrepreneurial control.
3. Employees' dominant entrepreneurial control is split into two radically different cases according to whether control is exercised by employees individually holding a smaller share of equity than of

---

* This paper originated in a discussion on employee ownership at an ILO seminar held in Budapest in February 1997. I owe much to the seminar participants and in particular Felix FitzRoy, Derek Jones, Mark Klinedinst, George Lajtai, Niels Mygind, Charles Rock, Milica Uvalić, Daniel Vaughan-Whitehead – though many of them should be credited with views different, sometimes opposite, to those expressed here. While my views on employee participation, over time, have diverged from those of Branko Horvat (as exemplified, for instance, in Horvat, 1982) and other staunch supporters of self-managed and worker-owned enterprises, I still share Branko's values and I regard him as an important intellectual stimulus and source of inspiration. I therefore hope that he will accept this somewhat heretical text as a token of esteem and affection.

labour, in which case the possibility of employee exploitation of other shareholders arises (a possibility which lies outside the Ben-Ner and Jones framework).
4. Some combinations of the two forms of participation are shown to be impossible or at any rate unstable, such as dominant control without profit participation, or substantial participation in returns without substantial control rights.
5. James Meade's (1993) Agathotopian model is included in the taxonomy.

Classification discontinuities and gaps are revealed by this approach. These are shown to have significant implications for the impact of participation on productivity and other aspects of enterprise performance. The case for public policy support for participation is accordingly much weakened, if not altogether destroyed.

6.2 Employee participation: the standard framework

In a conventional capitalist enterprise all rights to entrepreneurial control and returns belong to the firm's owner or owners, or to shareholders in the case of a joint-stock company. Departures from this benchmark, in the guise of various degrees of employee participation in enterprise control and/or returns, occur frequently for different reasons, such as paternalism, profit maximization especially in the long run, inducements or obligations set by public policy. Traditional taxonomy of enterprise types according to degrees of employee participation envisages a continuous field of variation for both forms of participation in control and/or returns. In its most developed form, this approach is exemplified by the work of Ben-Ner and Jones (1995), who use it as a theoretical framework to investigate the continuous (though not necessarily monotonic) impact of both forms of participation on labour productivity.

Ben-Ner and Jones place types of enterprises on a grid by increasing degrees of participation (see Table 6.1). Their grid is limited to a 4x4 size only by practical constraints; employees' control rights go from zero to participation in control, sharing of control, and dominant control; return rights go from zero to small, moderate and majority degrees. However, the idea is that of a continuous spectrum of actual or possible enterprises graded by the intensity of both participation forms. Ben-Ner and Jones (1995) distinguish between participation's impact on individual and on organizational productivity – a distinction which we neglect here in looking at the overall impact regardless of sources.

Return rights held by employees	Control rights held by employees			
	None	Participation in control	Sharing of control	Dominant control
None	OA_1 Conventional firms	OA_2 Quality circles involving majority of workers	OA_3 Employee representation on board of directors	OA_4 British Industrial Common Ownership; e.g. Scott Bader
Small	OA_5 Profit sharing; ESOPS; e.g., Occidental Petroleum; Kimberly Clark	OA_6 Profit Sharing with participation programs	OA_7 Co-determination with another program; e.g., in Sweden co-determination sometimes exists with convertibles	OA_8 British Retail Coops[a]
Moderate	OA_9 ESOPS;[b] e.g., Proctor and Gamble; Corning Rucker Plans	OA_{10} Scanlon Plans; John Lewis; Lincoln Electronics; Polaroid; Japanese Mfg.	OA_{11} Producer Cooperatives;[c] e.g., U.K. Clothing Denmark	OA_{12} Producer Cooperatives,[d] e.g., U.K. footwear
Majority	OA_{13} ESOPS; e.g., Vermont Asbestos; Harcourt, Brace and Ivanovich; Lincoln S & L	OA_{14} ESOPS: e.g., Brooks Camera; Hyatt Clark; Ruddick	OA_{15} ESOPS: e.g., Weirton Steel; Rath; French building PCs	OA_{16} Producer Cooperatives; e.g., Mondragon; Italy; French Consulting; U.S. Plywood

[a] In some cases, workers constitute a majority of the decision-making board and employees have tiny amounts of profit sharing and ownership. See Jones (1987).
[b] Information on ESOPS is largely derived from Blasi and Kruse (1991: 14–20, and chap. 4) and Rosen, Durso, and Rothblatt (1990).
[c] Workers share control and other organizations, such as labour unions and consumer cooperatives.
[d] Workers have majority control of decision-making bodies, but modest amounts of profit sharing and/or individual ownership.
Source: Ben-Ner and Jones, 1995

94 *Employee Participation in Enterprise Control and Returns*

On its own, employee participation in enterprise returns is believed, by Ben-Ner and Jones, to have an uncertain impact on labour productivity. Employees are exposed only fractionally to the consequences of increasing or decreasing their own work effort; the increase in income uncertainty might bring risk-averse employees below the efficiency wage;[1] managers might be induced to neglect control in presence of employee participation in returns. In their view, these negative effects might reduce or even more than offset the direct positive impact of participation in returns.

Employee participation in control, again on its own, is believed by Ben-Ner and Jones likely to have a small positive effect when it affects employees' immediate work environment, with an otherwise uncertain impact for power sharing, and a negative impact when employees' voices become dominant.

The combination and interaction of both forms of participation, however, is believed to produce productivity effects which exceed the sum of the separate effects and may even be of the opposite sign. In particular, with the parallel rise of participation in returns, dominant employee participation in control reverses its effects from negative to positive, indeed to highly positive, in what turns out to be a superior organizational alternative: 'On balance, we expect that the organizational productivity of employee-owned firms will exceed that of firms with other ownership arrangements' (Ben-Ner and Jones, 1995: 547). Before we reach this peak, along the diagonal in Table 6.1 the commensurate rise of both control and return rights is presumed to have positive though less strong effects, although the complex balance of individual and organizational productivity effects may cause the relationship between participation and productivity to be non-monotonic (this is what Ben-Ner and Jones mean though they call it non-linear instead).

Using zero, (+) and (−) for small positive and negative effects, up to +, ++, +++ and down to −, the productivity impact of the participation schemes outlined in Table 6.1 according to Ben-Ner and Jones can be summarized thus:

0	(+)	+ or −	−
+ or −	+ +	+	+
+ or −	+	+ or −	+
+ or −	+	+	+ + +

If this were the case, Ben-Ner and Jones would have provided, without realizing it, an exceedingly strong case for treating employee participation in control and returns as a public good worthy of government education campaigns, direct subsidy and/or fiscal support. Without such support, enterprises experimenting with participation formulas, either only in control or only in returns, or with some forms of participation in both, might experience a negative impact on productivity or, at best, weak net benefits; participation is needed in both dimensions, and with a critical mass, before its full benefits can be reaped.

This paper takes the Ben-Ner and Jones framework as a useful point of departure but it introduces drastic changes in both the analytical approach and the conclusions reached.

6.3 Minor and major objections

A number of minor and major objections can be raised against this formulation. First, it is questionable that participation in returns on its own might have negative effects. Presumably, mutual monitoring of employee effort (which Ben-Ner and Jones confuse with 'emulative behavior') gets rid of individual incentive to slack; profit-maximizing enterprises would not allow incomes to fall below the efficiency wage through higher uncertainty; it is not at all clear why managers should reduce their monitoring efforts simply because of employee participation in returns (presumably it is a matter of indifference to managers whether they share the product of their monitoring with owners or with other employees). The productivity impact of employee participation in returns may not necessarily be large enough to induce companies to introduce it, but is unlikely to be negative. At the same time, there is no reason why voice – beyond industrial democracy which might decrease productivity – should necessarily enhance the impact of participation in returns: quite the contrary, a great supporter of profit sharing such as Weitzman (1984) specifically rules out any form of participation in entrepreneurial control, in order to prevent insiders from keeping out outsiders *à la* Ward (1958).

Secondly, there can be no difference between 'participation in control' and 'sharing of control' seeing that neither are 'dominant'. We propose a distinction instead between control over work organization, that is, 'industrial democracy', and entrepreneurial control – whether in a minority or dominant position – over basic decisions such as those on price, output, employment, wages, investment, finance.[3] Effective industrial democracy will have an indeterminate impact on productivity; the impact may be negative, as employees may be 'feather-bedding' their jobs more than is justified by accompanying productivity increases. Participation in entrepreneurial control, unless dominant, will be largely ineffective; if dominant, it will sooner or later lead to participation in returns, whether informally through salaries and employment higher than is compatible with profit maximization, or formally through the introduction of participation in enterprise returns; enterprise owners will be unlikely to allow employee dominant participation in control. It follows that enterprises with dominant employee control and zero or little participation in returns can only exist, if at all, as a transient phenomenon.

Thirdly, strictly speaking, what matters is not whether employees have 'dominant' control, in the sense of a majority position, but whether they have 'effective' control. This may require more than 50 per cent of the votes plus one, if employees are absent or intimidated, while substantially less than 50 per cent of the votes may yield effective control if a sufficient number of other shareholders are absentees. In order not to complicate matters, we retain the notion of 'dominant control' – understood as 'effective control'. The only significant difference is that the point beyond which control is effective will vary from one enterprise to another, according to the degree of dispersion and involvement of its shareholders.

Fourthly, it is immaterial whether or not employees obtain a 'majority' share in enterprise returns. While a majority voice in enterprise control makes a world of difference, it makes no difference at all whether employees have somewhat more or somewhat less than majority returns. Moreover, presumably, the same share in return may be high or low according to capital intensity of output.

Two aspects of participation in returns, on the contrary, make a vital difference:

1 It matters a great deal whether returns are simply a share of current profits (or even current dividends), in which case employees will have a short time horizon and a justified reluctance to reinvest, or whether returns also include the increase in the capital value of the enterprise as a going concern due to its success.[3] It is, in any case, inconceivable that there could be substantial participation in returns (especially if they include capital gains) without substantial control rights.
2 It also matters a very great deal, when employees have dominant control, whether such control is in the hands of individuals holding a smaller share of equity than of labor supply. In such case employees stand to gain more from higher wages as employees than they stand to lose as shareholders. Therefore they will have an incentive

to decide higher wages, or to sustain higher employment, than would be warranted by profit maximisation in the same market conditions. Such case lies outside the Ben-Ner and Jones framework (see Nuti, 1997). (The same opportunity to exploit other shareholders arises also for stakeholders other than employees, when shareholders who have an individual share smaller than their proportional stake have a controlling interest.)

6.4 An alternative framework

The minor and major objections raised in the previous section, plus some additional considerations developed below, are summarized in Figure 6.1. This figure also visualizes a pattern of enterprise types that emerges from the proposed conceptualization of participation schemes. Enterprises are bunched into distinct groups which are strictly separated from each other. In Figure 6.1, employee participation in control along the horizontal axis goes from zero to industrial democracy to entrepreneurial control (non-dominant control becoming dominant beyond a point which is enterprise-specific). The top left hand cell contains the traditional capitalist enterprise (OA1 in Table 6.1); on its right, up to the threshold between non-dominant and dominant control, we find Mitbestimmung and equivalent arrangements (OA2 and OA3). The top right cell is labeled 'desert' to stress the non-sustainability of dominant entrepreneurial control and lack of participation in returns (see above).

Along the vertical axis, participation in returns goes from zero to participation only in net profit, to participation in both profit and capital gains. A value of one signifies full participation in both; another 'desert' labels the unlikely combination of significant participation in returns without some participation in control. Participation in profits only takes the form of profit-sharing (without control or, at any rate, with non-dominant control, with OA6, OA7, OA10). Dominant control plus participation in profits only is to be found in traditional cooperatives (OA4, OA8, OA11, OA12, OA16), as well as in 'Illyrian' enterprises (that is Yugoslav type 'associationist' firms which Ben-Ner and Jones 1995 unduly exclude from their taxonomy); strictly speaking, all cases of non-transferable capital rights of employees find their place in this cell. There remains the bottom right cell for various degrees of entrepreneurial control, and up to 100 per cent participation in profit and capital gains. This is the standard case of shareholding employees, as long as a controlling interest is exercised by individuals holding a smaller share of equity than labour (including OA5, OA9, OA13, OA14,

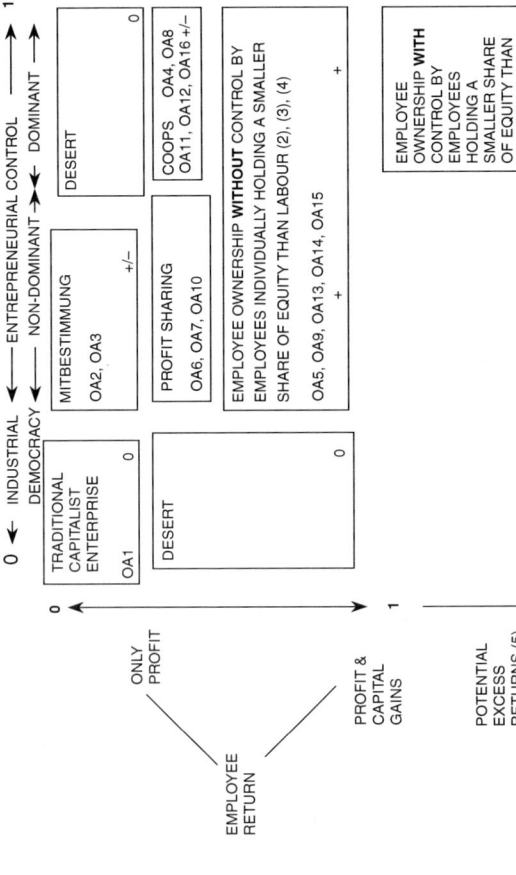

Figure 6.1 An alternative view of employee participation in enterprise control and returns

1 This involves, exclusively, decisions about labour organization and work conditions.
2 Participation through shareholding means that participation in results is normally no greater than participation in enterprise equity; it can be less if there is profit sharing with non-shareholding employees; hence this area ought to have a triangular shape, with the 90 degree angle at the top right end. Here, the area is drawn as a rectangle to allow for the possibility that some of the company shares may be privileged, that is, non-voting.
3 James Meade's Agathotopia (the 'Good Place' not shown in any map) is not represented here either; it can be imagined as a segment within an area beyonded by the diagonal sloping down from the top left end to the bottom right end corner. In Agathothopia, employees share net value-added and capital gains; their share is exactly proportional to their total shares (of both labour shares and, possibly also, capital shares) – hence the location along the diagonal.
4 Russia lies across the two areas of employee ownership.
5 That is, potential expropriation of other shareholders.
6 Probably institutionally unstable, as shareholding employees cease to be employees or shareholders, or acquire a larger equity share than their labour share; or the enter-

OA15). Outside the space considered by Ben-Ner and Jones, below the line of 100 per cent participation in profit and capital gains, there is another area, where employee ownership is accompanied by control in the hands of employees individually holding a smaller share of equity than labour – in which case the exercise of dominant control leads to potential excess returns, right down to the expropriation of other shareholders. This cell is not empty: it contains a large proportion of Russian enterprises privatized in 1994–8.[4]

This class of 'below the line', potentially exploitative enterprise is institutionally unstable: it is likely to be 'eaten up' by employees distributing its net assets among themselves; it will be refused credit and equity capital. The type of enterprise in the top right cell, if it temporarily existed, would be doubly institutionally unstable, first moving to this class of 'below the line' potentially exploitative enterprises, then vanishing as such for the reasons given in the previous paragraph.

An additional possibility is the utopia, or rather the 'Agathotopia' (etymologically a 'good place') proposed by James Meade (1993). Meade's Agathothopian enterprise is a 100 per cent participatory enterprise with ordinary capital-shares and temporary labour-shares for employees, commanding equal dividends. Employees receive a dividend in lieu of wages, and therefore the whole value added net of rentals and interest is distributed instead of net profit. Each employee is issued, at the time of hiring, with as many shares as would yield the going wage rate, and thereafter throughout his/her employment gains or loses from enterprise performance being better or worse than anticipated. By definition, net value added is distributed according to the number of shares owned by employees and by outsiders, thus avoiding the kind of conflict illustrated in the previous paragraph – though there may be residual problems in the treatment of pension rights or the possible periodical revision of individual employee shares (Meade, 1993). The scheme has the advantage of transforming employees into entrepreneurs – at the cost of additional risk which therefore requires additional arrangements such as part-time non-wage labour, or a citizenship income. In Figure 6.1 Meade's Agathotopian enterprise corresponds to a segment of the diagonal going from top left to bottom right, located within the bottom right hand rectangle (not represented).

6.5 Policy implications

This kind of classification and accompanying reflections place employee ownership in a more sobering light and weaken the case for public policy support for participation schemes. The signs of productivity effects, expected of the various types of employee participation in control and returns regrouped according to Figure 6.1, instead of Table 6.1, form a smaller matrix than for Table 6.1, of the type:

$$\begin{array}{ccc} 0 & + & - \\ 0 & + & +/- \\ 0 & + & +/- \end{array}$$

It does not justify public encouragement for moving in a top left/bottom right direction – lest enterprises are pushed into inferior areas in which employee control and return rights become too much of a good thing. The bottom line of this alternative approach is that the discovery and implementation of positive effects of participation on productivity and other aspects of economic performance is best left to spontaneous market forces: 'se son rose, fioriranno'.[5]

Notes

1. For instance, if total earnings of risk-averse employees remained unchanged and a part of them was now volatile (though even that may be at least partly offset by a higher probability of continued employment).
2. This distinction is recognized, but not used, by Ben-Ner and Jones (1995).
3. Participation in profits includes deferred distribution of profits accumulated over time as in Mondragon cooperatives. The distinction between return as net profits and as capital gains escapes Ben-Ner and Jones because they do not include among ownership rights the right to transfer; they talk of temporary or contingent property rights – in which case, of course, temporary or contingent owners cannot cash in any of the increment in enterprise value. But this is wrong both in law and economic conceptualization: there is simply no such thing as a temporary or a contingent property right. Usufruct is a part of a property right, not a temporary property right.
4. Jones (1996) suggests that 'in transition economies privatisation does not produce fundamental changes in inherited patterns of corporate governance but rather has served to strengthen managerial control. There is no strong evidence that the key obstacle to enhanced performance is employee ownership'. At the same time, it seems premature to dismiss dominant employee ownership as a major factor explaining the low degree of capacity and employment restructuring in the Russian economy to date.
5. 'If they are flowers, they will blossom' (Italian proverb).

References

Ben-Ner, A. and Jones, D. C. (1995) 'Employee Participation, Ownership, and Productivity: a Theoretical Framework', *Industrial Relations*, 34(4): 532–44.

Blasi, J. and Kruse, D. (1991) *The New Owners*, New York: Harper Business.
Horvat, B. (1982) *The Political Economy of Socialism: A Marxist Social Theory*, Armonk, N.Y.: M. E. Sharpe, Inc.
Jones, D. C. (1987) 'Productivity Effects of Worker Directors and Financial Participation by Employees in the Firm: the Case of British Retail Cooperatives', *Industrial and Labour Relations Review*, 41: 79–82.
Jones, D. C. (1996) 'Privatisation and Restructuring in Russia: a Review and Micro Evidence from St. Petersburg', LBS Conference Paper, 19–20 September.
Meade, J. E. (1993) *Liberty, Equality and Efficiency – Apologia pro Agathotopia Mea*, London: Macmillan.
Nuti, D. M. (1997) 'Employeeism: Corporate Governance and Employee Share Ownership in Transition Economies', in M. I. Blejer, and M. Škreb (eds.), *Macroeconomic Stabilisation in Transition Economies*, Cambridge: Cambridge University Press, pp. 126–54
Rosen, C., Durso, G. and Rothblatt, P. (1990) *International Developments in Employee Ownership*, Oakland: National Centre for Employee Ownership.
Ward, B. (1958) 'The Firm in Illyria: Market Syndicalism', *American Economic Review*, 48: 566–89.
Weitzman, M. L. (1984) *The Share Economy*, Cambridge, Mass: Harvard University Press.

7
Employee Involvement and the Modern Firm*

Tea Petrin and Aleš Vahčič

7.1 Introduction

In the early 1970s the topic of workers' participation attracted great attention among economists and also among other social scientists. Undoubtedly, professor Horvat has been the leading economist who devoted his rich scientific work to the development of the concept of workers' self-management in the Marxist tradition. He has also popularized the concept among the Western and Eastern socialist economists and has had a significant number of followers particularly among his students. He presented his ideas in a large number of works published in the West as well as in the East. Here we will refer mainly to his seminal work *The Political Economy of Socialism* (Horvat, 1982).

With the fall of socialism it may seem that his work was lost. This, however, is not the case. There are at least two reasons for that. First, Professor Horvat stressed that certain conditions must be fulfilled for the implementation of workers' self-management: '(i) Long industrial tradition..., (ii) Long tradition in political democracy..., (iii) High personal incomes..., (iv) Short working week..., and (v) High level of education...' (Horvat, 1982: 218). He stressed that the implementation of self-management, due to the highly demanding set of factors, is possible only in highly developed societies. This is obviously the old Marxist conclusion that socialism can potentially be successfully introduced in the most developed countries.

---

*This contribution is based on the paper presented at the 9th Conference of the International Association for the Economics of Participation, Clifton Hill House, University of Bristol, Bristol, 26–8 June 1998.

Secondly, when they started to liberalize, the so-called socialist countries did not choose the democratic form of market socialism (that is, self-management) but instead opted for a radical variant of capitalism; in those countries in which workers' participation was practiced, it was not completely abolished and today it continues to be practiced at least as some form of co-determination. In highly developed countries, which are also the most successful global economies, workers' involvement in different forms not only survives, but is increasingly becoming one of the factors determining the success of companies. In this respect Horvat's analysis on the prospects of self-management proved to be correct. This article is the contribution to the elaboration of this idea in the following framework.

First, we discuss the economist's approach in studying the world from the point of view of economic welfare. In this respect, the question – how can economic agents be induced to allocate scarce resources for the greater benefit of the population – is in the center of our interest. The field of workers' self-management and participation offers one possible solution to this problem. The hypothesis is that under certain conditions, workers' control of firms and/or participation in the management of firms will lead to superior results. Not only will the efficiency of allocation be higher but also there will be additional benefits of a more egalitarian distribution of income and a higher degree of freedom.

Secondly, we examine how other disciplines such as management, political science, sociology, engineering, deal with the above question. While economists traditionally deal with the economy as a whole, they have been only marginally interested in the actual functioning of firms.[1] Other disciplines focus on different aspects of the same fundamental question, namely: in what way is the manner in which people are involved in economic activities important for maximization of economic welfare?

Thirdly, we consider the possible benefits of cooperation among different disciplines in order to arrive at better policy solutions for people's involvement in economic activities for attaining a higher level of welfare.

Throughout the paper, lessons from Yugoslavia before its disintegration as well as from Slovenia are drawn. The reason is that both countries practiced self-management based on collective and social ownership. They illustrate whether workers' control of firms and/or participation in the management of firms did or did not lead to superior results, as hypothesized. They also illustrate why we foresee increased workers' (employee) participation in the future as the consequence of the change in management paradigm triggered off by the Deming's quality movement.

7.2 Three approaches to economic welfare

Economists study the world within the paradigm of welfare economics. A practical goal of studying economics is to learn something that will be useful for policy advice: how to put in place economic institutions and policies that would lead to higher economic welfare. In the past there were three main approaches to attaining maximum economic welfare:

1. a centrally planned economic system, based on state ownership;
2. a free market system based on private ownership; and
3. a self-management market economic system based on social or collective ownership.

When the centrally planned system collapsed, the hope of market-oriented socialist economists that reforms in the socialist countries would go in the direction of the third way, was not fulfilled. Before the collapse of the communist system, the expectation of market-oriented socialist economists was that the transition to the democratic socialist market economy would change state ownership into social or collective ownership, with the control given to the employees. On the macro policy level, it was hoped that countries would be open to international competition and, internally, the creation of new firms would be promoted.

The third way looked ideal. The field of Workers' Self-management and Participation offers one possible solution to this problem. The hypothesis is that, under certain conditions, workers' control of firm and/or participation in the management of firms will lead to superior results. Not only will the efficiency of allocation be higher but also there will be additional benefits of a more egalitarian distribution of income and a higher degree of freedom. In particular, competition would ensure efficiency, social ownership would ensure egalitarian income distribution and workers' control would ensure workplace democracy. Normal macroeconomic policy would ensure stable prices and a stable balance of payments and budget. Yugoslavia was expected to lead the way because it had many of the elements of this system already in place.

This did not happen. The self-management model did not work well under the old regime because the efficiency assumptions were not fulfilled. When the socialist countries decided to make the transition to the market economy, there was a chance to correct for the inefficiencies and implement this model. However, even Slovenia, which had the most open and the least rigid communist regime, opted for the fully capitalist solution and never really considered continuing and further developing the self-management system. The last attempt to save at least some elements of the self-management system in Slovenia were the privatization proposals that favoured management-employee buyouts.

In all 27 new East European countries the free market system based on private ownership was, with few exceptions, faithfully implemented. So, the free market system, based on private ownership, is the winner. Although it is the winner, it is still far from ideal, and serious problems, like those we shall discuss below, persist.

First, the concentration of income and wealth is occurring at an accelerated pace on a global scale. The ultimate consequence of this system under the present institutional arrangements is that the winner takes all. This has become a topic of serious discussion among influential government and academic circles throughout the world (Stiglitz, 1998).

Secondly, in a large number of countries there is large-scale corruption and appropriation of income by the privileged classes. This is characteristic not only of the underdeveloped market economies, but also of advanced democracies like Italy, Japan, Mexico, USA, and so on.

Thirdly, the free market approach has consequences for workplace democracy. Here, the results are rather contradictory. On the one hand, we are witnessing increased employee participation within companies. Increased employee involvement has become a prerequisite for attaining competitiveness. On the other hand, competitiveness requires a high degree of flexibility not only regarding production processes but also regarding workforce. In the past decade, this has created the wave of layoffs during the downsizing periods of large companies. Workforce flexibility, another prerequisite for attaining competitiveness, is hampering workers' participation because job security is no longer assured.

Are we then witnessing an era of increasing or decreasing workplace democracy on a global scale? This question is addressed in the next section.

7.3 Employee involvement and competitiveness

Separate from a largely ideological discussion on the three systems (for example, which one is the best, or which system assures greater justice), a new perception of how firms should be run has gradually been emerging. This new perception is not a result of political or academic discussion on the relative merits of different economic systems. Instead, the new approach to management emerged from the pragmatic day-to-day running of corporations and companies. The two major changes, which deeply influenced management science, are described below.

First, there is a revival of entrepreneurship. Entrepreneurship has become accepted as one of the central forces of economic growth. The entrepreneurial firms are defined by two elements. First, they pursue continuous improvement in methods, products and processes. And second, they are firms in which entrepreneurial activity is transformed from its traditional individualist activity into collective activity (Best, 1990).

Economists have noticed this change towards entrepreneurship, and the promotion of new firm formation became an important part of proposed policies as it is still within the economists' conceptual framework. However, most of the new literature on entrepreneurship is coming from the field of management (Drucker, 1985, 1991; Stevenson, Roberts and Grousbeck, 1985; Timmons, 1990), an area unfamiliar to most economists. There is now a vast literature on entrepreneurship and there are about 20 professional journals specializing in this field. The entrepreneurship bibliography currently contains over 30 000 entries.

The second major change was the replacement of hierarchical management models by models with different degrees of decentralization of management decision-making (Nadler, 1977; Peters and Waterman, 1982; Walton, 1987; Sengenberger and Loveman, 1987; Cole, 1989; Kanter, 1989; Kochan and Useem, 1992; Hamel and Prahalad, 1994; Nonaka and Takeuchi, 1995).

Economists have largely ignored changes concerning company management because those changes fell outside the economists' conceptual framework. In our view, the key changes have actually occurred in this sphere. This change in the management paradigm was triggered off by the quality movement (continuous changes in product, processes, and being first on the market). It was started by W. Edwards Deming and Joseph M. Juran in Japan. The movement then spread to the US and is now rapidly proliferating throughout the world (Deming, 1982). A small group of economists working in the area of Industrial Organization followed this development and have identified these major changes in global competitive conditions. Their work has become known through Michael Best's writings as the 'new competition' (Best, 1990; see for example also Lazonick, 1991; Piore and Sable, 1984; Porter, 1990).

The policy advice developed from these ideas encouraged the government to speed up the dissemination of knowledge on how to adapt to the new competition through introduction of new principles that include focus on quality, focus on customers, continuous improvement, reducing waste and work in progress, just in time operations management, flexible specialization and inter-firm relationship, networking and benchmarking (Spendolini, 1992; Watson, 1993; Cox, Wolfram, Mann, and Samson, 1997).

Numerous successful firms have implemented such systems. Moreover, all major consulting companies have helped to develop consulting programs for the introduction of quality approach to management.

In Europe, the quality movement is primarily associated with the introduction of ISO 9000. These quality focused management systems were initially associated with operations management and manufacturing systems. It is now increasingly recognized that the general principles of the new approach can be applied through the whole organization, including administration and management. The introduction of this system requires a total change in attitude. It can only be implemented as a long run and continuous project.

Because these systems were historically implemented on the shop floor, the technology of introducing and implementing them was primarily developed by engineers (Deming, 1982; Shingo, 1983, 1985; Kobayashi, 1995). Eventually, academics in the field of management started to appreciate the cost reduction and productivity gains resulting from these systems, but only after a substantial delay. The new management system was running contrary to the practice of traditional departmentalized organizations.

7.4 Lessons from Slovenia

As already mentioned, the practical purpose of the study of economics is to develop a foundation for policy advice. Already during the mid-1980s, it was felt in Slovenia that something would have to be done to increase the efficiency of a stagnating economy. In the liberal circles of the Communist Party, there was also a readiness to discuss major changes. In Slovenia as well as the rest of Yugoslavia, the market-oriented economists started to gain influence over the direction of structural change in the economy.

One of the ideas that became widely accepted was to speed up entry of new firms, to boost the number of entrepreneurs in order to dynamize the highly concentrated and stagnant industrial structure. The theoretical basis for this was the Marshallian concept of competition, where the entry of new firms is a necessary condition for efficiency. A further theoretical impetus came from the economics of self-management, where entry was crucial for ensuring allocative efficiency (Vanek, 1972).

Gradually, national action programs were defined and budgetary sources were allocated for the systematic promotion of new firms. Programs to support the entry of new firms, private or social, were introduced on the national scale. It was expected that each republic would establish an agency for the development of small and medium-sized enterprises as well as entrepreneurship based on models from the USA and West Germany (Petrin, Vahčič and Denda, 1990).

This first experience revealed some interesting features of self-managed and private firms. The immediate reaction of existing large firms was to block entry in order to protect their monopoly position. After some time, when it became clear that entry was primarily from small firms, the resistance came from the existing small firms. Resistance to competition came not only from the orthodox Communist dogma but also from vested interests of both self-managed enterprises and small private businesses. However, this did not block the activities for the development of entrepreneurship as the main source of entry of new firms.

The new entry promotion activities were initially dominated by economists who based their views on Schumpeter's writings on the role of entrepreneurship (Schumpeter, 1934). At the very beginning, there was little knowledge about entrepreneurship as an academic field, or practical entrepreneurship promotion schemes as practiced in the West. Gradually, this knowledge was acquired and entrepreneurship as an academic field was promoted. Practical entrepreneurship promotion schemes, as developed in the West, were put in place (Petrin and Vahčič, 1987; Petrin, 1989; Vahčič; 1996). The entry of new firms through the promotion of entrepreneurship brought an end to the former dominance of bureaucratic entrepreneurship. It also increased the number of active decision-makers to carry out entrepreneurial functions. In the past, this function was concentrated in the same people, whether on enterprise or bureaucratic level, year in and year out. Although we will not discuss this issue further here (see for example Petrin, 1989), it is important to stress that in our view, entrepreneurship is not hindered by employee participation in decision making. On the contrary, employee participation may be the only way for the entrepreneurial firms to survive in the future under the conditions of new competition.

The entry of new firms was viewed as only one source, although a very important one, of increasing competitiveness of the Slovene economy (D'Andrea Tyson, Petrin and Rogers, 1994). To reverse the economic decline, the entry of small, new firms, which satisfied local demand, was not the only thing needed. A development of export-oriented production firms was also necessary. Otherwise, the entry of small, new firms would have only a short-term effect on economic growth and competitiveness of the Slovene economy. To achieve export competitiveness, the restructuring of existing enterprises was needed. The restructuring would follow the pattern of industrial restructuring in those countries which were the most successful competitors in the world. This further implied that entrepreneurs and managers, as well as workers' collectives and policy makers, would have to concentrate on strategies that were best suited for gaining international competitive advantage. This meant that Slovene companies would have to restructure according to the organizational and production principles of the new competition. Whereas the old production paradigm was based on minimizing the costs of producing standardized products, the new production paradigm was based on establishing the competitive advantage through superior product design and permanent innovation.

There were several attempts to stimulate restructuring of Slovene enterprises in order to gain international competitiveness. Two such projects[2] were based on the principles of new competition (see Petrin, 1992, 1995, 1996). In reality, it meant the introduction of total quality management in the enterprises as well as cooperation among enterprises in the form of strategic groups. The first of the two projects, which was carried out in 1989–90 and 1990–92, will be discussed here from the point of view of employee involvement.

The project revealed clearly the importance of employee involvement. It was found that any meaningful restructuring demanded the involvement of everyone in the enterprise. It was crucial that everybody gained an understanding of the new production and organizational principles on which the internal restructuring would then be based.

Programs of this type depend, to a great extent, on the methodology used. Because this means a deep change of enterprise culture, a thoroughly tested approach should be used and the results cannot be obtained in a short period of time. In the wood-processing industry, we found that the main cause of low international competitiveness was low operational efficiency. For the introduction of the new management system, we chose a well-tested system of '20 keys' – a system developed by the Japanese management consultant Iwao Kobayashi (Kobayashi, 1995).

The twenty areas of the 20 Keys system cover all aspects of enterprise operations. The areas are cleaning and organizing, management by objectives, team activities, reducing inventories, quick change-over technology, value analysis, zero monitoring, coupled manufacturing, maintenance of equipment, time control, quality assurance, developing suppliers, eliminating waste, empowering workers to make improvements, skill versatility and cross training, production scheduling, efficiency control, using information systems, conserving energy and materials, and technology.

From this list it is obvious that the system ties together practically everything which the productivity consultants have identified as important for increasing efficiency of production. This system stresses that long lasting improvements cannot be achieved by concentrating only on parts of the areas listed. Improvements in these areas support each other, and the movement to higher levels of achievement in any of these areas requires simultaneous improvement in all others.

This is, however, impossible to achieve without the total involvement of everyone in the organization, from the janitor to the top level of management. This further requires detailed information on the operation of the enterprise both at the strategic and the process level. This program, if consistently implemented, leads to a coherent workers' collective where improvements are both performance oriented and people oriented. This means that the improvement of working conditions, interpersonal relationships, safety, personal development (people oriented improvement) is as important as the achievement of lower cost, better quality and faster delivery to customers (performance oriented improvements). Complex systems of performance improvement like this one cannot function at all without achieving full employee participation in team-based improvement activities.

The 20 Keys system, when firmly adopted in an enterprise, creates a long lasting environment. That is beneficial for everyone. Employees at all levels recognize their interdependence and work together towards common goals. Frequently, the employees in companies that successfully implement these systems develop after-work activities where employees get to know each other better and thus further boost the cooperative spirit in the work place.

In coping with the problem of how to acquire the know-how for the implementation of 20 Keys, enterprises developed inter-firm relations previously unknown to them. In spite of the self-management system, which theoretically promotes cooperation, the companies viewed each other as competitors, competing for domestic customers. Each company produced similar wood products because of the low product specialization in the industry. As a result, the doors of the factories were firmly closed to each other and there was no cooperation established along the production chain.

However, during the implementation of 20 Keys, every company included in the project soon recognized that they could all benefit substantially if they established a consultative relationship among themselves. As a result, the networking hub KONLES (Consortium for wood processing) was established, including ten companies which were implementing 20 Keys, to facilitate the acquisition of the necessary knowledge on a shared basis. They also began to develop cooperation in production, marketing and so on, and to share knowledge on how to ensure enterprise adaptability through project teams and other relevant employees.

This new organizational form encouraged companies not only to compete on a higher quality base, but also to cooperate in order to turn the paradox of competition into an advantage. It was foreseen that this relationship would eventually form a base for the development of a sector strategy through which independent firms would realize Schumpeterian non-price forms of competition. Strategically managed inter-firm associations can promote the long term development and competitiveness of a sector due to the utilization of organizational innovations that emerge among firms.

The case of the 20 Keys approach is just one of several successful systems of implementation of the new approach to management through quality and inter-firm relations. In Slovenia today, the introduction of such systems in companies is being implemented through the network of external and in-company consultants – mainly within the framework of the Slovene Quality Association, supported by the Chamber of Commerce – and through the implementation of computer based business re-engineering projects.

What did we learn from these projects with respect to both past experiences of self-management, and the future of workers' participation and its contribution to workplace democracy and firm competitiveness?

In our view, the failure of the past self-management system was not only due to the fact that people associated self-management with the undemocratic Communist regime, but also the system really did not work. The operational rules of self-management were prescribed from outside and were very rigid, leaving little scope for creativity. In addition, the right to participate in decision making processes was not accountable. Neither workers nor managers were responsible for the outcomes of their decisions.[3] This is the reason why self-management, as practiced in the past, is viewed by managers trying to implement management based on quality, as a hindering factor. Many workers, however, see the type of involvement, that a management based on quality is demanding, as less liberal compared to the previous regime.

Not only was individual activity thwarted because of the regulation of the entry of new firms, it was also regulated by the management within existing firms. Empirical evidence showed that workers' creativity, and in particular their incentives to change, to improve production processes or products, although in principle central to self-management, were chronically neglected (Petrin, 1986; Glas *et al.*, 1987). Inside the enterprise, self-management was largely limited to the sphere of income distribution and conditions of work, and was not incorporated into the issue of how production should be organized and carried out. These questions were held to be a prerogative of management, whose position in the firm depended mainly on good connections with the State and political bureaucracy. Those connections actually kept them away from making entrepreneurial decisions and from adopting entrepreneurial behaviour. Not surprisingly, then, Yugoslav self-managed firms lacked the team-work and collective atmosphere which is so characteristic of successful Japanese firms and world class firms elsewhere that have adopted a quality approach to management. In this way, the development process was limited by the dominance of bureaucratic entrepreneurship mainly geared at the establishment of big enterprises that produced low quality, mass-produced products for protected domestic markets (Petrin, 1989).

The question that remains to be discussed here is whether the old system was a good base for real employee participation which could simultaneously achieve both performance and personal improvements.

It is our view that the achievement of both goals, company competitiveness and personal satisfaction through employee involvement, cannot be achieved without significant technical know-how, since it requires a complete change in organizational culture and people's behaviour. This is why the selection of the best suitable procedure for the implementation of required changes is of crucial importance.

In spite of good intentions, the introduction of quality-based management into a company frequently fails. This occurs when the introduction of the organizational change is perceived by employees as manipulative or is associated with competitive, rather than cooperative goals (Tjosvold, 1998; Tung-Chun, 1997). The more fundamental question still remains, namely, whether any such systems will have a lasting effect if the workers are not the owners or do not have significant stakes in the business performance of the company. Two possible directions can be foreseen.

First, with increased worker involvement in business processes, greater investment in employee knowledge and the improvement of working conditions as the companies move into knowledge-based production processes and product development areas, the transparency of company operation increases and workers become better placed to participate in business decision-making. Therefore, one solution may be to establish a closer connection between business results and workers' involvement. Such a system, for example, is the open book management system (Case, 1998) which has lately become popular in the US. Under this system, workers are given detailed cash flow information, and over time develop a remuneration system which links the individual or team contribution to cash flow. This is one form of profit sharing, but it is also very close to the original intention of the self-management system in the former Yugoslavia.

The second solution may lie in the fact that people will become motivated out of self-interest to acquire skills such as team work, cross department collaboration, multiple technical skills and so on, which are characteristic of firms with a quality based management, even when they do not expect that they will work permanently in such a company. The reason is that world class companies will increasingly expect these skills from newcomers and even temporary workers. Cooperative skills can become a basic requirement for being hired. We can foresee the situation where workplaces, as a result, will be much more cooperative and democratic than they are today. This development, we should stress, will come as a result of collective learning from world class companies and not from political or academic sources.

7.5 Conclusion

There is no simple model of the organization of the firm that can describe the complexity of rapidly changing production modes. Coexistence of solutions, depending on branch, technology, culture, habits and so forth, will prevail. The view of the firm as a collective of homogeneous individuals, with equal interests in the long-term survival of the firm, is no longer valid. Governments are gradually abandoning the full responsibility for the social security of people and, increasingly, individuals and their families have to take responsibility for their income and wealth. We are witnessing not only the globalization of firms but also the globalization of individual/family income sources and wealth. Therefore, loyalty to one firm, which is an implicit assumption of the self-management model, is increasingly becoming questionable. Also, with new trends of models of systems integration (Best, 1997), people are increasingly required to understand what other firms are doing, in greater detail.

What are the implications for workers' participation? It is quite obvious that there will be ever less worker and employee participation of the type foreseen by the traditional self-management model. The basic reason is that fewer and fewer firms conform to the organization according to the assumptions of the traditional theory of the firm. However, there will be an increased trend towards much greater flexibility in the ways people are included in the operations of the firm. Although loyalty of a worker may be limited, efficiency will require that the minimum time be spent on the full inclusion of a newcomer in the work process of any company. This will require, on the company's part, the development of an efficient and transparent information system which will clearly show the relationship between the company's performance and the contribution of the employee. Such a system should describe the company's business process in a way that enables the employee to understand his/her role in this process quickly. On the employee's part, this will require cooperative skills. There will be more democratic and open decision-making in the companies and this will gradually lead to the achievement of welfare goals: higher income, fairer distribution and more creative work environment.

These developments will not be based on political and ideological considerations. This seems to be a natural consequence of profound technological change which we are witnessing today. The information and knowledge-based economies require open societies with political democracy and increasingly higher investment in life-long education and training. Increased efficiency will lead to higher personal incomes, which will enable people to choose shorter working weeks (witness Germany and France). Changes will be the fastest in the countries with a long industrial tradition (such as in Western Europe). But are these not familiar points which professor Horvat stressed as conditions for the implementation of workers' self-management? After all, Professor Horvat's and Marxist insight into the dynamics of human society may not be so far from a future reality.

Notes

1 Rather, they have been mainly interested in the macroeconomic consequences of different assumptions of the firm's behaviour.
2 (1) 'Restructuring the Wood Processing Industry According To the Principles of New Competition and Networking of Firms in Notranjska and Primorska Regions and the Community of Ljubljana', 1989–92, carried out by T. Petrin, M. Best and R. Vitez, and supported by the Ministry of Science and Technology of the Republic of Slovenia. (2) 'Revitalization of Enterprises',

the project of the Government of Slovenia, directed by T. Petrin and R. Vitez, 1993-4.
3 Prevailing opinion among Slovene managers is that in comparison to, for example, Poland, self-management gave only short-run advantages to Slovenian firms – workers were used to take decisions – but not the long-un advantages, since qualitative changes in the workplace are much harder to achieve. Persistence by workers not to become accountable for their decisions is very high. (Quoted from the director of the wood processing company *Javor*, which was also included in the above mentioned project).

References

Best, M. (1990) *The New Competition: Institutions of Industrial Restructuring*, Cambridge MA: Polity Press.
Best, M. (1997) *'System Integration'*, Center for Industrial Competitiveness, University of Massachusetts, Lowell.
Case, J. (1998) *The Open-Book Experience*, Cambridge, MA: Parseous Books.
Cole, R. E. (1989) *Strategies for Learning: Small-Group Activities in American, Japanese, and Swedish Industry*, Berkeley: University of California Press.
Cox, J., Wolfram, R., Mann, L. and Samson, D. (1997) 'Benchmarking as a Mixed Metaphor: Disentangling Assumptions of Competition and Collaboration', *Journal of Management Studies*, 34(2): 287-314.
D'Andrea Tyson, L., Petrin, T. and Rogers, H. (1994) 'Promoting Entrepreneurship in Eastern Europe'. *Small Business Economics*, 6(3): 165-85.
Deming, W. E. (1982) *Quality, Productivity and Competitive Position*, Cambridge, MA: MIT Center for Advanced Engineering Study.
Drucker, P. F. (1985) *Innovation and Entrepreneurship: Practices and Principles*, London: Heinemann.
Drucker, P. F. (1991) 'The New Productivity Challenge', *Harvard Business Review*, Nov.–Dec.: 69-79.
Glas, M. *et al.* (1987) 'Analiza vzrokov učinkovitosti in neučinkovitosti gospodarjenja v družbenem sektorju', Raziskovalni center Ekonomske fakultete, Ljubljana.
Hamel, G. and Prahalad, C. K. (1994) *Competing for the Future*, Cambridge MA: Harvard Business School Press.
Horvat, B. (1982) *Politička ekonomija socijalizma*, Zagreb: Globus.
Kanter, R. M. (1989) *When Giants Learn to Dance: Mattering the Challenge of Strategy, Management, and Careers in the 1990s*, New York: Simon and Schuster.
Kobayashi, I. (1995) *20 Keys to Workplace Improvement*, revised edition, Portland, OR: Productivity Press.
Kochan, T. A. and Useem, M. (1992) *Transforming Organizations*, Oxford: Oxford University Press.
Lazonick, W. (1991) *Business Organization and the Myth of the Market Economy*, Cambridge: Cambridge University Press.
Nadler, D. A. (1977) 'Concepts for the Management of Organizational Change', in R. Hackman, E. Lawer and L. Porter (eds), *Perspectives on Behavior in Organizations*, New York: McGraw Hill.

Nonaka, I. and Takeuchi H. (1995) *The Knowledge Creating Company*, Oxford: Oxford University Press.
Peters, T. J. and Waterman, Jr., R. H. (1982) *In Search of Excellence*, New York: Harper & Row.
Petrin, T. (1986) 'Vzroki učinkovitosti gospodarjenja v drobnem gospodarstvu družbenega sektorja', Raziskovalni center Ekonomske fakultete, Ljubljana.
Petrin, T. (1989) 'Restructuring the Yugoslav Economy through Entry of New Firms', Program in Soviet and East European Studies Occasional Papers Series no. 19, University of Massachusetts, Amherst.
Petrin, T. (1992) 'Medpodjetniška mreža povezav in prestrukturiranje podjetij pohištvene industrije notranjske regije in ljubljanskega območja – 2.faza', Raziskovalni center Ekonomske fakultete, Ljubljana.
Petrin, T. (1995) 'Industrial Policy Supporting Economic Transition in Central-Eastern Europe: Lessons from Slovenia', The World Bank EDI Working Papers, no. 95–07.
Petrin, T. (1996) 'Industrial Policy and the Restructuring of Firms in Post-Socialist Slovenia', *Review of Industrial Organization*, 11: 325–37.
Petrin, T. and Vahčič, A. (1987) 'Razvoj drobnega gospodarstva, ključni element strategije razvoja slovenskega gospodarstva v naslednjih desetih letih', Raziskovalni center Ekonomske fakultete, Ljubljana.
Petrin, T., Vahčič, A. and Denda, A. (1990) 'Program prestrukturiranja jugoslovenske privrede sa ulaskom novih poduzeća razvojem poduzetništva: predlog za uspostavljanje savezne Agencije za mala i srednja poduzeća i poduzetništvo', Agencija za mala i srednja poduzeća i poduzetništvo, Beograd.
Piore, M. and Sabel, C. F. (1984) *The Second Industrial Divide*, Basic Books, New York.
Porter, M. (1990) *The Competitive Advantage of Nations*, New York: The Free Press.
Schumpeter, J. (1934) *The Theory of Economic Development*, Cambridge, Mass.: Harvard University Press.
Sengenberger, W. and Loveman, G. (1987) 'Smaller Units of Employment: A Synthesis', Report on Industrial Reorganization in Industrial Countries,' Discussion Paper no. 3, International Institute for Labour Studies, New Industrial Organization Programme.
Shingo, S. (1983) *A Revolution in Manufacturing: The SMED System*, Japan Management Association, Tokyo (English translation, Cambridge, MA: Productivity Press, 1985).
Shingo, S. (1985) *Zero Quality Control*, Japan Management Association, Tokyo (English translation, Cambridge, MA: Productivity Press, 1986).
Spendolini, M. J. (1992) *The Benchmarking Book*, New York: American Management Association.
Stevenson, H. H., Roberts, M. J. and Grousbeck, H. I. (1985) *New Business Ventures and the Entrepreneur*, Homewood, IL: Irwin.
Stiglitz, E. J. (1998) 'Economic Science, Economic Policy, and Economic Advice', paper prepared for the Annual World Bank Conference on Development Economics. Washington, DC, April 20–21.
Timmons, J. A. (1990) *Entrepreneurship in the 1990s*, Homewood, IL: Irwin.
Tjosvold, D. (1998) 'Making Employee Involvement Work: Cooperative Goals and Controversy to Reduce Costs', *Human Relations*, 51(2): 201–21.

Tung-Chun, H. (1997) 'The Effect of Participative Management on Organizational Performance: The Case of Taiwan', *The International Journal of Human Resource Management*, 8(5): 677–89.

Vahčič, A. (1996), 'The Future of Self-management: Reflection', in D. Fink-Hafner and J. R. Robbins (eds.) (1996), *Making a New Nation: The Formation of Slovenia*, Aldershot: Dartmouth.

Vanek, J. (1972) *The Labor-Managed Economy – Essays*, Ithaca: Cornell University Press.

Walton, E. (1987) *Innovating to Compete: Lessons for Diffusing and Managing Change in the Workplace*, San Francisco: Jossey-Bass.

Watson, G. H. (1993) *Strategic Benchmarking*, New York: John Wiley and Sons.

8
Uneasy Symbiosis of a Market Economy and Democratic Centralism: Emergence and Disappearance of Market Socialism and Yugoslavia*

Jože Mencinger

8.1 Introduction

The Yugoslav economic system served as the only example of a socialist market economy, even though the system evolved through many reforms. The motives for the reforms and, what I call, counter-reforms, differed. These systemic changes also differ from similar attempts in other socialist countries of Eastern Europe. In Yugoslavia, the changes brought by reforms were greater, their scope was not limited by external powers, and they were not related to changes in political leadership. The reforms, however, remained 'half-hearted efforts to implement policies promoting free market exchange of goods and services' (Katz, 1987). They, in particular, failed to delimit political power from economic power; counter-reforms were enacted when the market became too destructive to political monopoly of the Party and to the principle of democratic centralism.

In the theory of economic systems, the Yugoslav economy served as the only example of what is called *the self-managed, the participatory, the labour-managed or the socialist market economy*. Benjamin Ward's Illyrian firm, Evsey Domar's producer cooperative, Jaroslav Vanek's labour-managed market economy, and Branko Horvat's realistic model were all directly or indirectly inspired by the particular features of the Yugoslav institutional setting. This setting, however, was not particularly stable and often differed considerably from its theoretical blueprints.

---

*The original version of the paper was written before political and systemic change. Section 8.6 was added afterwards.

Since 1945, four distinct types of economic system in Yugoslavia can be distinguished:

1. administrative socialism, or a Soviet-type economic system (1945–52);
2. administrative market socialism (1953–62); which gradually led to:
3. market socialism (1963–73); and
4. contractual socialism (1974–88), followed by the collapse of socialism and the breakdown of the country.

The starting years of each period coincide with newly passed constitutions. Such periodization can be subject to criticism. First, it creates the notion that abrupt changes occurred in those years when actually they did not. Secondly, some far reaching institutional changes preceded constitutional changes; some followed them in subsequent years. Thirdly, the gaps between the ideology, embodied in constitutions, which really set out norms of behaviour, and the reality were always wide. Fourthly, some economic policy changes had a much greater impact on actual economic development than systemic changes. The 1965 economic reform, which was dominated by macroeconomic policy change (Bajt, 1984; Burkett, 1983), has even been considered the turning point between the more successful and the less successful period of labour management (Horvat, 1971; Sapir, 1980). The same is true with respect to the 1980s, when the change in economic policy forced by the country's indebtedness caused a similar turning point in all measurable performance indicators. The periodization is, however, closely related to changes in the formal allocation of decision-making in the economy.

What were the reasons for these systemic changes? If we reject the view that the changes reflected the rather mystical concept of the 'increasing development of productive forces', the answer must be that the predominant reasons were either economic or political. Later in the paper, I shall argue that *political factors were dominant in the abandonment of the Soviet-type, centrally planned system in the early 1950s, and in the adoption of the associated labour concept in the early 1970s, while the reforms in the early and mid-1960s were prompted predominantly by economic considerations.* Economic collapse in the early 1980s can be considered the reason for the reform attempts in the late 1980s.

The rest of the paper is divided into five sections. The main features of the economic systems before the 1970s are summarized in Section 8.2. An attempt is made to identify the reasons for their reform. Section 8.3 describes and comments on systemic settings contemplated in the course of the 1970s. The normative setting of the so-called 'contractual

120 *Market Socialism in Yugoslavia*

socialism' is sketched, and the reasons for the gaps between norms and reality are considered. Section 8.4 discusses economic performance within systemic periods, and the effects reforms might have had on both economic performance and structural change. Section 8.5 deals with the prospects of the Yugoslav economy for the 1990s, as they were seen in the 1980s, and discusses the prerequisites for a new economic reform. It will be noted that economic reforms were enacted within the existing political system and rather easily adaptable ideology. The persistency of the overwhelming crisis in the 1980s indicated, however, that to be effective, a new reform would require the abandonment of the basic orientations in the economic sphere, the leading role of the Party in the political sphere, and the Marxian ideology in the ideological sphere. Finally, the developments leading to the collapse of the socialist economic system and the breakdown of Yugoslavia are presented in Section 8.6.

8.2 Systemic changes 1945–73

8.2.1 Administrative socialism, 1946–52

The major goal of administrative socialism was to transform the underdeveloped, predominantly agricultural, capitalist society into an industrial socialist society. Basic reasons for this objective were ideological and political; economic and social issues were comparatively less important. A rigidly planned economy was at the time believed to be the only viable socialist model, and the transformation of Yugoslavia into such an economy was to be achieved by nationalizing most of the means of production, collectivizing the agricultural sector, and establishing a planning apparatus. The principle of control over the private sector was included in the Constitution of 1946 by stipulating that private property could be expropriated if so required by an extendable 'common interest'. In the agricultural sector, the anti-peasant policy was brought forward by compulsory deliveries and forced collectivization. The organization of the economy was modeled on the Soviet pattern; all basic economic problems such as valuation, organization of production, income distribution, savings, and investment were to be solved by centrally planned solutions. Enterprises were agents of the planners obliged to fulfill their instructions.

The specific means employed to bring about the transformation can be attributed only in part to the faith of the new political elite in the supremacy of the new system over a market economy; they were also in part intended to eliminate political competition and social pluralism.

The period was to be dominated by the First Five Year Plan (1947–52), an ambitious program of rapid Soviet-type growth, giving priority industry over agriculture, to heavy industry over light industry, and the production of the means of production over the production of consumer goods. Even though it was extended for a year, the plan was never completed. In 1948, when the Communist Party of Yugoslavia was accused of revisionism and expelled from the communist movement, a complete economic boycott by communist countries followed. For two years, Yugoslav leaders tried to prove that the accusations were unjust; they therefore strengthened the efforts for rapid transformation to complete administrative socialism. The efforts peaked in the early part of 1950 and then were rapidly disbanded so that 'by the end of 1951, the centrally planned economy belonged to history' (Horvat, 1971).

8.2.2 Administrative market socialism, 1953–62

After 1952, Yugoslavia started to move away from the centralized economic planning, by reducing administrative constraints and making enterprises more independent. The official birth of the new system can be traced to the *Law on Management of Government Business Enterprises and Higher Economic Associations by Workers' Collectives*, enacted in 1950, which proclaimed self-management as its foundation. However, its basic legal and political features were explicitly defined in the *Constitution Act* of 1953. These features were clearly summarized by Bićanić (1957). He enumerated the differences between the new and the old system as follows:

- social ownership of the means of production as opposed to state ownership
- reliance on the market mechanism for the allocation of goods and services as opposed to the administrative mechanism
- increased use of financial instruments as opposed to the adoption of simple administrative rules
- free distribution of available income by workers' councils as opposed to administratively fixed wages
- decentralized and functional budgeting at all administrative levels as opposed to an all-embracing state budget
- the rehabilitation of consumer sovereignty as opposed to the treatment of personal consumption as a residual
- and the acceptance of independent farmers as opposed to compulsory collectivization.

The reasons for the first, and by far the most radical, reform have not yet been fully explained. According to official beliefs, shared by some western scholars, the reform was contemplated by the Yugoslav political leaders long before the break with the Soviet Union. The opinion that workers' self-management was 'in the air before it was officially introduced by the government' (Gurvitch, 1966) can hardly be proven by actual developments before or after the break. On the contrary, the organization of the economy, the overwhelming nationalization of practically every economic activity (including non-capitalist forms of production) and the increased pressure for forced collectivization in agriculture after the break with the Soviet Union, all suggest the opposite. Yugoslav political leaders were fully engaged in recasting the Yugoslav economy into a Soviet-type planned economy until the time of the break. To Boris Kidrič, who dominated economic thought and was one of the architects of the administrative system, state ownership was, up to 1950, 'the highest form of the ownership of the means of production, and planning was the fundamental law of socialist development' (Kidrič, 1949 and 1950a). In less than one year, the standing of state ownership became 'only the first and the shortest step of the socialist revolution; the building of socialism requires the transformation of state socialism into a free association of direct producers' (Kidrič, 1950b). Very soon, similar statements were repeated by practically all Yugoslav social scientists. The ability of both Yugoslav politicians and social scientists to reread and reinterpret Marx according to daily needs was thus established for the first time and certainly not the last.

A convergence of circumstances – such as the fact that the war for liberation was in large part an independent effort and that the Soviet model was voluntarily adopted – did exist, making rejection of the Soviet model feasible. Bad economic results and the need to adapt to the new environment were certainly important, but ideological and political factors were decisive in searching for new, non-Soviet, forms of socialism. The opinion that something had to be invented quickly to give the break a symbol rather than, at least at first, to engage in a full-fledged systemic reform (Rusinow, 1977) appears to be close to the truth. It might also have been a way for the regime to build popular support during difficult times.

At first, self-management was rather limited even in the normative setting, and much more so in practice. In principle, workers were to take over the managerial function, but in reality both the distribution of enterprise income and the investment decisions remained centralized. Self-management as such had little impact on resource allocation. The development strategy remained essentially of the Soviet-type, that is, based on a high share of investment in GNP and priority given to heavy industry. In short, two of the basic economic decisions, namely the decision on income distribution and investment, remained under strict government control, while consumers were to decide what to produce, and enterprises were to decide how to organize production and combine productive factors.

The political system and the policy of no social pluralism remained firm. For example, while catastrophic results in agriculture compelled the strategic decision to abandon forced collectivization, the socialist transformation of the countryside as an ultimate aim was not given up. Only the method was changed – under the *Agricultural Land Pool Act* of 1953, the maximum land allowed to individual peasants was reduced to ten hectares, and the *Constitution Act* of 1953 proclaimed this restriction as a constitutional principle. The principle has since become the major obstacle to the development of the private agricultural sector.

8.2.3 Market socialism, 1963–73

Market socialism was initiated by the *Program of the League of Communists* of Yugoslavia in 1958, which defined socialism as:

> the social system based on socialized means of production in which social production is managed by associated direct producers, in which income is distributed according to the principle to each according to his work, and in which, under the rule of the working class, itself being changed as a class, all social relations are gradually liberated from class antagonisms and all elements of exploitation of man by man.
>
> (Savez Komunista Jugoslavije 1958: 133)

In fact, the entire systemic development during the 1950s and the 1960s was a process of permanent reforms. All imaginable solutions were tried, often in a very uncoordinated manner (Čičin-Šain, 1985). Numerous and varied economic instruments were used, and each new economic instrument tended to change the given structure and the system as such. Nevertheless, throughout this period, the economy was gradually becoming market-based, although neither the labour nor the capital market were officially sanctioned, and both remained rudimentary.

Among permanent changes, two reforms, in 1961 and in 1965, should be noted as those that decisively reduced central control and considerably increased the autonomy of economic units. In the 1961 reform, wage control was abolished, foreign trade was liberalized and the economy, which was virtually closed, was to be made susceptible to the influences of the world market. The monetary and banking system was radically overhauled. However, 'the three reforms of 1961 were poorly prepared, partly inconsistent and badly implemented' (Horvat, 1971: 83), and even more elaborate systemic changes, with macroeconomic policy changes that were to be designated as the 1965 Economic Reform, took place in 1964–7. Changes affected the investment mechanism, the foreign trade system, the monetary and banking system, the tax system, and the price system. General investment funds of governments at all levels were abolished and assets and liabilities transferred to banks. The banking system was restructured, and banks could now be established and managed by groups of enterprises. The National Bank was transformed into a monetary institution. The reform of the investment system included tax cuts that, it was hoped, would enable enterprises to finance more of their investment. The turnover tax, which had been levied at various rates in different sectors, was replaced by a general retail sales tax. Prices were restructured to more closely resemble world prices. Foreign trade liberalization included reducing tariff rates and abolishing licensing.

In short, with the abolition of wage controls in 1961, and with the changes in the investment system in 1965, the remaining two basic types of economic decisions – to whom and when – were, at least formally, transferred to independent enterprises. The Yugoslav economy was to become a market economy.

Market liberalization, combined with restrictive macroeconomic policy, produced predictable, though not anticipated, results: economic growth slowed down. The social and political consequences of rapidly-increasing unemployment were eased by a massive exodus of workers. Cost-push inflationary pressures emerged from the combination of increased freedom of enterprises in income distribution and the increased softness of their budget constraints. The balance of trade worsened, and the Yugoslav share in world exports started to decline. In short, the aspirations of the reformers were not realized, and the reform was soon considered a failure, marking an end of the 'Yugoslav economic miracle' (Sapir, 1980).

Poor economic performance in 1966–70 was accompanied by even less desirable developments in the social and political domains. Social property, defined as property of 'no-one and everyone', degenerated into group property (Bajt, 1980). Inequality among individuals and regions increased, causing social and political tensions. Furthermore, the concentration of economic power in the hands of the managerial elite and technocrats, though predominantly members of the Party, did not only endanger workers' control but also threatened to deprive the Party bureaucracy of political control. This threat, it appears, was the most important reason for the counter reform.

By the early 1970s, the counter-reform began. Institutional changes started with the *Constitutional Amendments* of 1970. They were to be the blueprint for the so-called associated labour concept of the self-managed economy. Although formally the basic elements of the socialist market system were to be retained, changes were so far-reaching that the market character of the Yugoslav economy was put into question. The associated labour concept rejected two key concepts of the market economy: the market as the basic mechanism for resource allocation, and macroeconomic policy and indicative planning as the means of indirect regulation of economic activities. It insisted that these were to be substituted, to the greatest extent possible, by mechanisms of social contracts, self-management agreements, and social planning. In short, the lines of responsibility for making economic decisions became blurred, a recipe for indecision and bureaucratic bargaining.

The changes in the 1970s were officially introduced to strengthen the basic elements of the system of a self-managed socialist economy. Actual motives can be grouped as economic, social, or political. Among the economic motives, the developments following the 1965 reform were important. However, more important were the social and political ones. The economic reforms of the 1960s reached the Rubicon, the crossing of which would lead to the land of democratic market socialism. The counter reform was seen as inevitable if the political power of the League of Communists of Yugoslavia (LCY) and its actual control of social, political, and economic developments, especially at the enterprise and community levels, were to be saved.

8.3 Contractual socialism, 1974–88

8.3.1 The normative setting

The solution was found by inventing a new version of a socialist economy, one that would preserve its basic orientations permanently. The new economic model was shaped by Edvard Kardelj, the politician-ideologue who dominated economic and political thought in Yugoslavia for more than twenty years. Again, there was no problem in finding the explanations in Marx's teaching, and again, the Yugoslav social scientists were quick in applauding these explanations. Doubts about its functioning and performance were rare and were pushed aside. The system was legalized by the 1974 *Constitution* and by the 1976 *Associated Labour Act*. In subsequent years, parts of the system were gradually adapted to conform with these laws. Every single part of the economic system was affected, and an entirely new and rather awkward terminology was invented. The most important new organizational forms were: the so-called 'income relations' and 'pooling of labour and resources', the institutions of 'free exchange of labour', and the system of social planning.

The Basic Organization of Associated Labour (BOAL) became the basic economic unit. According to the Constitution and the Associated Labour Act, a BOAL is the form in which workers directly and on terms of equality exercise their economic and self-management rights. The official proclamation that maximization of income is the basic objective of BOALs, as well as Working Organizations (WOs, or enterprises) and Composite Organizations of Associated Labour (COALs), allegedly resolved an old debate. This debate had started when Ward's 'natural and rational' objective (Ward, 1958), although accepted by most foreign economists (Domar, 1966; Vanek, 1970; Sapir, 1980) was criticized in Yugoslavia (Horvat, 1972; Dubravčić, 1970).

It was assumed that social property and self-management promoted cooperation rather than competition. This required an invention of a new instrument which was to replace contracts between the parties in a market economy. A Self-Management Agreement (SMA) was considered to be an appropriate name for it. An SMA was a binding contractual agreement, signed by two or more parties, for the realization of a specific project with a view to maximizing their income. The agreements were supposed to serve as microeconomic devices for inter-enterprise and inter-BOAL communication, replacing in that role the planning agencies under Soviet socialism and price signals under capitalism. The SMAs were supplemented by the system of Social Contracts (SC), agreements among political communities (governments at different levels), or between such communities and other agents in the economy, including chambers of commerce, trade unions, and Self-Managed Associations of Interest (SMAIs). SMAIs were the organizational form that linked the interests of those who used the services and those who produced them, for example, in housing, education, and health care. SCs were used to state policy objectives in areas such as planning and income distribution. They were thus typical macroeconomic devices to regulate or to help promote laws regulating economic activity.

The institution of both vertical and horizontal pooling of labour and resources was to be another cornerstone of the system. It served above all as a replacement of the usual demand-supply market relations. Secondly, it could be used for channeling investment resources to their most profitable uses. It was also a medium through which wider policy objectives could be achieved. SMAs concerning investment projects were supposed to play the functions of the capital market. It was hoped that such SMAs could cope with low mobility of capital and encourage the circulation of investible resources between surplus and deficit enterprises, without the mediation of banking institutions which had become ideologically suspect.

The concept of Free Exchange of Labour (FEL) was an innovation in the system of social finance that dealt with the formation and the use of resources for the satisfaction of social and individual needs that could not be met through market mechanism. Two basic categories of social needs distinguished were: general and collective. The general needs are those of the entire community and are to be funded through taxes. The collective needs are those of specific social groups using particular services. Funding of these was to be ensured through self-imposed contributions.

The disappointment with the market in the late 1960s revived confidence in planning. Because neither directive nor indicative planning could be adapted to the new system, social planning was invented. It consisted of microeconomic planning by economic units (BOALs, WOs, COALs), and of macroeconomic planning by sociopolitical communities. There was an obligatory exchange of information among all these economic units. The coordinated plans were to be codified into legally binding agreements: SMAs and SCs. All affected parties were to be consulted and their agreement secured before the codification. The basic plan was the midterm five-year plan with annual assessments and revisions.

The attempt to socialize the countryside was renewed. This time, socialization was to be based on the following principles: (1) farmers are free to decide on association and to retain ownership of the land; (2) the status of associated farmers should, in principle, be the same as the status of workers, but they should be entitled to a share of income based on their ownership of land, mechanized equipment and other farm facilities. The Associated Labour Act provided various possibilities for farmers to cooperate and associate among themselves, and with the socialized sector.

8.3.2 The laws and the reality

The new system introduced in the 1970s quickly disintegrated. The statutes regulating the behaviour of economic units that were introduced after 1976 were in fact explicitly or implicitly abolished soon after their appearance and replaced by new statutes or administrative measures. Other statutes, for example the planning act or the act on compulsory pooling of labour and resources of commercial and manufacturing enterprises, remained irrelevant for the actual functioning of the economy.

Explanations of the wide gap between the blueprints and the reality differed. Two groups, nevertheless, can be distinguished, one blaming the inappropriate behaviour of economic units, the other, the blueprints themselves. However, it may be argued that economic units behave rationally, given the system. If such rational behaviour produces undesirable results, or if economic units do not behave in accordance with the premises of the system, the problem is most likely within the system itself. The system appeared to have at least three important deficiencies. First, it was based on ideologically-inspired self-serving perceptions of the reality, which led to unrealistic performance expectations. Secondly, the principles of economic theory were simply overlooked or ignored. Thirdly, the system was overloaded with institutions.

Scepticism about the functioning of the system was rejected by appealing to the peculiarities of the socialist self-managed economy. The problems that should have been dealt with were, instead, 'resolved' by ideological statements. For example, the problem of the *wage vs. accumulation dilemma* could and should have been discussed in the framework of wealth maximization behaviour (Furobotn and Pejovich, 1972). It was instead pushed aside by proclaiming that it was the responsibility of associated labour to reproduce capital in an expanded way. The consequences of a monopolistic economic structure promoted by the pooling of labour and resources, were overlooked. The institutions of free exchange of labour produced additional administration at enormous costs to those who were wasting time in 'decision making' to run its course. The planning system, which to some economists was highly appealing as a theoretically promising way to obtain an *ex ante* general equilibrium solution (Ardalan, 1980), could not work in practice due to massive information barriers.

Inoperative blueprints, together with undesirable results of the system, required government intervention. Suspended or irrelevant rules of the game were replaced daily by an enormous number of administrative measures and incessant changes in legislation. As a consequence, the system gradually acquired many characteristics of the administrative system, such as, inflexibility, slowness, inconsistency of administrative measures, distrust of economic units by administrators, and the application of non-economic means for the implementation of economic goals. Slowness and inconsistency were amplified by the need to compromise in order to obtain conformity of regional governments and cartelized economic groups. The distrust of economic units by administrators emerged from the differences between their expected and actual behaviour. Economic units responded to administrative measures in a way which, while rational, was considered socially undesirable. Moreover, responses often would have to be considered irrational by the standards of a market economy. The irrational, in this latter sense, and socially undesirable responses of economic units therefore constantly required *ad hoc* administrative measures, leading to systemic instability. Attempts to correct the behaviour of economic units could be made only through political persuasion, which strengthened the links between the economic and political system.

8.4 The economic effects of the reforms

To evaluate adequately the impact of economic reforms on the performance of the Yugoslav economy is not possible, since we do not know how the economy would have performed in the absence of these reforms. My remarks in this section are therefore necessarily somewhat speculative.

Most studies analyzing performance of the socialist self-managed economy focus on micro-economic issues. Performance has been judged predominantly by deductive analysis, comparing the worker-managed firm's behaviour to that of the capitalist firm under different assumptions concerning objective functions, production functions, institutional constraints on labour and capital supply, and environmental conditions. Macroeconomics of the labour managed economy has been analyzed much less, though both theoretical and empirical studies of macroeconomic performance do exist (Tyson, 1980; Estrin and Bartlett, 1983; Burkett, 1983; Bajt, 1986).

The two most prominent scholars in the field of labour-managed economy, Vanek and Horvat, stressed its macroeconomic advantages. Vanek's conclusions about the expected performance of the self-managed economy were extremely favourable:

> Comparatively – leaving aside the Soviet-type model as a basically inefficient one (except perhaps when it comes to income distribution) – there is every reason to believe that the participatory economy is, all other things considered, superior to the western

capitalist economy. In the sphere of how well it allocates resources in production, it has both advantages and disadvantages compared to western market alternative. It has a definite advantage in generating full employment, long-run price stability, and growth.

(1970: 38)

Horvat (1972) arrived at similarly favourable macroeconomic implications. According to him, high rates of growth are assured by a higher propensity to invest due to reduced risk and uncertainty, full employment by the reluctance of workers to dismiss fellow workers, and price stability by the absence of the fundamental employee–employer conflict.

The above three macroeconomic propositions of Vanek and Horvat were tested against the Yugoslav reality in the 1971–7 period (Mencinger, 1979). Only the proposition of stability in employment and short term growth rates was confirmed, but the promotion of long run growth and price stability were not. On the other hand, evidence of strong economic performance was provided by early empirical studies (Balassa and Bertrand, 1970). The performance was often described

Table 8.1 The main performance indicators of the Yugoslav economy, 1946–88

Period	46–53[1]	52–62	63–73	74–88	80–88
(average annual rates of growth, in per cent)					
GNP	2.3	8.2	6.5	3.3	0.6
Industry	12.9	12.2	8.6	5.0	2.4
Agriculture	−3.1	9.2	3.1	2.1	0.0
Employment	8.3	6.8	2.4	3.4	2.2
Exports in US$	−3.1	12.0	14.0	11.3	8.0
Imports in US$	3.6	10.1	16.6	11.3	−0.8
Investments		11.5	5.3	0.7	−8.0
Consumption		6.5	6.4	2.2	−1.0
Prices		3.6	13.0	42.3	80.2
(ratios, in per cent, except rows 3 and 4)					
Unemployment rate		5.01	7.58	13.29	14.24
Export/import ratio		64.44	69.44	67.96	87.81
Labor/output ratio[2]		3.87	2.42	1.87	1.90
Capital/output ratio		2.28	2.23	2.68	2.97
Investment/GDP rate		41.99	38.87	35.21	28.60

[1] Horvat, 1971.
[2] Number of workers per 1 million dinars in 1972 prices.
Source: Statistical Yearbook of Yugoslavia, various years.

as impressive before 1965, and the declines after 1965 were attributed to changing external conditions and to relative weights given to various economic objectives, and only partly to the system which weakened macroeconomic policy making (World Bank, 1979). Performance indicators for the Yugoslav economy under the four systems are summarized in Table 8.1. Simultaneous movements over time of the capital/output and labour/output ratios indicate that the dynamic efficiency of the economy is related to systemic changes (Mencinger, 1986). In the period of administrative socialism (1946–52), economic growth was achieved by enormous increases in inputs, with both ratios increasing rapidly. When rigid planning was abolished, and the dominance of planners was replaced by that of consumers and independent producers, (1953–62), the two ratios decreased rapidly. In the third period (1963–73), the capital/output ratio started to grow again, while the labour/output ratio decreased slowly. The changes that made relatively abundant labour expensive, as the majority of taxes and contributions were levied on wages, and scarce capital a virtually free good, with real interest rates negative, appear to be important causes of this deterioration. The situation worsened further in the period of contractual socialism when the capital/output ratio started to increase rapidly and the labour/output ratio first stagnated but after 1980, began to increase.

Growth rates in Table 8.1 appear satisfactory when compared to those of developed market economies. A comparison with countries at a similar level of development, however, suggests that growth performance was fairly normal, except for the excellent agricultural results in the period 1953–62, following the abandonment of the forced collectivization policy. Faster growth of industrial production in the second period is partly the fruit of huge investment in the first period in projects with long lead times.

Large shares of investment in GNP suggest that the cost of growth in Yugoslavia was high and, indirectly, that despite reforms, the country retained the Soviet pattern of development. The increase of GNP per unit of investment during 1960–80 period was only 70 per cent of the corresponding increase in comparable market economies of Southern Europe (Bajt, 1987).

What was the impact of economic reforms on the economic structure? This could be established, to some extent, by comparing patterns of structural change in Yugoslavia with other countries, both market-based and centrally-planned. To avoid problems created by differences in relative prices among the countries, employment structures are more appropriate.[1]

The share of labour force in the material sectors is inversely related to the per capita GNP, and there is a significant difference between the two systems. The estimated share of the labour force in the material sectors for Yugoslavia would be 69.0 per cent if the Soviet pattern of development was assumed, and 54.2 per cent for the capitalist pattern of development. The actual figure of 62.4 per cent placed Yugoslavia almost precisely in the middle between the two systems.

8.5 Was an effective reform feasible?

In the 1980s, reforms and economic laws were again on the central stage in Yugoslavia, as in most other socialist countries. An illusion that reforms would quickly transform Yugoslavia into a welfare state was created. The continuous economic crisis, dysfunctional institutions, and growing ethnic and social tensions required changes, but Yugoslavia found it difficult to move in any direction. The number of commissions, meetings, resolutions and words devoted first, to 'open questions and serious difficulties', then to 'economic crisis', and finally, to 'overwhelming economic, political and moral crisis' grew rapidly. In the process, the assumed premises of the society became increasingly more open to question. Was an effective reform feasible? What were the major obstacles to it? What was the price to be paid?

8.5.1. The political and ideological stalemate

In the 1970s, the criticism of contractual socialism on efficiency grounds was vigorously refuted as hostile to self-management and socialism. However, when the economic situation deteriorated into the most profound economic, social, political and moral crisis, this prompted attempts at a new reform. The first such attempt was in 1982, with the *Long Run Stabilization Program* (Savezni društveni savet, 1984), which consisted of seventeen documents (over 1000 pages) dealing with all aspects of the economy. The Program was highly eclectic and inconsistent in its approaches to economic problems. It drew ideas from all schools of economic thought, from extreme monetarism to orthodox Keynesian, often nicely cloaked in Marxian terminology. Its main orientation was nevertheless clear: the reintroduction of the market and a reduced role of institutions. Enormous conceptual differences between this new attempt to revive market socialism and the old Associated Labour Act, the cornerstone of contractual socialism, deterred neither politicians nor some social scientists from applauding both at the same time. The Program remained the single proclaimed answer to the crisis in most of the speeches at Party and trade union congresses in the second half of the 1980s. As a reform proposal, the Program tried to increase economic efficiency by introducing or restoring the *modus operandi* of capitalist market economies in the framework of social ownership and self-management. The Program did not demand radical changes and, in contrast to the situation in the early 1950s when administrative socialism had been quickly abandoned, the dismantling of contractual socialism was slow, hesitant, and uncertain. The Program soon appeared to share the fate of economic reforms in other socialist countries: ideological obstacles and fears about the unacceptable weakening of the Party's political monopoly being the most decisive determinants of the actual extent of reforms.

The stalemate can be easily illustrated by reference to another official document, the *Critical Analysis of the Functioning of the Political System of Socialist Self-Management* (Savezni društveni savet, 1985). The document differs markedly from its predecessor and can be considered as an alternative program. Its basic idea was that the breakdown of the system with accompanying catastrophic economic results was caused by the inappropriate behaviour of economic units, and not by deficiencies in the systemic blueprints. Therefore indoctrination and changes of attitude were called for, rather than a change in the system itself.

The stalemate was also apparent on the constitutional and legislative level. While the number of previously unacceptable ideas multiplied after the decision to change the Constitution, ideological and political stalemate permitted only modest changes. They did not touch on essential problems and were not sufficiently concrete. Inconsistency marked new systemic statutes – some reintroduced the rules of the game intended to restore market socialism, while others strengthened the transition to administrative socialism.

The variety of ideas concerning the best way out of the overwhelming crisis became particularly wide in academic debates. A number of solutions were suggested and, in the process, most of the taboo topics were opened (Horvat, 1985; Jerovšek *et al.*, 1985). These included recognition of labour and capital markets as indispensable segments of the market economy; calls for changes in the principles of self-management (Goldstein, 1985); the questioning of the concept of social property and suggestions to replace it with collective property (Bajt, 1986 and 1988); and the restoration of a truly mixed economy (Popović, 1984).

While Party ideologists and economists speculated about other types of socialism, the government, maintaining its inability to deal with economic problems within the existing economic system, established a commission that launched a new program of economic reform in 1988 (Savezno izvršno veće, 1988). Contrary to expectations, the reform proposals of the so called *'Mikulić Commission'* were extremely radical, although theoretically confused and inconsistent. Had they been realized, they would have devastated the basic premises of the economic system and shaken the premises of the political system. In many respects, the economy would have been transformed into a capitalist economy. In particular, the proposals commenced from the premise that ownership of the means of production, as practiced, constituted the essence of Yugoslav economic problems. They urged abandonment of the so called non-property philosophy of social property, by which everybody and nobody is the owner, and insisted, instead, that 'the subject' (titulus) of social property be determined. They also demanded that the principle, according to which management was related to labour only, be replaced by the principle according to which those who provide capital are also entitled to management and profit-sharing. They required an integral market consisting of product, labour and capital markets, and abandoning social planning, one of the cornerstones of contractual socialism. However, while recognizing the need for property pluralism, proposals insisted on social property remaining the predominant form, and proposed compulsory amortization and minimal rates of accumulation to protect it.

The degree of theoretical confusion can easily be seen by inspecting some of the provisions of the proposed reform. Firstly, there is hardly any other concept of social property but the non-property concept. By determining the subject, social property degenerates into collective or state property.

Secondly, the essential problem of social property is its inefficiency, which results from differences in management philosophy when social property is involved, compared to management philosophy when private property is involved. It seems unlikely that social property could therefore persist as the predominant form if property pluralism were established. The introduction of compulsory amortization and compulsory minimal rates of accumulation demonstrate that degeneration of social property to collective and private cannot be prevented except by administrative measures – they are intended to assure that the economic actors behave in a proper way.

Thirdly, profit and management for those who provide capital constitute the essence of capitalism. Introduction of equity requires the solution of many theoretical and practical problems that arise from the need to reconcile the principle of one-worker – one-vote, to the principle one-share – one-vote.

Fourthly, while capital and labour markets existed in a rudimentary form, they were not accepted on the ideological and theoretical level. Their official introduction requires the recognition of the consequences; the proclaimed premises of the system – social property and self-management – cannot coexist with labour and capital markets. A labour market with self-management can operate well when employment in an enterprise is increasing, but not when there is a need to reduce employment. In the first case, workers looking for jobs appear as sellers of labour services and enterprises as buyers; there are no problems. The labour market breaks down when enterprise employment is to be reduced. Workers, who by definition become managers by entering the firm, would in this case be forced to dismiss themselves or to decrease wages voluntarily, which is not likely. If some workers are dismissed by their fellow workers, this contradicts the notion of self-management. The second solution, that is, the voluntary decrease of wages that emerges from the solidarity of workers and which should soften the downward rigidity of wages, is rejected in practice – strikes confirm that workers do not consider themselves managers.

These proposals, therefore, did not only indirectly question the premises of the Yugoslav economic system: they reopened the old dilemma – socialism or efficiency (Mencinger, 1988b). The *Enterprise Law*, passed in January 1989, formally ended the period of contractual socialism and set the stage for nothing else but a return to capitalism.

While political and social obstacles and ideological dilemmas appeared important determinants of the limits to reforms, the state of the economy, leaving aside the interdependence with systemic changes, should not be overlooked.

8.5.2 The state of the economy in the 1980s

Macroeconomic performance in the period of contractual socialism is characterized by the break in 1980 when acute difficulties started. However, the fact that yearly inflows of foreign capital were greater than increases of the gross domestic product indicates that the success before 1980 was fictitious. The Yugoslav economy was doomed to stagnate for a decade in the absence of net foreign capital inflows. When the possibilities for development based on foreign financing ended, and the servicing of accumulated debts, which amounted to 20 billion US dollars, required an enormous outflow of capital, the fictitious success dissolved. Two previous attempts to restore external balance, in

1972 and in 1975–6, were followed by deterioration of the domestic economy and quickly abandoned. Only when, after 1979, indebtedness became excessive, did economic policy shift towards the restoration of external balance. At this point, the price for achieving external equilibrium was high. It consisted of stagnation coupled with decreased efficiency, represented by the increase in the capital/output and labour/output ratios, a rising level of unemployment, inflation, and increased interregional disparities. Deterioration turned to stagflation and, after 1983, to a kind of hyper-stagflation. The annual growth of GNP decreased from 5.7 per cent in the period 1974–80 to stagnation in the 1980s. The unemployment rate reached 16.4 per cent at the end of 1988. The average inflation rate increased from 20 per cent in the 1974–80 period to 200 per cent in 1988. Real wages dropped to two thirds of those in 1979, and interregional differences increased. The pressure of excess demand on the economy was softened in the 1970s by persistent deficits in the current balance of payments. When the supply of foreign credits became inadequate to cover the deficit in the 1980s, both the balance of payments crisis and the acceleration of inflation became inevitable. The only alternative to inflation was the Romanian policy of shortages and rationing. Both inflation and administrative restrictions, the latter only in 1982 and 1983 when

Table 8.2 Performance of the Yugoslav economy in the 1980s

	Internal balance			External balance	Efficiency	
	I	II	III	IV	V	VI
1974–80	5.7	20.1	13.3	55.6	2.64	1.86
1981	1.5	44.8	13.5	70.2	2.69	1.79
1982	0.5	31.0	14.1	77.8	2.82	1.84
1983	−1.0	38.1	14.6	81.6	2.96	1.89
1984	2.0	56.3	15.3	84.5	2.95	1.89
1985	0.5	75.4	16.0	87.2	2.97	1.91
1986	3.5	88.1	16.2	84.1	2.95	1.91
1987	−1.0	118.4	15.7	91.3	3.01	1.97
1988	−2.0	198.8	16.4	96.5	3.13	2.01
1989	0.8	1255	17.9	90.3		
1990	−9.8	588	20.2	75.8		

I – GNP growth, II – inflation rate, III – unemployment rate, IV – export/import ratio, V – capital/output ratio, VI – labour/output ratio.
Source: Statistical Yearbook of Yugoslavia, various years.

shortages appeared in many sectors and rationing was used in some, were used to reestablish external balance. Certainly, inflation in Yugoslavia was not used deliberately as an instrument of an austerity program, which was apparently the case in Hungary (Kornai, 1986). The Yugoslav government simply lost macroeconomic control. While acceleration of inflation was initiated by the squeeze of domestic supplies, other factors contributed as well. Cuts in imports reduced competition, and devaluation of the Dinar led to increased production costs which were readily passed along to domestic prices. Producers increased domestic prices as the real value of exports declined. Unpaid foreign credits to the Soviet Union and Iraq were monetized by the National Bank. After 1983, inflationary expectations set in, and became the single most important factor sustaining high inflation.

Inflationary cycles were shaped predominantly by government interventions in the form of direct price controls, the drawbacks of which are well known. They accelerated inflation for three reasons: (1) creating persistent imbalances in the price structure; (2) causing global imbalance; and (3) increasing inflationary expectations. Furthermore, government intervention increased the ability of the economy to socialize inefficiency since both credit and foreign currency remained undervalued. The practice of not paying bills, a specific manifestation of the soft budget constraint, reduced the power of monetary policy. Unpaid bills at the end of 1986 amounted to twice the amount of outstanding bank credits.

Unemployment was the next important economic obstacle to radical reforms. The economic, social and political implications of high unemployment set Yugoslavia apart from developed industrial countries in many respects. Unemployment was basically a long-term and regional problem. Labour supply was influenced by the relatively high birth rates, a high percentage of agricultural population and specific ownership structure: the predominantly socialist nonagricultural sector and the predominantly private agricultural sector. The spread of technological progress in agriculture, differences in real wages and status, and economic policy inspired by ideological biases, caused a quick one-way flow of labour from agriculture to other sectors. Agriculture became not only the most important source of labour but also a buffer against the social and political effects of unemployment. On the other hand, demand for labour was limited by the scarcity of capital. The effect of this was amplified by underpriced capital which favoured capital intensive development, as well as by ideological biases regarding ownership of the means of production – this was reflected in legal constraints that induced the transfer of private capital into consumption and nonproductive investments such as housing.

The growth of domestic employment in the 1970s and 1980s was nearly autonomous, almost independent of the ups and downs in production. This caused large underemployment. Approximately 20 per cent of those employed in the socialist sector should have been, at the end of 1982, considered redundant owing to zero marginal productivity (Mencinger, 1983). Underemployment had increased since then and, by the end of 1987, a total of about 1.7 million workers had to be added to the 1.08 million of registered job seekers when estimating unemployed labour resources (Mencinger, 1988a). The changed structure of job seekers, mainly skilled and young people concentrated in industrial centres rather than unskilled workers dispersed in villages, only increased the social and political dimensions of the problem.

Regional disparities were also one of the major obstacles for future economic development, and even more so, for effective economic reform. These disparities had increased despite government efforts to redistribute development throughout the country. The gap in GNP per capita between Slovenia and Kosovo, for example, widened from 5:1 in 1955 to 7:1 in 1988. An attempt to reduce disparities would require massive transfers of resources from the North to the South through administrative measures, a policy that was meeting increasing resistance in the North.

During 1986–8 the economic situation worsened, partly due to eccentric economic policy pursued by the government of Mr. Mikulić. When it took power in 1986, the stand-by agreement between the IMF and Yugoslavia expired, and the government promptly separated the interest and inflation rate, hoping to bring down inflation by price freezes and other 'inventive' measures. This was opposed by the more developed regions which were, however, too weak to thwart the government. The increasing hyper-stagflation and inability to service the foreign debt soon forced the government to ask for a new stand-by agreement and debt rescheduling. In May 1988, a completely opposite and market-oriented economic policy was finally agreed upon. It was to be based on three liberalizations – prices, imports and foreign exchange market, and on three anchors – restrictive fiscal and monetary policy, and wage control. However, it soon became apparent that the government was unable to control fiscal and monetary policy, and in October, the last of the three anchors, the wage control, slackened and urgent measures were added to ease social tensions and prevent further declines of real wages. Before the end of the year the government resigned, after losing the support of the less developed regions.

It was succeeded by a new government led by Mr. Ante Marković who eagerly continued economic reforms and launched a new stabilization program. At that time, nobody could have presumed that his was to be the last Yugoslav government.

The real prospects for the Yugoslav economy in the 1990s, however, were not encouraging. An interesting question was whether poor economic performance would help or hinder systemic transformation. The social and political implications of slow growth could, above all, easily result in a counter-reform. Administrative solutions might be favoured for at least three reasons. First, because of fear that the reintroduction of the market would increase social differences among individuals and regions to unacceptable dimensions. Secondly, the energy of the population was exhausted during the years of continuous economic crisis. Thirdly, economic efficiency could only be increased by giving up many unquestioned premises about social property, self-management, the political monopoly of the Party, Marxian ideology and so on. A simple tinkering with the 'capitalization of socialism' was not enough any more.

In principle, federalism, decentralization of political power and its concentration at the local and republican levels, as well as the fact that the Yugoslav League of Communists was less dominant and more diverse in values and interests than other communist parties in Eastern Europe, could have been both advantageous and disadvantageous for radical reforms. Such pluralism could have eased the steps towards a market economy, but it could have prevented the reforms from arriving at any kind of solution too.

8.6 The collapse of the system and the breakdown of the country

Economic reforms had enabled Yugoslavia to adapt to global structural changes more rapidly than other socialist countries. Thus, an optimist could have argued that the proven ability to change systems, re-evaluate Marxism, and redefine socialism, could again push the trade-off between ideology and economic efficiency in favour of the latter. But the flexibility that the country had shown in the past was no longer there. The problem was that, despite many reforms in the economic sphere, the political sphere, dominated by the monopoly of the Party and by the principle of democratic centralism, remained rather stable. Numerous institutional changes had been adopted to preserve rather than to weaken links between the economic and political system. A radical economic reform would, on the other hand, require above all a separation of political and economic power. To put it bluntly, the leading subjective force, the nomenklatura, and the determined ways of development, were all superfluous in a market-based economy. The commitment of Yugoslav politicians and of the LCY to the concept of market economy could therefore be considered insincere or shortsighted.

In 1988, Yugoslavia reached the point at which any economic reforms, if unaccompanied by political reforms, could only increase the inconsistency between the economic and the political system. It could sustain the stalemate indefinitely or transform the economic system back to an administrative system. The ability to reread and to reinterpret Marx, which had characterized the past so profoundly, did not suffice any more. New changes of the economic system that would remain within the bounds of Marxist ideology were no longer feasible. The situation required that the ideology be abandoned. The rather peculiar economic system came to its end after continuous economic crisis, ideological disintegration, dysfunctional institutions, growing ethnic and social tensions, and political stalemate.

The latest and the last Yugoslav economic reform launched in 1988 before introducing political changes, was based on the idea of creating an 'integral market' consisting of product, labour, and capital markets. However, it very soon became clear that it required *transition* rather than reform. The constitutional preconditions for the transition were created by a set of amendments to the Constitution and by the document containing a general outline of the reform *The Principles of the Economic System Reform*, elaborated by the federal government's commission. The two systemic laws – *The Foreign Investment Law* and *The Enterprise Law* – passed in late December 1988, in fact reintroduced capitalism. At that time, Yugoslavia had, despite rather peculiar systemic features, many advantages compared to other East European countries, and therefore had chances for a successful transition into a market economy. Most of the so-called essential features of economic transition – decentralization of decision making, price reform, openness to the outside world, and diversification of ownership – were at least partly met before political and ideological change.

There was no need for decentralization and reorganization of central institutions. Directive planning was dismantled in the fifties, and financial autonomy was given to the enterprises in the sixties when diversification of the banking system was also introduced. The enterprises were autonomous, planning did not exist, and government used standard fiscal and monetary policy tools. Basic market institutions existed, although the notion of the so-called 'integral market' encompassing product, capital, and labour markets was not inaugurated until 1988.

Extensive price reform was not needed either. The liberalization of prices for certain products, considered the first stage of price reforms in Eastern Europe, was the core of the economic reform of 1965. Since then, price controls (including the exchange rate policy) have only been used as anti-inflationary measures.

Yugoslavia was a relatively open economy. The nature and the extent of Yugoslavia's links with the rest of the world through commodity, factor and financial markets, and the structure of its foreign trade and exchange rate systems resembled those which characterized developing market economies rather than centrally planned economies. Exports to countries with convertible currencies by far exceeded exports to the clearing areas. The opposite was the case in other East European countries – CMEA mutual trade was predominant in them. Less was achieved in the diversification of the ownership structure, although land was predominantly privately owned, and the private sector grew fast in services.

The systemic reform was accompanied by a 'shock therapy' stabilization program launched in December 1989. Fixed exchange rate, tight monetary policy, and wage control, were to be the pillars of the program. In fact, initial overvaluation of the Dinar, weakness of the wage controls and fiscal overhang existed from the very beginning. In the first two quarters of 1990, economic performance was satisfactory: in April 1990, the rate of inflation was even negative. In June, fatal mistakes were added to those of December 1989 which made price stability unsustainable. Policy makers started to pump money through selective credits for the agricultural sector and nearly doubled the wages of federal employees. The program was thus left without consistent built-in nominal anchors except for the fixed exchange rate. Private consumption and public sector spending increased dramatically in the summer and stayed on the same level till the end of 1990, while economic activity dropped to less than 90 per cent of 1989 economic activity. In the last two quarters of 1990, prices jumped up again. Severe monetary restrictiveness that followed in the last quarter pushed the economy into critical illiquidity, large scale bartering, and recession without deflation. With a fixed exchange rate at a highly overvalued Dinar, exports were left without support, imports were pushed up, and the trade deficit started to grow. In October, politically incited speculative attacks on foreign exchange deposits started. Finally, foreign currency reserves, the last resort of the stabilization program, started to vanish.

The federal government tried to stop further deterioration of economic performance by undertaking institutional changes. They were blocked by the republics; however, even without this blockade, systemic changes could not have had significant effects on economic performance in the short run. In autumn 1990, Yugoslavia actually ceased to exist as an economic entity – taxes were not collected, money was 'printed' elsewhere, tariffs and special levies were introduced for 'imports' from other republics. In addition, the republics started to build up their own economic systems which differed considerably from the very beginning. The collapse of the economic reform and of the stabilization program, which were launched in an acute economic crisis and carried out during a political crisis, was unavoidable.

The agony of the political system became evident during 1988. Then, public demonstrations that were more or less organized began to escalate dramatically, both in number and ferocity, expounding contradictory economic, social and political demands.

In Vojvodina and Montenegro, the political demonstrations in favour of a stronger Serbia caused the resignation of the entire Party and government leadership; overthrow of the party leadership was, however, for a short time only, prevented by similar public demonstrations in Kosovo.

The political demonstrations in Slovenia were in support of political pluralism emerging in the republic: demands for the abolition of the one party system were growing. The Peasants' Party, the Slovene Democratic League and the Social-Democratic Party were established. The legalization of political parties in 1989 created necessary conditions for free elections and parliamentary democracy. Pre-election campaigns and elections were peaceful and the transition of power from the old to the new governments was similar to the best traditions of European democracies.

The outcome of these elections, as well as elections held in other republics, divided Yugoslavia into two parts: one part remained a system of the communist/socialist type (Serbia and Montenegro), and another (the rest of the country) emerged with the Western-type systems. This, together with emergence of nationalistic governments and the collapse of economic reform, finally led to the civil war and to the breakdown of the country.

Notes

1 The combined employment in manufacturing, mining, construction, and transportation, or in the so called material sectors, as a share of total non-agricultural employment (sL) were regressed against the per capita GNP and a dummy variable D for the economic system, where D equals 0 for a capitalist and 1 for a socialist country. Data for 22 European countries, Yugoslavia excluded, in 1980 produce the following equation:

$$sL = 58.79 - 0.1816 * GNP/cap + 14.90 * D \quad R^2 = 0.86$$
$$(16.9) \quad (-3.46) \quad (7.47) \quad SE = 3.61$$

t values are in the parentheses, R2 is the adjusted coefficient of determination, and SE is the standard error of the estimate.

References

Ardalan, C. (1980) 'Workers' Self-Management and Planning: The Yugoslav Case', *World Development*, 8: 623–38.
Bajt, A. (1980) 'La propriété sociale en tant que propriété de tous et de chacun', *Revue d'Etudes Comparatives Est-Oest*, 11: 41–72.
Bajt, A. (1984) 'Trideset godina privrednog rasta', *Ekonomist*, 38: 1–20 (German translation in *Socialistische Theorie und Praxis* 13 (1986): 34–62).
Bajt, A. (1986) 'Preduzetništvo u samoupravnoj socijalističkoj privredi', *Privredna kretanja*, 159: 32–46.
Bajt, A. (1987) 'Stvarni i potencijalni društveni proizvod 1980', *Privredna kretanja*, 171: 42–52.
Bajt, A.(1988) *Samoupravna oblika družbene lastnine*, Zagreb: Globus.
Balassa, B., and Bertrand, J. (1970) 'Growth Performance of Eastern European Countries', *American Economic Review* (Proceedings), 60: 314–20.
Bićanić, R. (1957) 'Economic Growth under Centralized and Decentralized Planning: Yugoslavia – A Case Study', *Economic Development and Cultural Change*, 5: 63–74.
Burkett, J. (1983) *The Effects of Economic Reform in Yugoslavia, Investment and Trade Policy, 1959–1976*, Berkeley: IIS University of California.
Čičin-Šain, A. (1985) 'The Development and Role of the Major Economic Policy Instruments in Yugoslavia 1952–1972', in Gey *et al.* (1985), *Sozialismus und Industrialisierung*, pp. 175–96, Frankfurt: Campus Verlag.
Domar, E. D. (1966) 'The Soviet Collective Farm', *American Economic Review*, 56: 734–757.
Dubravčić, D. (1970) 'Labour as Entrepreneurial Input, An Essay in the Theory of the Producers Cooperative Economy', *Economica*, 37: 297–310.
Estrin, S., and Bartlett, W. (1983) 'The Effects of Enterprise Self-Management in Yugoslavia: An Empirical Survey', in D. C. Jones (ed.) (1983), *Participatory and Self-Managed Firms*, pp. 83–109, Lexington Books.
Furobotn, E. and Pejovich, S. (1972) 'Property Rights and Economic Theory: A Survey of Recent Literature', *Journal of Economic Literature*, 10: 1137–62.
Goldstein, S. (1985) *Prijedlog 85*, Zagreb: Scientia Yugoslavica.
Gurvitch, G. (1966) 'Les conseils ouvriers', *Autogestion*, no. 1: 50–57.
Horvat, B. (1971) 'Yugoslav Economic policy in the Post-War Period: Problems, Ideas, Institutional Developments', *American Economic Review* (supplement), 61 (2): 71–169.
Horvat, B. (1972) 'Critical Notes on the Theory of the Labour-Managed Firm and Some Macroeconomic Implications', *Economic Analysis*, 6: 291–4.
Horvat, B. (1985) *Jugoslovensko društvo u krizi*, Zagreb: Globus.
Jerovšek, J. *et al.* (1985) *Kriza, blokade i perspektive*, Zagreb: Globus.
Katz, A. (1985) 'Growth and Regional Variations in Unemployment in Yugoslavia: 1965–1980', in D. Jones, and J. Svejnar (eds.) (1985), *Advances in the Economic Analysis of Participatory and Labour-Managed Firms*, Vol. I.
Katz, A. (1987) 'The Adaptability and Feasibility of Market Socialism: Lessons from Yugoslavia', University of Pittsburgh, mimeo.

Kidrič, B. (1949) 'Kvalitet robnonovčanih odnosa u FNRJ', *Komunist*, no. 1: 33–51.
Kidrič, B. (1950a) *Privredni problemi FNRJ*, Beograd.
Kidrič, B. (1950b) 'Teze o ekonomici prelaznog razdoblja u našoj zemlji', *Komunist*, no. 6: 1–20.
Kornai, J. (1986) 'The Hungarian Reform Process: Vision, Hopes and Reality', *Journal of Economic Literature*, 24 (4): 1687–737.
Lydall, H. (1984) *Yugoslav Socialism – Theory and Practice*, Oxford: Clarendon Press.
Macura, M. (1986) 'Dugoročna stabilizacija i problem zaposlenosti', MCCK Srbije, Beograd, mimeo.
Meade, J. E. (1972) 'The Theory of Labour-Managed Firms and Profit Sharing', *Economic Journal*, Supplement, 82 (1): 402–28.
Mencinger, J. (1979) 'Theoretical and Actual Performance of the Worker-Managed Economy', *Economic Analysis*, 13: 253–65.
Mencinger, J. (1983) 'Otvorena nezaposlenost i zaposleni bez posla', *Privredna kretanja*, no. 128: 27–40.
Mencinger, J. (1986) 'The Yugoslav Economic Systems and Their Efficiency', *Economic Analysis*, 19: 31–43.
Mencinger, J. (1988a) 'Verižni učinki zastojev v gospodarstvu na "brezposelnost" zaposlenih in izrabo kapacitet', *Gospodarska gibanja*, no. 180: 34–49.
Mencinger, J. (1988b) 'Reforme socializma in paradoks izkoriščanja', *Ekonomska revija*, no. 4: 319–22.
Popović, S. (1984), *Ogled o jugoslovenskom privrednom sistemu*, Beograd: Marksistički centar.
Rusinow, D. (1977) *The Yugoslav Experiment 1948–1974*, Berkeley: University of California.
Sapir, A. (1980) 'Economic Growth and Factor Substitution; What happened to the Yugoslav Economic Miracle?', *Economic Journal*, 90: 294–313.
Savez Komunista Jugoslavije (1958) *Program Saveza Komunista Jugoslavije*, Belgrad: Komunist.
Savezni društveni savet (1984) *Dugoročni program ekonomske stabilizacije*, Beograd.
Savezni društveni savet (1985), *Kritička analiza funkcionisanja političkog sistema socijalističkog samoupravljanja*, Beograd.
Savezno izvršno veće (1988), *Osnove reforme privrednog sistema*, Beograd.
Tyson, L. (1980) *The Yugoslav Economic System and its Performance in the 1970s*, Berkeley: University of California.
Vanek, J. (1970) *The General Theory of Labour-Managed Market Economies*, Ithaca: Cornell University Press.
Vanek, J. (1972) 'The Macroeconomic Theory and Policy of an Open Worker Managed Economy', *Economic Analysis*, 6: 255–69.
Ward, B. (1958) 'The Firm in Illyria: Market Syndicalism', *American Economic Review*, 48: 566–89.
World Bank (1979) *Yugoslavia: Selfmanagement Socialism and the Challenges of Development*, Baltimore: Johns Hopkins University Press.
World Bank (1984) 'Yugoslavia: Employment Strategy and Manpower Policies for the 1980s', Washington, mimeo.

9
Self-Management, Employee Ownership and Transition*

Saul Estrin

9.1 Introduction

The process of economic reform and transition from plan to market has created unprecedented opportunities for the development of a significant employee owned or controlled sector in large parts of the globe. But these developments have also highlighted some fundamental weaknesses and deficiencies in the traditional self-management literature (see, for example, Ward, 1958; Vanek, 1970; Meade, 1972; Bonin, Jones and Putterman, 1993). These questions were not resolved in the 1970s and 1980s, when the main focus of attention was on producer co-operatives in Western Europe and the United States, and the self-management experiment in Yugoslavia. The issues continue to plague us in our analysis of how to take employee ownership forward in the transition context. My aims in this paper are to highlight the opportunities for employee ownership in this region and to provide some direction as to where I think new research will be needed to yield an appropriate model for this emerging self-managed sector.

The main themes of this paper derive from a single unanswered question. What is the appropriate institutional model for a labour-managed sector in a transition economy? I believe that there are four aspects to this question. The first concerns the appropriate ownership form. Much of the traditional labour-management literature focused on social or collective ownership (see for example, Horvat, 1976; Ward, 1958;

---

*An earlier version of the paper was presented at the 9th Conference of the International Association for the Economics of Participation, Bristol, 1998. The author acknowledges helpful discussions with Will Bartlett, Derek Jones, Mario Nuti, Milica Uvalić and Michael Keren. Any errors remain, however, his own.

Vanek, 1970). In practice, most of the transition economies have introduced structures in which, while employee ownership is widespread, it takes the form of individualistic holdings. This raises the key moral issue at the core of labour-management: that each worker should have an equal vote rather than operate within an arrangement which yields one vote to each share. If the moral superiority of the labour-managed system comes from its democracy, it will not be delivered by individual ownership.

The second issue concerns the appropriate institutional arrangements for the labour-management sector. There was much research on this matter in the 1980s and the 1990s (see, for example, Ben-Ner, 1984; Estrin and Jones, 1983; Perotin, 1987). These authors were trying to understand what the legal features were of Mondragon and the French and Italian producer cooperatives that made these sectors work so well and survive for so long. There was also a great concern as to whether these arrangements were replicable (see, for example, Bradley and Gelb, 1981). The answers relate to the potential role of a centralized funding authority, to ownership-transfer rules and to voting rules. It is not clear how much of this analysis can be transferred to the transition context.

The third big issue concerns the relationship between a labour-managed firm and the capital market. The original work by Ward and Vanek assumed that capital markets were perfectly competitive and that the supply of debt was perfectly elastic at an exogenously determined cost. There was also some work on internally financed labour-managed firms (see Stephen, 1980). But, the literature has never adequately tackled the question of debt versus equity finance and the moral hazard problems raised by external financing when a factor of production controlled the surplus. This has left the issue open to discussion by unsympathetic authors such as Hansmann (1990).

The final topic is the question of what particular advantages and disadvantages labour-management might bring to the problems of enterprises in transition. This links to the key issue in the research agenda of the producer co-operatives literature during the 1980s. The question we need to consider now is: what are the sectors, the ownership arrangements and so forth, conducive to the success of labour-management firms in transition economies. In this chapter I want primarily to raise the first three points, but to focus in some detail on the fourth. The structure of the chapter is as follows: in the following section I summarize the opportunities for labour-management in transition economies, by providing evidence on the emergence of the private sector and on the scale of labour-management that is already in place. In the subsequent section I analyze the potential role of labour-management in transition and consider the appropriate ownership form and institutional structure.

9.2 The opportunities for labour-management in transition economies

The opportunities for the speedy growth of a labour-managed sector in transition economies arise for a very simple reason. Excluding the former Yugoslavia where, as Horvat has stressed, ownership was social, the vast majority of industrial firms in the former communist block were state owned. I have argued elsewhere (Estrin, 1994) that, for political reasons primarily, reform governments sought very rapid privatization. This was done to prevent the de-cumulation of state owned assets by theft or through consumption. It was also explicitly intended to create a new middle class and thereby to provide political underpinnings for the reform process. Among others, Stiglitz (1994) has questioned whether the economic arguments alone would support such speedy ownership transformation, rather than allowing first a sharpening of competitive forces.

To achieve widespread private ownership very quickly, in a context of poorly developed or non-existent capital markets and with very limited private savings, there are only two options for the bulk of industrial firms:

1. To sell the industrial sector to foreign firms or investment funds. This has been, to a significant extent, the inner strategy in Hungary and in Estonia (see Estrin, 1994). However, this approach has profound domestic political ramifications and is, anyway, hardly a viable strategy in larger economies such as Russia or even Poland.
2. To give the industrial sector away to the domestic population. If this strategy is being followed, there are only three avenues to follow: first, one could distribute the shares to the population as a whole, as was done in the Czech Republic, Slovenia and Poland. The second way would be to distribute shares to workers and managers, as was in effect done in Russia and Ukraine. Finally, one might give ownership rights back to the former owners – restitution – an important phenomenon in East Germany.

The various options are summarized in Figure 9.1, with examples of countries that predominantly followed particular methods.[1] Some data

148 *Self-Management, Employee Ownership and Transition*

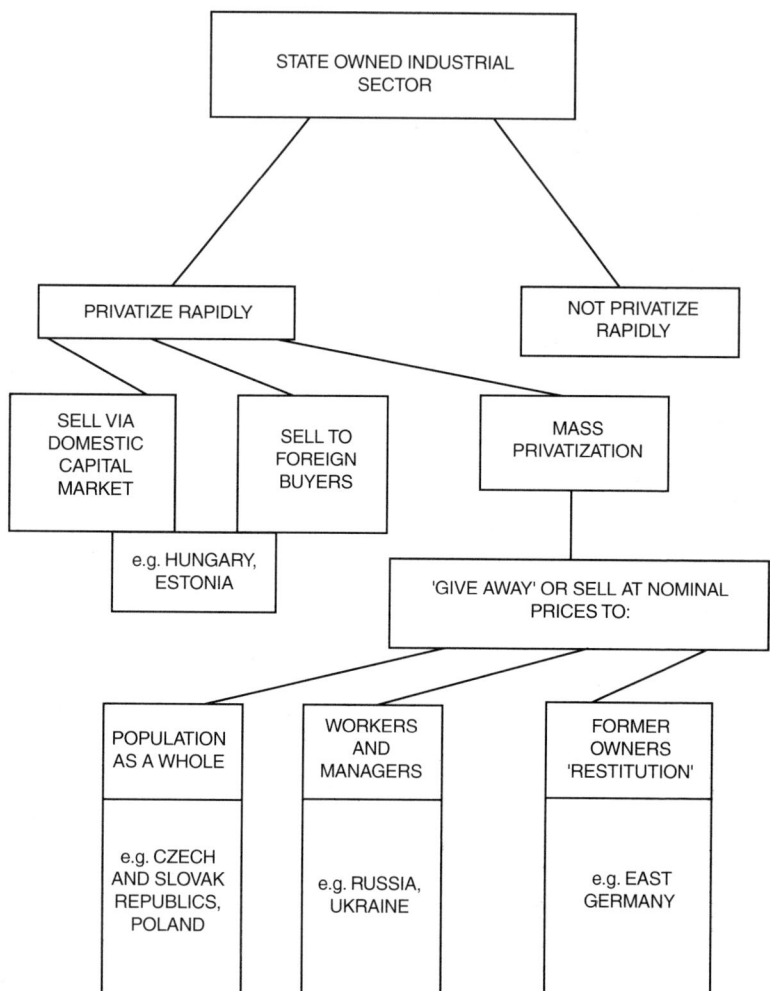

Figure 9.1 Privatization options for state sector

may be helpful to establish the potential scale of the labour-managed sector in these economies. The pace of privatization has been extraordinarily rapid in most transition economies. In the most advanced countries (the Czech Republic, Slovakia, Poland and Hungary), well over 50 per cent of GDP was in private hands by 1996, increasing to 70–75 per cent by 1998. Even in the countries where privatization has been more modest, such as Ukraine or Azerbaijan, the private sector share has grown very rapidly and covers more than a quarter of gross domestic product. Thus the desire by governments to undertake very speedy privatization has in most of the region been realized. Interestingly, the countries of former Yugoslavia, with the exception of Slovenia, have lagged in this privatization process – in part because their ownership form, social ownership, has made the process of privatization much more complicated.

In Table 9.1, we present the main methods of privatization employed in the region for medium size and large firms. It immediately becomes clear from the figure that in seven of the leading transition countries, sales to outside owners (the predominant privatization form in the West and in other emerging economies) were relatively insignificant. As noted above, the only exceptions are Estonia and Hungary. Voucher privatization and management-employee buy-outs have been the main mechanism for privatization in the countries covered and have been more general. Table 9.2 goes on to discuss in greater detail the operation of mass privatization schemes. It can be seen that almost every country in the region, except Hungary and the former Yugoslavia, has used mass privatization as part of their privatization program. In countries like the Czech Republic, Russia, Slovakia and Romania, mass privatization has been the predominant privatization form. In other countries, such as Poland and Ukraine, it has been one form amongst several. Nonetheless, mass privatization has been the great invention of the transition process and it is because of mass privatization that such widely defused ownership holdings have emerged in so many transition economies. It is when we turn to the outcomes of these mass privatization program, and the broader privatization efforts, that the prospects for a significant employee ownership sector become clear. We find the widespread emergence of employee ownership almost everywhere in the region. This is true not only in Russia, Ukraine and Romania, but also even in Hungary and Poland where it was not a planned or desired policy outcome. This is because almost everywhere insiders have been given ownership rights, and the insider group comprises the coalition of workers and managers. In some countries, managers have managed both to retain control over firms and to get for themselves a predominant ownership stake. However, in practice, this is usually very hard to accomplish because, though firms were being sold for a fraction of what they were worth, managers still could not generate sufficient funds among themselves and therefore needed also to rely on the savings of their much larger labour forces. Table 9.3 gives some very rough estimates of the ownership outcome in some key countries.

Table 9.1 Methods of privatization for medium-size and large enterprises in seven transition economies (percentages of total)

Country	Sale to outside owners	Management-employee buyout	Equal access voucher privatization	Restitution	Other[a]	Still in state hands
Czech Republic						
By number[b]	32	0	22[c]	9	28	10
By value[d]	5	0	50	2	3	40
Estonia[e]						
By number	64	30	0	0	2	4
By value	40	12	3	10	0	15
Hungary						
By number	38	7	0	0	33	22
By value	40	2	0	4	12	42
Lithuania						
By number	<1	5	70	0	0	25
By value	<1	5	60	0	0	35
Mongolia						
By number	0	0	70	0	0	30
By value	0	0	55	0	0	45

Poland					
By number	3	14	6	0	23	54
Russia[c]					
By number	0	55	11	0	0	34

Data are as of the end of 1995.

[a] Includes transfers to municipalities or social insurance organizations, debt-equity swaps, and sales through insolvency proceedings.

[b] Number of privatized firms as a share of all formerly state-owned firms. Includes parts of firms restructured prior to privatization.

[c] Includes assets sold for cash as part of the voucher privatization program through June 1994.

[d] Value of firms privatized as a share of the value of all formerly state-owned firms. Data for Poland and Russia are unavailable.

[e] Does not include some infrastructure firms. All management buyouts were part of competitive, open tenders. In thirteen cases, citizens could not exchange vouchers for minority shares in firms sold to a core investor.

Source: World Bank (1996), From Plan to Market – World Development Report 1996, Table 3.2, p. 53.

Table 9.2 Mass privatization programmes in Central and Eastern Europe and the Commonwealth of Independent States

Country	Year voucher distribution began	Are shares issued in waves or continuously?	Are vouchers bearer, tradeable, or nontradeable?	Is investment in funds allowed, encouraged, or compulsory?
Albania	1995	Continuously	Bearer	Encouraged[a]
Armenia	1994	Continuously	Bearer	Allowed[b]
Belarus	1995	Continuously	Bearer	Encouraged[c]
Bulgaria	1995	Waves	Nontradeable	Encouraged
Czech Republic	1992	Waves	Nontradeable	Encouraged
Estonia	1993	Continuously	Tradeable[d]	Allowed[e]
Georgia	1995	Continuously	Tradeable	Allowed[b]
Kazakstan	1994	Waves	Nontradeable	Compulsory
Kyrgys Republic	1994	Continuously	Bearer	Allowed[f]
Latvia	1994	Continuously	Tradeable	Allowed[e]
Lithuania	1993	Continuously	Nontradeable	Allowed[e]
Moldavia	1994	Waves[g]	Nontradeable	Encouraged
Poland	1995	Waves	Tradeable	Compulsory
Romania[h]	1992	Continuously	Bearer	Compulsory[i]
Romania	1995	Waves	Nontradeable[j]	Allowed
Russia	1992	Continuously	Bearer	Encouraged
Slovak Republic	1992	Waves	Nontradeable	Encouraged
Slovenia	1994	Continuously	Nontradeable	Allowed
Ukraine	1995	Continuously	Nontradeable	Allowed

[a] By July 1966 only one or two funds had applied to receive vouchers.
[b] Although a legal entitlement exists to invest vouchers in funds, in practice this option was limited.
[c] The results of the first voucher auction were cancelled in March 1995, and fund licences were suspended from then until August 1996.
[d] Vouchers were nontradeable at the outset of the programme, but cash trading was legalized in the spring of 1994.
[e] Citizens could also exchange vouchers for other things such as apartments or land.
[f] Citizens could invest their vouchers in housing as well as shares. They can sell their vouchers to funds, but no formal mechanism exists for them to subscribe to funds.
[g] Although the design of the Moldavian programme was based on the offer of companies in waves, the waves were small in the early stages, and thus had many of the characteristics of a continuous issue.
[h] In 1991, Romania introduced a scheme based on the distribution of certificates of ownership in five private ownership funds. In 1995, a supplementary mass privatization programme was introduced involving the distribution of coupons that could be exchanged for company shares or fund shares, after which the funds are to be transformed into financial investment companies.
[i] Under certain circumstances, certificates of ownership in funds could be exchanged for company shares.
[j] Certificates of ownership were bearer, coupons were registered and nontradeable.
Source: Estrin and Stone (1997).

We find that only in the Czech Republic has mass privatization not led to a significant degree of majority employee control. Table 9.3 was derived from Earle and Estrin (1996) and shows that in Romania, employees hold around 65 per cent of shares, and managers just 32 per cent; while in Hungary, workers own around 28 per cent. Earle and Estrin (1996) report that Hungary and Romania both have significant employee stock ownership plan (ESOP) schemes that have a trust structure and include some elements of collective ownership. In Poland, the sample of 200 firms in 1994 suggested that around 35 per cent of private firms have significant employee stakes.

Tables 9.4 and 9.5 provide information for what are probably two largest employee owned sectors in transition economies: Russia and Ukraine. We find in Table 9.4 that the Russian privatization process led to around 77 per cent of shares in privatized firms being held by insiders: of these 50 per cent were held by workers. This has led to a situation in which some 37 per cent of all Russian firms are majority worker owned. The situation is almost as striking in Ukraine. We find that workers' and managers' shareholding is around 51 per cent, with workers' holding around 43 per cent. Once again, of all old firms, workers' shareholding is around 40 per cent. Thus in summary, there is a lot of employee ownership in the region. It is concentrated in the former Soviet Union, but is also widespread elsewhere. The scale is extraordinary in comparison with the levels of employee ownership which have emerged through *de novo* foundation. It is also interesting that widespread employee ownership has emerged as a by-product of other government privatization policies (mainly, the urge to privatize quickly), and the process of mass privatization. Reformed governments did not plan to create employee ownership. However, they have done so and the question to be addressed is how to make these sectors survive and

Table 9.3 Ownership consequences of privatization

Country	% Privatizations with majority employee control	Number of firms with employee control	Average per cent held by employees
Czech Republic (1993)	1	3	–
Hungary (1993)	43	187	42
Poland (1993)	75	1478	51
Romania (all large privatizations) (1994)	98	600	95

Source: Earle and Estrin (1996).

Table 9.4 Dominant owner type in Russia, 1994

Dominant owner Type	Privatized firms (unweighted)	Privatized firms (weighted)	All old firms (unweighted)	All old firms (weighted)
SO column %	8.3	20.3	32.5	38.1
PO column %	91.7	79.7	67.5	61.9
IO column %	76.7	58.7	56.4	45.6
WO column %	50.4	44.5	37.1	34.6
MO column %	14.6	8.3	10.7	6.5
INO column %	10.0	4.7	7.4	3.7
OO column %	8.8	12.1	6.4	9.4
NO column %	5.8	8.8	4.3	6.9
N	241	241	327	327

The category 'All old firms' includes enterprises that were partially or fully privatized and enterprises that had not begun privatization and were still held by state. 1994 employment was used to weight firms in the columns labelled 'weighted'. SO = state-dominated, PO = private-dominated, IO = insider-dominated, WO = worker-dominated, MO = manager-dominated, INO = insider-dominated, but not clearly by workers or managers, OO = outsider-dominated, NO = private-dominated, but unclear whether by insiders or outsiders.
Source: Author's work on enterprise surveys.

thrive. The alternative is that they gradually disappear, reverting to managerial or outsider ownership in a degenerative spiral (see, for example, Boycko, Shleifer and Vishny, 1995).

9.3 Policies for employee owner firms in transition?

In this section, I want to consider three areas in which labour-management could help the transition process. These are: ownership and investment, productivity and labour incentives, and enterprise restructuring.

9.3.1 Ownership and investment

Ownership of capital assets implies two fundamental rights. The first is the control over the production process; and the second *usus fructus*, the right to allocate the surplus generated. When employees control the production process, they are in a position to reallocate expenditure between cost and surplus so as to squeeze out other equity or debt holders. This fundamental agency problem needs to be addressed. Horvat has always held the view that the appropriate solution to this problem is social ownership, as defined in the Yugoslav self-managed system. In principle, this may be correct. However, in the current transition countries, social ownership is clearly not now on the political

Table 9.5 State ownership in Ukraine, 1996

Shareholding	Privatized firms (unweighted)	Privatized firms (weighted)	All old firms (unweighted)	All old firms (weighted)
Total state	10.9	21.2	17.6	25.5
Total private	89.1	78.8	82.4	74.5
All insiders	50.7	41.7	46.9	39.4
Workers	42.8	35.5	39.6	33.6
Managers	7.9	6.2	7.3	5.9
All outsiders	38.4	37.1	35.5	35.1
Firms	9.9	10.1	9.2	9.6
Banks	7.8	7.4	7.2	7.0
Citizens	15.9	13.4	14.7	12.7
Foreigners	1.1	2.5	1.0	2.4
Other	3.8	3.7	3.5	3.5
Valid *n*	123	123	133	133

Source: Estrin and Rosevear (1998).

agenda. As we have seen, there is widespread individualistic ownership with some trust holding or collective ownership in a few countries. We need therefore to consider the appropriate rules that might be introduced to address this problem, if employee owned firms are to have access to the large investment funds that would be needed to implement deep or strategic restructuring and accelerated transition.

It is important to note that individual ownership stakes held by workers do not necessarily yield control over management. This is because employee holdings are typically highly dispersed and there are significant transaction costs of monitoring and controlling managers. This is especially true if the combined employee stake is relatively large but not controlling. Earle and Estrin (1996) argued that the situation that might emerge would be one of an MCEO – 'Managerially Controlled Employee Owned Firm'. Such firms would quickly revert back to the capitalist form. Therefore, if individualized employee ownership is to be made into something meaningful in the transition context, we need to see one of two things emerging. The first is a move to some element of collective ownership, along the lines of producer cooperative sectors in Italy or France. The second is to ensure institutional mechanisms that convert employee ownership into real control over enterprise decision making. Such governance mechanisms might include, for example, direct elections by the workers of representatives to company boards, with democratic systems to mandate the worker-directors. This would allow employee ownership to evolve along the lines of German co-determination (see, for example, Cable and FitzRoy, 1980).

The question of investment, which is so crucial in transition economies, raises a further dilemma for employee owned firms. Democracy in decision making is one of the key elements of labour-management, and arguably is an important reason for the productivity benefits from employee ownership. But on the other hand, employee ownership can be associated with problems of under-investment. These may arise because the workers' ownership stakes are not tradable if ownership is collective, so income-maximizing workers seek to obtain the return from their investment in the firm through finer but relatively more productive capital projects. It may also derive from unwillingness of capital market institutions to lend to labour-managed firms, partly because of the agency problems discussed above, but also because of the bias against worker run organizations (see Vanek, 1975).

Fresh thinking is needed about the appropriate balance between individual and collective ownership particularly in the transition context. This is because the key long-run issue for restructuring firms in transition is investment and the implementation of new technologies and new products. It seems clear from books of the theoretical literature (see, for example, Furubotn and Pejovich, 1970) and from the empirical evidence (see, for example, Bartlett *et al.* 1992) that employee ownership may have problems in generating sufficient investment.

9.3.2 Incentives and productivity

There is a large amount of literature on this subject, both theoretical and empirical (see, for example, Bonin, Jones and Putterman, 1993 for a survey). As is well known, there is a conflict in theory: on one hand, there are those who argue that labour-management will worsen corporate performance because of the slow process of decision making, corporate governance problems, and the cost of the worker-owners reaching agreement on the strategic developments (see, for example, Jensen and Meckling, 1979; Hansmann, 1990). On the other hand, there is a group who argues that employee ownership and workers' management will sharpen incentives, strengthen performance and raise productivity (see, for example, Cable and FitzRoy, 1980; Cable, 1984; Sertel, 1982; Bradley and Gelb, 1981). The evidence, however, establishes unambiguously that employee ownership acts to raise company productivity and efficiency (see, for example, Defourny, Estrin and Jones, 1985; Jones and Svejnar, 1985; Bonin, Jones and Putterman, 1993).

Low productivity and weak employee morale is at the very heart of the transition problem. Socialist ownership combined with central planning and hierarchical managerial structures acted to de-motivate the labour force and led to very low growth productivity in most firms. One of the key aspects of the changes required in the transition economies is therefore to address the labour productivity question and labour-management may be the best way to change this environment. However, it is important to note that there is very little evidence that this has been achieved as yet. A series of studies (see, for example, Belka et al., 1995; Earle and Estrin, 1997; Frydman, Gray, Hessel and Rapaczynski, 1997) have found little evidence that indicators of labour productivity, for example, are associated with ownership, or that privatization is leading to enhance company performance (see, for example, World Bank, 1996). Case studies suggest that even when workers do own firms, they exercise relatively little control or influence (see, for example, Brada, Estrin, Gelb and Singh, 1995; Earle, Estrin and Leschenko, 1996). One explanation for this disappointing result may be that privatizations have not been the platform for the real employee involvement underlying productivity gains; either MCEOs have predominated or the workers themselves have therefore not been empowered by the changes in ownership.

9.3.3 Enterprise restructuring

One key characteristic of transition economies is that most enterprises need to reduce employment, at least in the short term and possibly permanently. This is because the planning system created incentives to hold a labour surplus in order to meet production needs at the end of each plan period. Moreover, since company targets were focused primarily on output, to a lesser extent on profit and hardly at all on cost, there were clear benefits in raising employment to above normal needs in order to facilitate meeting the prime target.

In addition, the opening of the transition economies to relatively free trade, in a situation of (typically) fixed exchange rates, led to fundamental changes in relative prices (notably for energy, capital and foreign exchange) in ways that massively reduced labour demand in most industrial sectors, and therefore created structural unemployment or labour hoarding.

Hence, actual employment in most firms in transition is some way to the right of the labour demand equilibrium level implied by cost minimization, or even that implied in a labour-managed (or a utility maximizing labour-managed) firm. It seems likely that in most circumstances, the first task of new owners of transition firms will be to address the labour hoarding problem.

Personally, I am very nervous about the establishment of any sort of employee ownership in this context. The workforce is placed in the situation of resolving potentially irresolvable problems, without recourse to any new capital which might ease the path or point to a new strategic direction. Worker ownership has much less to offer a firm in this situation; the problems are in the area of what the firm sells, how it sells it, and how it makes the product. The workers might be able to contribute by proposing process improvements, but if these are labour productivity increasing, they will merely add to the problem of overmanning if the ultimate constraint is on the product demand side. Worker owners might also assist the short-term survival of the enterprise by offering wage cuts (or wages arrears, as has occurred across the former Soviet Union). But long-term solutions will almost certainly require the injection of new capital and, as discussed above, employee ownership is not the ideal form to deliver this.

I am also worried by the demonstration effects from employee ownership of slowly-dying firms. We can imagine a dismal picture of worker owners implementing wage cuts or refusing to pay wage arrears, then cutting employment to keep a non-viable enterprise afloat. These actions will ultimately reduce solidarity, undermine morale and prevent exploitation of productivity gains. Cut off from capital markets because of agency problems, such employee owned firms would go on a downward spiral of slow exit. This is a clear danger under labour-management because, as Vanek (1970) noted, it is hard to define the exit point for a labour-managed firm because labour costs are determined endogenously. In principal, provided workers will accept zero wages, the firm can survive if revenues exceed or equal non-labour costs. The firm will therefore only close when earnings are driven below the level available through other sources, for example unemployment benefits, income in hand from working on private plots, and so on. The exit process for the labour-managed firm is therefore likely to be long and protracted, driven by the pace of quitting by disenchanted workers. This contrasts with the capitalist case, where exit is likely to follow when price falls below average variable cost (including wage costs set at a market level). Because average variable costs by definition exceed average non-labour variable costs, such exit is likely to be sooner as well as being determined by an external set of owners rather than the dwindling residue labour force. The negative demonstration effects from employee ownership presiding over widespread enterprise collapse of this sort could do untold damage to the labour-management movement in transition economies; a nation-wide version of the reputation of employee-owned firms gained from the so-called 'Benn co-operatives' in the UK in the 1970s, and the Scottish Daily News (see, for example, Bradley and Gelb, 1980).

9.4 Conclusions

I have argued that the transition process creates an exciting opportunity for those interested in the development of an employee owned sector. This is because, as a consequence of mass privatization, many workers in Central and Eastern Europe now own shares in the companies where they work: taken together, this often forms a majority or strategic stake.

However, this is not enough to ensure that labour-management emerges as a significant form in these countries. The employee ownership which has developed is individual and highly dispersed: there are no mechanisms to convert ownership into control and many of the firms are non-viable. I have argued that the opportunity for labour-management should nonetheless be seized, at least in (probably a minority of) the firms that have a long-term potential. But to succeed, we need to learn the lessons from successful employee owned sectors in Western Europe and North America to formulate the legal framework, institutional rules and supporting agencies and structures to assist the evolution of these employee holdings into an effective labour-managed sector (see Uvalić and Vaughan-Whitehead, 1997). The lessons from the Yugoslav self-management experiment need also to be drawn and digested. This has become an urgent agenda for policy orientated research in this field, before the significant employee owned sector in these countries disappears either via bankruptcy or reversion to the capitalist form.

Note

1 Of course, in practice almost all the countries applied all the methods. The figure refers to the main method of privatization.

References

Bartlett *et al.* (1992) 'Labor-Managed vs. Private Firms: An Empirical Comparison of Cooperatives and Private Firms In Central Italy', *Industrial and Labor Relations Review*, 46(1): 103–18.

Belka, M., Estrin, S., Schaffer, M. E. and Singh, I. J. (1995) 'Enterprise Adjustment in Poland: Evidence from a Survey of 200 Private, Privatised and State-Owned Firms', CEP Discussion Paper, no. 233.

Ben-Ner, A. (1984) 'On the Stability of Cooperative Type of Organization', *Journal of Comparative Economics*, 8(3): 247–60.
Bonin, J., Jones, D. C., and Putterman, L. (1993) 'Theoretical and Empirical Studies of Producer Cooperatives: Will ever the Twain Meet?', *Journal of Economic Literature*, 31: 1290–320.
Boycko, M., Schleifer, A. and Vishny, R. (1995) *Russia Privatizing*, Cambridge MA: MIT Press.
Brada, J. C., Estrin, S., Gelb, A. and Singh, I. (1995) *Restructuring and Privatization in Central Eastern Europe*, Armonk: ME Sharpe.
Bradley, K. and Gelb, A. (1980) 'Worker Cooperatives as Industrial Policy: the Case of the Scottish Daily News', *Review of Economic Studies*, 47: 665–78.
Bradley, K. and Gelb, A. (1981) 'Motivation and Control in the Mondragon Experiment', *British Journal of Industrial Relations*, 19(2): 211–31.
Cable, J. (1984) 'Employee Participation in Firm Performance: A Prisoner's Dilemma Framework', Florence, European University Institute Working Paper, no. 126.
Cable, J. and FitzRoy, F. R. (1980) 'Productive Efficiency, Incentives and Employee Participation: Some Preliminary Results for West Germany', *Kyklos*, 33: 100–21.
Defourny. J., Estrin, S. and Jones, D. (1985) 'The Effects of Workers' Participation on Enterprise Performance – Empirical Evidence from French Cooperatives', *International Journal of Industrial Organization*, 3(2): 197–217.
Earle, J. S. and Estrin, S. (1996) 'Employee Ownership in Transition' in R. Frydman *et al.* (eds.), vol. 2, pp. 1–61.
Earle, J. S. and Estrin, S. (1997) 'After Voucher Privatization: The Structure of Corporate Ownership in Russian Manufacturing Industry', CEPR Discussion Paper, no. 1736.
Earle, J. S., Estrin, S. and Leshchenko, L. (1996) 'Ownership Structures, Patterns of Control and Enterprise Behaviour in Russia', in S. Commander, Q. Fan and M. Schaffer (eds.), *Enterprise Restructuring and Economic Policy in Russia*, EDI Development Studies, Washington, DC: The World Bank, pp. 205–52.
Estrin, S. and Jones D. (1983) 'The Effects of Worker Participation upon Productivity in French Producer Cooperatives', Florence, European University Institute Working Paper, no. 68.
Estrin S. and Rosevear, R. (1998) 'Enterprise Performance and Corporate Governance in Ukraine', Paper presented at the Workshop on Corporate Governance in Russia, London, London Business School, June.
Estrin, S. and Stone, R. (1997) 'A Taxonomy of Mass Privatization' in I. W. Liberman, R. M. Desai and S. S. Nestor (eds.), *Between State and Market – Mass Privatization in Transition Economies,* Washington DC: World Bank; also in *Transition*, 7(1996, 11–12): 8–9.
Estrin, S. (ed.) (1994) *Privatization in Central and Eastern Europe,* London and New York: Longman.
Frydman, R., Gray, C., Hessel, M. and Rapaczynski, A. (1997) 'Private Ownership and Corporate Performance: Some Lessons from Transition Economies', Economic Research Report 97-28, CV Starr Center for Applied Economics.
Frydman, R., Gray, C. and Rapaczynski, A. (eds.), (1996) *Corporate Governance in Central Europe and Russia,* Budapest: CEU Press.

Furubotn, E. and Pejovich, S. (1970) 'Property Rights and the Behavior of the Firm in a Socialist State: The Example of Yugoslavia', *Zeitschrift fur Nationalökonomie*, 30: 431–54.

Hansmann, H. (1990) 'The Viability of Worker Ownership: an Economic Perspective on the Political Structure of the Firm', in M. Aoki, B. Gustafsson and O. E. Williamson (eds.), *The Firm as a Nexus of Treaties*, London: Sage.

Horvat, B. (1978) *The Yugoslav Economic System: The First Labor-Managed Economy in the Making*, New York: International Arts and Sciences Press.

Jensen, M. H. and Meckling, W. H. (1979) 'Rights and Production Functions: An Application to Labor-Managed Firms and Codetermination', *Journal of Business*, 52(4): 459–506.

Jones, D. and Svejnar, J. (1985) 'Participation, Profit-Sharing, Worker Ownership and Efficiency in Italian Producer Cooperatives', *Economica*, 52(November): 449–65.

Meade, J. (1972) 'The Theory of Labor-Managed Firms and Profit Sharing', *Economic Journal*, 82(March): 402–28.

Perotin, V. (1987) 'Conditions of Survival and Closure of French Cooperatives: Some Preliminary Findings', in D. Jones and J. Svejnar (eds.), *Advances in the Economic Analysis of Participatory and Labor-managed Firms*, vol. 2 Greenwich CT: JAI Press pp. 201–25.

Sertel, M. R. (1982) *Workers and Incentives*, Amsterdam: North-Holland.

Stephen, F. H. (1980) 'Bank Credit and the Labor-managed Firm: A Comment', *American Economic Review*, 70(4): 796–9.

Stiglitz, J. E. (1994) *Whither Socialism?*, Cambridge MA: MIT Press.

Uvalić, M. and Vaughan-Whitehead, D. (eds.), (1997), *Privatization Surprises in Transition Economies – Employee Ownership in Central and Eastern Europe*, International Labour Organization and Cheltenham: Edward Elgar.

Vanek, J. (1970) *The General Theory of Labor-Managed Market Economies*, Ithaca: Cornell University Press.

Vanek, J. (ed.) (1975) *Self-Management, Economic Liberation of Man*, Baltimore: Penguin.

Ward, B. (1958) 'The Firm in Illyria: Market Syndicalism', *American Economic Review*, 48(4): 566–89.

World Bank (1996) *From Plan to Market – World Development Report 1996*, New York: Oxford University Press.

10
Privatization and Enterprise Performance: Evidence from Estonia*

Derek C. Jones and Niels Mygind

10.1 Introduction

The relationship between different organizational forms and economic efficiency has long attracted the interest of many influential economists including Mill, Marshall, Pigou and Keynes.[1] Important contributions which led to a widening of this debate to include labour-managed firms have also been made by Branko Horvat, including an early survey of theoretical and empirical evidence which pointed to the better performance of labour-managed firms compared to firms that were either state-owned or capitalist (Horvat, 1982: ch. 6). Since the collapse of the command economies, the main issue that has emerged in this realm of comparative organization and efficiency concerns the effects of the different forms of private ownership upon economic performance. The main aim of this paper is to provide fresh empirical evidence on this matter for the interesting case of the transition economy of Estonia. In considering the effects of privatization on economic performance, most economists expect that privatization *per se* will have favourable economic effects. In addition, economic outcomes are expected to vary

---

*In facilitating this work, the authors acknowledge support from ACE Phare, NSF SES 9511465, the Danish Research Council for Social Sciences and the National Council on Soviet and Eastern European Studies. In addition, the paper has benefited from research assistance by Lindsey Culbertson and comments from J. Bonin, J. Pliskin, P. Kalmi, L. Tikla, E. Peev, and participants at the 9th Conference of the International Association for the Economics of Participation, Bristol, June 1998; the workshop on corporate governance, London Business School, June 1998; the first International Conference on Economic Restructuring and Corporate Governance, Copenhagen Business School, August 1998, and a seminar at UNWIDER, Helsinki, August 1998.

with the specific *form* of private ownership with most contemporary economists viewing employee ownership as a form of privatization that is much less efficient than other forms (for example, Boycko *et al.*, 1996; Frydman *et al.*, 1997). However, not all theories lead to adverse predictions concerning employee ownership (for example, Sertel, 1996). Moreover, as forcefully argued by Horvat (1969), the beneficial economic effects of employee ownership are to be expected only if ownership is accompanied by institutional arrangements that provide for real participation.

The theoretical issues raised concerning new forms of enterprise ownership are all the more salient because, unexpectedly, employee ownership has proven to be a widespread feature of the privatization process in several transition economies (Uvalić and Vaughan-Whitehead, 1997; Nuti, 1997). In addition, the empirical evidence on ownership issues for transition economies is quite slim and what there is often presents a mixed picture. Thus for Visegrad countries, while most early studies on economic performance concluded that the economic effects of these new structures of ownership have been difficult to discern, more recent studies of firms often conclude that effects of privatization are apparent and that employee ownership is not the best way to privatize.[2] Also, studies which include *de novo* private firms find that privatization has beneficial effects (for example, Barberis *et al.*, 1996). By contrast, studies of newly privatized Russian firms (for example, Earle *et al.*, 1996) seldom find strong evidence that the form of private ownership affects economic outcomes, though Jones (1998) finds mixed evidence on this point.

Apart from differences in institutional settings, one potential reason for the apparent discrepancy between findings on the effects of ownership on economic performance for former state-owned Russian firms and for Visegrad countries is that the available data often have been quite restricted, not only in terms of sample size and number of years but also in the range of information that has been available on key variables such as 'ownership'. Consequently, researchers have been required to estimate models which differ in key respects. Thus despite a rapidly changing environment, many researchers have had access only to cross-sectional data which, amongst other things, means that they have been unable to consider the impact of *changes* in ownership subsequent to privatization. Also, some researchers estimate models using the growth rate of economic performance (when several indicators of performance are used and key variables are measured in 'privatization time', for example, Frydman *et al.*, 1997), while others estimate key variables in different ways and use econometric approaches that are essentially cross-sectional (for example, Earle and Estrin, 1996).

By contrast, in this paper, new data from a large panel of Estonian firms are used to investigate these issues. The use of a large panel for one country enables us to progress beyond previous work on this topic – for example, to generate estimates of the influence on economic performance of *levels* of ownership, more reliable than is contained in studies which pool small samples for different countries. In addition, since in transition economies many firms may have similar ownership structures at a particular time but may have very different transition paths towards those current ownership configurations, it is arguably important to examine the consequences of these ownership *changes*. Hence in this paper, the impact on economic performance both of *changes* in majority ownership as well as *minority* stakes for different groups, are investigated.[3] Before presenting these findings however, in the next section we consider the theory on the case for privatization, and its preferred form.

10.2 Conceptual framework

The theoretical case for privatization rests on several arguments (for example, Boycko *et al.*, 1996) including an alleged need for depoliticization and the view that it is only non-state forms of ownership that will produce an environment conducive to nurturing financial discipline in firms. While not everyone accepts these views and there is also empirical evidence, both for China as well as for state and non-privately-owned firms in former communist countries in transition (for example, Pinto *et al.*, 1993 for Poland; Bim *et al.*, 1993 for Russia), which suggests that the issue is not as clear cut as proponents believe, in this section we accept the need for privatization and a large private sector and instead discuss the arguments for the preferred form of private ownership.[4]

To consider these issues, the dominant approach in the corporate governance literature classifies firms by *ownership* (see for example, Schleifer and Vishny, 1997). For reasons including allegedly superior solutions to agency problems, it is argued that ownership by outsiders is to be preferred and that when insiders dominate, the most efficient form of insider ownership is managerial (rather than worker) ownership (for example, Boycko *et al.*, 1996). However, there are several reasons why these conclusions may not always be most appropriate for transition economies.

Critics question whether stock markets actually perform their intended functions effectively, especially in the context of formerly centrally planned economies with very underdeveloped capital market institutions. Aoki and Kim (1995) note that much of the traditional analysis assumes an idealized view of advanced market economies and that the argument for the promotion of outside ownership and efficient securities markets ignores crucial matters such as inherited factors and assumes competitive product and labour markets. Especially in the context of transition economies, Earle and Estrin (1996) argue that the effects of employee ownership may be dependent on a host of factors such as market conditions and that, in particular cases, some forms of employee ownership may be the best feasible solution to the choice of ownership structure.

Moreover, arguably the mainstream view uses a framework that is quite narrow in its conception of organizational processes.[5] While in the discussion of the desired institutional set-up for a labour-managed economy, Horvat (1982: ch. 8) identifies many ways in which this is so, in the contemporary debate on transitional economies, there has been, in particular, a tendency to identify ownership with control. Even if it is assumed that it is appropriate to focus on ownership alone, there is a tendency to take an overly static view. In the context of transition economies, where firms which have similar ownership structures at a point in time may have very different transition paths to these ownership configurations, it is arguably important to examine the causes and the consequences of these ownership changes.

In addition, some have posited the potential existence of ownership complementarities and the potentially important roles of minority ownership stakes. For example, Smith *et al.* (1997) point to possible synergies when the dominant owner is an outsider (for example, foreign owners with access to high technology) but insiders (such as non-managerial employees) have a significant minority ownership stake. Also there is abundant theoretical and empirical evidence which points to the potential benefits to organizational performance that arise when groups such as employees or managers have minority stakes.[6]

In sum, from the perspective of effects on economic performance, formal economic theory yields no clear cut predictions concerning the preferred form of ownership neither in the sense of the preferred main owner, nor on the relationship of that owner to other minority owners, nor on the role of ownership dynamics. The ambiguous nature of predictions is especially apparent when the special circumstances confronting transition economies are taken into account. Thus in contexts of embryonic stock markets, evolving and often underdeveloped institutional infrastructure, heterogeneity and confrontation amongst owners might mean that majority owners are especially unlikely to act in unison.[7] In addition, in a context that, initially at least, was heavily politicized (for example, with extensive concessional pricing of shares during early privatization), then initial configurations of ownership in those firms are most unlikely to represent equilibrium outcomes. While this point may not apply as strongly to firms privatized later, in accounting for the time patterns of performance after privatization, potentially it is important to also take into account the possible effects upon enterprise behaviour (and thus enterprise performance) of *changes* in ownership (as well as the initial configurations of ownership).

10.3 Institutional framework[8]

For several reasons, the Estonian case is a particularly interesting one to examine ownership issues in transition economies. Since Estonia was formerly a constituent republic of the USSR, it was most unlikely to have experienced as comprehensive and as rapid a process of institutional change as had occurred in the independent states (for example, Visegrad countries) before transition began in earnest. Notwithstanding this missing prehistory of reforms, Estonia is generally regarded as a successful transition economy with, compared to many countries, impressive macro indicators (Fischer *et al.*, 1996). One indication of this good track record is Estonia being the sole Baltic Republic which was invited to sign the Association agreement with the EU. In part, this success is attributed to Estonia being judged as, overall, having made considerable progress in transition to the market. For example, Estonia quickly introduced a set of (liberal) polices – including a very free economy with no trade barriers – and Estonia has a fairly sophisticated banking sector (EBRD, 1997). In addition, Estonia's program for large scale privatization was virtually complete as of 1997 (and small scale privatization was finished in 1994); consequently, compared to many other countries, the extent of the Estonian private sector is quite large. Moreover, surveys reveal that Estonia has made considerable progress in indicators of legal transition such as the existence and implementation of bankruptcy laws. Hence, one would expect that what might be called the 'institutional structural preconditions' (which are often assumed when generating some of the theoretical propositions discussed above) would at least be as likely to have been met in Estonia as, for example, in the other constituent republics of the Soviet Union, particularly Russia, though perhaps less so than in the Visegrad countries.

At the same time, it is important to remember that the large scale of the private sector has not been achieved by one set of privatization initiatives but rather has been accomplished, as in many countries, by a series of initiatives. In the main, these privatization measures do not reflect a consistent approach to privatization but instead changing attitudes and political contexts. Thus, in the first stages of privatization in Estonia many concessions were made to insiders. For example, between 1987 and 1989 in several cases, so-called people's enterprises were transferred to employees free of charge. While this strategy was soon ended – and in 1990 management buyouts became a much more common way of privatizing – employees were able to buy up to 20 per cent of shares at reduced prices. But by 1991–2, the sale of enterprises to employees with special rights was ended. Since then, the emphasis has been on selling off large firms via a Treuhand-like arrangement, though since 1994, a system of vouchers has been used to enable Estonian citizens to obtain minority positions in privatized firms. Overall, it is estimated that 90 per cent of privatization transactions have occurred through cash tenders, with 30–40 per cent of those assets held by foreigners (EBRD, 1997).

The upshot is that formerly state owned firms that are now privatized are not a homogeneous set but rather one reflecting an array of 'privatization vintages' as well as differing privatization policies. Also, not all 'privatized' firms are equally 'privatized'. In some, the state continues to retain an ownership interest that is sometimes substantial, other times not.

We would expect that these policy and institutional differences might modify some of the theoretical propositions discussed above. For example, concerning the effects of ownership on economic performance, the motivational effects of insider ownership may be expected to be blunted somewhat when shares are gifted (rather than bought by insiders who risk some of their own savings). At the same time the existence of many different ownership packages (and often in the same industry) provides an unusual opportunity to test some of the key propositions – for example, in the possibility of ownership complementarities. In designing our empirical strategy, we will attempt to take some of these institutional considerations into account, namely, the timing of privatization and also whether or not the state continues to own a part of the privatized firm.

10.4 Data and ownership patterns

An important strength of our study is the use of rich new panel data for a large sample of firms. With the cooperation of the statistical authorities, annual economic and financial data were extracted from company records for 666 firms for the period 1993–7. These standard economic data (for example profits, assets and employment) have been merged with special surveys that collected detailed data on ownership at the time of privatization and for three years during this period.[9]

It is important to stress that these data enable us not only to estimate diverse specifications, but also to construct measures of key variables that often improve on those used in previous studies. Since there is much disagreement over the relevant analytical categories to use with which to describe patterns of ownership (especially the dynamics of these processes), questions were included in the surveys in order to provide for several options. In particular, information on the extent of ownership for major ownership groups (managers, non-managerial employees, foreigners, domestic outsiders, and the state) was collected on an annual basis from 1995 to 1997. Thus, we are able to classify firms by either dominant or majority ownership (compared to most studies that use only dominant share, for example, Frydman *et al.*, 1997; Jones, 1998; and Earle *et al.*, 1996). In addition, some information was collected on the dispersion of ownership within firms which enabled us to construct other measures – for example, the extent of inequality of ownership within insider-owned firms and also the percentage of employees who own shares.

When the economic and ownership data for the sample of 666 firms were merged, sufficient data were available to enable ownership structures to be analyzed on 601 firms from 1995 (the first year for which detailed annual data on ownership and economic data were collected) through to 1997.[10] Examination of these data (reported in Jones and Mygind, 1998) reveal that there is enormous variation across Estonian firms in their ownership structures. Thus, there are examples of firms in which *majority* ownership lies with insiders (in some cases, employees, in others, managers) and also firms in which the majority owners are outsiders (in some cases, foreigners, in other instances individuals who do not work in the firm.) At the same time, there have been important *changes* in ownership configurations, in the sense of who the majority owner is. Equally, there is much inertia – more than three in four privatized Estonian firms did not switch their ownership category during a three-year period.

Furthermore, there are interesting patterns concerning *minority* ownership. Thus in 1995, foreigners were very rarely the largest minority group in firms owned by insiders. Similarly, insiders (and especially employees) were unlikely to be the largest minority in firms in which foreigners had majority ownership. From the perspective of minority ownership, there are strong indications that ownership structures are often inert. Thus in 1997 (as in 1995), large degrees of minority ownership by employees continued to be a relatively infrequent occurrence in firms in which most ownership lies overseas. At the same time, several changes were apparent between 1995 and 1997 in the relationship between majority owner and key minority owners. Most interestingly, perhaps, is the observed tendency for all minority groups to become more important in firms in which managers have the majority share.

10.5 Economic effects of privatization

To analyze relationships between structures of and changes in ownership and enterprise performance, we draw on an approach developed by Frydman *et al.* (1997) and also used and extended for the case of Russia (Jones, 1998). While the method of Frydman *et al.* (1997) is broadly comparable to approaches used in other studies (for example, Earle and Estrin, 1996), this particular empirical strategy has some novel attractions. Potentially most important, since the year of privatization varies across firms, an attempt is made to measure all key variables in privatization (rather than in calendar) time. Moreover, to deal with noisy data, performance is usually measured as an average (a growth rate) over a period of time (rather than for a single year). In addition, in an attempt to focus on the post-privatization performance of firms, a control for inherited pre-privatization differences in performance is included (namely, a measure of performance during the initial year of privatization). Then, the transition or marketization effect (which is common to all firms) is defined as the sum of the constant term plus the coefficient on the initial performance variable multiplied by average initial performance.[11] In some regressions, the coefficient on a privatization dummy measures the incremental performance effect specific to privatized firms,[12] whereas in other specifications a set of dummies for the largest owner (different forms of privatization) are included instead of the privatization dummy variable.

While the empirical strategies of Frydman *et al.* used in this approach are useful and innovative, as our earlier review indicated, other theoretical and empirical evidence suggests that when examining the effects of privatization upon enterprise performance, most studies of transition economies omit what are potentially important variables. For example, many empirical studies fail to examine the potential effects of what Horvat (1982: ch. 6) calls 'real participation' upon economic performance. In addition, most studies do not allow for *changes* in dominant/majority ownership, nor do they take into account the potential effects on performance of ownership by other (minority) groups.[13] Hence in our empirical work, we not only report findings from estimates which emulate some of the key strategies adopted by Frydman *et al.* (1997) but also estimate specifications which involve substantial extensions of that approach.[14] In addition, we always include dummy variables for industries and regions. Thus, they help to isolate the privatization effect and hopefully produce more reliable estimates of the privatization effect. However, one consequence of this extension is that the transition effect is no longer a unique number, but now differs by industry or region. Hence, when discussing our findings, we will not consider the transition effect in great detail.

In one set of specifications we use estimate equations of the form:

$$\text{AVPERF} = \alpha_o + \alpha \text{ INIPERF} + \beta \text{ PRV} + \Sigma_i \, \gamma_i \text{ IND} + \delta \text{ Tallinn} + \epsilon \quad (1)$$

where AVPERF is average performance computed for some measure of performance using annual data over the period 1994–7, except for those firms which were privatized during that period in which case it is measured relative to the year of privatization, INIPERF is a corresponding measure of the level of performance during the first year of privatization, and PRV is a privatization dummy.[15] For ease of comparability with Frydman *et al.* (1997), performance measurers are rates of growth and many of the measures of performance are the same set as those used in that study, for example, the growth in employment and the growth in labour productivity. In addition, our data enable us to construct the ratio of exports/sales, though other measures, notably costs, are not available for all years. We always include IND, which is a set of industry dummies, as well as a dummy variable for whether or not the firms are located in the capital district (Tallinn). In a related set of estimates, we replace the privatization dummy (PRV) by a set of dummy variable measures for ownership. This set of private ownership variables (hereafter the OL vector) contains measures of majority ownership (unlike most studies which use measures of dominant ownership). Also, as is the practice in the literature, the type of private ownership (which often changes during the period) is assessed in 1997 – that is at the end of the period of study.

However, to respond to some of the concerns which were raised by our discussion of the available theoretical and empirical evidence, we also draw on our data to estimate models which involve substantial augmentation of these approaches. In these preliminary exercises, we add to specification (1) at least one of two sets of other variables which are arguably of importance to economic performance: (i) OD, a vector of variables for *changes* in ownership; (ii) MO, a vector of variables for measuring the influence of a large minority ownership. Thus a specification which includes these two additional vectors is:

$$AVPERF = \alpha_o + \alpha \, INIPERF + \beta OL + \gamma \, OD + \delta \, MO + \Sigma_i \, \eta_i \, IND + \theta \, Tallinn + \epsilon \qquad (2)$$

Also, we report the results of F tests (which are used to select which specification from these augmented approaches best fits the data).

Findings from regression analysis are reported in Tables 10.1–10.3. The most obvious finding that emerges from these exercises is the low overall explanatory power of these estimates. The R^2 is always less than 0.1 (which is well below the fit obtained using similar specifications for samples of firms in other countries). The explanatory power of the specification for labour productivity is particularly poor.

Table 10.1A shows the first set of regressions, where the dummy variable for privatization measures the effect of privatization on performance.[16] The privatization effect, however, produced the expected direction of growth for only sales and employment. More importantly, privatization only had a statistically significant and positive effect on the growth in sales and exports/sales. Thus, contrary to the Frydman *et al.* (1997) study, the Estonian data do not provide strong evidence that privatization *per se* has favourable performance effects.

The magnitude of the privatization effects are also often surprisingly large. Thus for sales growth, the privatization effect is about 40 per cent per year. Privatization also had a statistically significant and negative effect on the growth rate of exports-to-sales, where privatized firms are expected to have a 48 per cent lower growth in this ratio per year relative to non-privatized firms. While this result appears to contradict the expectation that exports-to-sales would improve after privatization, it might be explained by privatized firms starting from a much higher ratio of exports-to-sales than state firms and the inadequacy of our control for initial performance. Additionally, the findings reported in Table 10.1A indicate that, relative to state firms, labour productivity fell. While this was only a small and statistically insignificant fall, this is still contradictory to the expected outcome. Also, according to this model, privatization led to an average 3 per cent fall per year in employment growth.

In all models, F tests reject the null hypothesis (and often at the 1 per cent significance level) that the joint effect of industries on performance is zero.[17] Surprisingly for all performance indicators, firms located in the capital district of Tallinn on average experienced slower

Table 10.1 Performance regressions: privatization and majority ownership

	Sales	Labour productivity	Export-to-sales	Employment
A Privatization				
Constant	−0.457	0.061	0.475	−0.017
	(0.293)	(0.178)	(0.623)	(0.092)
INIPERF	0.0000008	−0.0001	−0.000002	−0.000044
	(0.0000007)	(0.000089)	(0.000004)	(0.000035)
Tallinn	−0.307***	−0.114	−0.325	−0.023
	(0.1240)	(0.078)	(0.265)	(0.039)
PRV	0.393*	−0.04	−0.483**	−0.03
	(0.149)	(0.094)	(0.318)	(0.047)
Industry	Yes***	Yes	Yes**	Yes
n	481	471	481	466
Adj R^2	0.06	0.01	0.05	0.04
B Majority ownership				
Constant	−0.417	0.057	0.5	−0.025
	(0.301)	(0.181)	(0.628)	(0.094)
INIPERF	0.0000009	−0.0001	−0.000003	−0.00004
	(0.0000007)	(0.00009)	(0.000004)	(0.000035)
Tallinn	−0.337*	−0.114	−0.0274	−0.046
	(0.128)	(0.08)	(0.269)	(0.039)
MAJFOR	0.459***	−0.012	−0.101**	0.179**
	(0.197)	(0.127)	(0.042)	(0.062)
MAJDOM	0.354**	−0.027	−0.574	−0.054
	(0.18)	(0.11)	(0.37)	(0.055)
MAJMAN	0.351***	−0.191	−0.446	0.021
	(0.191)	(−0.098)	(0.40)	(0.059)
MAJEE	0.344***	−0.004	−0.118*	−0.002
	(0.213)	(0.13)	(0.045)	(0.065)
NOMAJ	0.361	−0.111	−0.25*	−0.064
	(0.396)	(0.242)	(0.084)	(0.12)
Industry	Yes***	Yes	Yes*	Yes
n	481	471	481	466
Adj R^2	0.05	0.01	0.04	0.02

* significant at the 1% level; ** significant at the 5% level; *** significant at the 10% level.

improvements in performance than other firms. However, the finding is statistically significant only for sales, though the size of the effect (almost 31 per cent) is unexpectedly large.

In Table 10.1B we implement the second stage of the analysis and estimate regressions in which a set of dummies for the largest owner (different forms of privatization) is included instead of the PRV variable. In the reported regressions, we see that the pattern of the coefficients on majority ownership usually resembles that found in the previous model (when a single privatization dummy was used). Thus in the growth in sales and the growth of exports/sales models, often the coefficients on the majority ownership variables are statistically significant. In fact, when performance is measured by either growth in sales or the growth of exports/sales, then F tests reject the hypothesis that the joint effect of majority ownership types on performance is zero.[18]

In addition, the direction of the majority ownership effects often is as expected, especially in the 'growth in sales' model. Then, in all cases, the coefficients are positive and significant indicating that firms with all forms of majority ownership enjoy superior growth in sales compared to state owned firms. In terms of the size of the effects, firms with all forms of private ownership have annual growth in sales that are at least 34 per cent better than in state owned firms. Amongst privately owned firms, firms in which there is majority ownership by foreigners have annual growth rates of sales that are about 10 per cent faster than other private ownership types.

By contrast, majority ownership variables are seldom statistically significant in the other estimates. One exception is in the exports-to-sales model where, surprisingly, firms with majority foreign ownership have significantly lower growth rates than do state owned firms. The other exception also concerns firms with majority foreign ownership which are found to have employment growth that is almost 18 per cent faster than in state firms.

The pattern of industry and regional effects is comparable to what was found when using the single privatization dummy.

In Table 10.2 we report our first attempt at extending the Frydman et al. approach by augmenting the regressions reported in the Table 10.1B to also include a vector of variables that capture different forms of minority ownership (and where minority ownership is defined as a group other than the majority owner, owning between 15 and 50 per cent of the total capital share). The key new finding that emerges from this exercise is that, if the specification reported in Table 10.1B is augmented to include a vector of 'largest minority variables', then for

Table 10.2 Performance regressions: majority and minority ownership

	Sales	Sales/L	Exp./Sales	Employment
INIPERF	−0.000001	−0.00001	−0.00001	−0.00001
	(0.00001)	(0.00001)	(0.00001)	(0.00001)
MAJDOMOUT	0.5503*	−0.0437	−0.6896***	−0.00001
	(0.2161)	(0.1417)	(0.4164)	(0.0691)
MAJFOR	−0.6860*	−0.0494	−1.311**	0.403***
	(0.2564)	(0.1688)	(0.5418)	(0.0805)
MAJEE	−0.5478	−0.1337	−0.2521	−0.1704
	(0.5628)	(0.4000)	(1.197)	(0.1945)
MAJMAN	−0.1042	−0.2192***	−0.1213***	0.0005
	(0.2330)	(0.1306)	(0.4918)	(0.0737)
NOMAJ	0.3941	−0.1889	−2.5739*	0.0645
	(0.3918)	(0.2498)	(0.8300)	(0.1217)
DMAJSMIN	−0.5468**			−0.3612**
	(0.3000)			(0.1757)
EMAJFMIN				0.5647***
				(0.3234)
EMAJDMIN	0.9679***			
	(0.6014)			
EMAJMMIN	−0.9760***			
	(0.5830)			
MMAJDMIN	0.5250***		−1.523**	
	(0.3265)		(0.6974)	
TALLINN	−0.3695**	−0.1209	−0.1432	0.0647***
	(0.1325)	(0.0863)	(0.2788)	(0.0414)
INDS	Y***	Y	Y	Y
R^2 adj.	0.02	0.003	0.01	0.01
n	450	438	450	438

* significant at 1% level; ** significant at 5% level; *** significant at 10% level. All models include a vector of 16 'large minority' variables. Thus, for firms in which employees are the majority owner, large minority variables are included for foreigners, domestic outsiders, managers, and the state, respectively EMAJFMIN, EMAJDMIN, EMAJMMIN and DMAJSMIN. For these variables, only estimates for which there is at least one statistically significant coefficient, are reported. (As shown, this happens for five variables in 7/64 cases.)

three performance measures, F tests reject the null hypothesis that the joint effect on performance of majority and minority variables is zero.[19] In addition, for every performance measure except labour productivity, at least one of the individual coefficients on the minority ownership variables is found to be statistically significant. However, overall, this is seldom found to be true – in only 7/64 cases are the individual coefficients on the minority ownership variables found to be statistically significant.[20]

Table 10.3 Performance regressions: majority ownership and changes in ownership

	Sales	Sales/L	Exp./sales	Employment
INIPERF	0.00001	−0.00001	−0.00001	−0.00001
	(0.0001)	(0.0001)	(0.0001)	(0.00003)
MAJDOMOUT	0.6822**	0.0778	−0.0991	0.0510
	(0.2816)	(0.1899)	(0.6364)	(0.732)
MAJFOR	0.4580	−0.0107	0.2113	0.1056
	(0.4305)	(0.2919)	(0.9857)	(0.1103)
MAJEE	0.7839*	0.0202	−0.6771	0.0518
	(0.3006)	(0.211)	(0.7000)	(0.0813)
MAJMAN	0.5207**	−0.1097	0.1744	0.0468
	(0.2932)	(0.1968)	(0.6617)	(0.0762)
NOMAJ	−0.0963	−0.6988***	−1.6800	0.0752
	(0.6769)	(0.4374)	(1.5486)	(0.1733)
KMAJD	−0.5018***			−0.1399**
	(0.2881)			(0.0745)
KMAJN		0.8380***		
		(0.5224)		
M95D97	−1.1398*	−0.9111*		
	(−2.858)	(0.2657)	−5.5032*	
M95N97			(2.298)	
E95D97				−0.2198**
				(0.1011)
E95M97	−0.9691**			
	(0.4515)			
S95D97				0.2388*
				(0.0848)
S95M97				0.2759**
				(0.1085)
N95M97	−6.2525*		5.3845**	
	(1.1498)		(2.6347)	
TALLINN	−0.3818*	−0.1899**	−0.3364	0.0596***
	(0.1226)	(0.0824)	(0.2724)	(0.0302)
INDS	Y	Y	Y	Y***
R^2	0.04	0.007	0.03	0.02

* significant at 1% level; ** significant at 5% level; *** significant at 10% level.

Moreover, the addition of the 'large minority ownership' variables yields some surprising results for the magnitudes of the ownership effects. For example, relative to a firm which has majority employee ownership and no large minority, the estimates imply that sales grow faster by an incredible 97 per cent in firms with large domestic minority ownership. Or relative to firms with majority state ownership, firms with majority employee ownership and a large domestic minority shareholding have faster sales growth of about 42 per cent (0.9679–0.5478).

In Table 10.3 we report the results of augmenting specification (2) with a vector of 'ownership dynamics' variables. For firms which do not change their majority owner, a set of 'constant' ownership variables are included, for foreigners, domestic outsiders, managers, employees and no majority – respectively KMAJF, KMAJD, KMAJM, KMAJE and KMAJN. (The base case is state majority ownership throughout the period.) For firms which do change ownership, variables for ownership transitions are included. For example, for firms which begin with majority ownership in foreign hands and ownership switches to domestic outsiders, managers, employees, and to no majority, the variables are F95D97, F95M97, F95E97, F95N97 respectively. Since there were no switches to state ownership and no switches from no majority to either foreign or employee ownership, there was a total of 28 variables in this 'ownership dynamics' vector. For these variables, only estimates for which there is at least one statistically significant coefficient are reported. The key new finding that emerges from this 'ownership dynamics' exercise is that, for all four performance measures, the null hypothesis that the joint effect of the 'ownership transition' variables on performance is zero, is supported by F tests. However, in a limited number of cases (in fact in 12/112), at least one of the individual coefficients on the ownership dynamics variables is found to be statistically significant. For example, firms which switch from majority state ownership to majority domestic ownership (S95D97) and majority management ownership (S95M97) have faster rates of employment growth. By contrast, firms which switch from employee majority ownership to domestic majority ownership (E95D97) have slower rates of employment growth.

10.6 Conclusions and implications

In this paper, we report evidence on the effects of different forms of ownership on enterprise performance. Since our data are for one country, our findings would not necessarily be expected to generalize to other countries. However, the Estonian case is of special interest since, by the many indicators, it is generally believed to be in the top tier of transition economies. Moreover, our findings are derived from a new and large panel that is representative of the whole economy. We are, therefore, able to assemble some of the first reliable evidence on these matters.

In our econometric work on the impact of privatization on performance, we construct several indicators of the growth rate of economic performance and estimate models in 'privatization' time. For the case of Estonia (and unlike findings for the Visegrad countries) this particular approach is not found to work very well – in the sense that the estimated models consistently have fairly low overall explanatory power. As such, this result is consistent with the hypothesis that the *key* influence on business performance is *not* ownership (for example, Horvat, 1982).

In terms of specific findings, when a privatization dummy is used, the effect on economic performance of the movement away from state ownership is found to be significant and in the expected direction only for the case of sales. This finding appears to be quite different from what has been found for Visegrad countries (Frydman *et al.*, 1997), though for the case of Russia the evidence (Jones, 1998) is that privatization *per se* had even weaker consequences for economic performance than we find here for Estonia. Thus, on balance, there is support for the hypothesis that private ownership does deliver improved performance, but when this particular empirical approach is used to study the effects of ownership upon economic performance, for Estonian (as for Russian) firms, it is difficult to conclude (as Frydman *et al.*, 1997 do for firms in Poland, Hungary and the Czech Republic) that 'the privatization effect may be a shock to the transition'.

When we account for differences in economic performance by introducing particular measures of majority ownership (rather than a single privatization dummy), we find that firms with all forms of majority ownership have faster growth of sales than do firms in which the state has a majority interest. This is consistent with the estimates that use a simple dummy. Also, for other performance measures, such as labour productivity, there are often no statistically significant differences between forms of majority ownership – including state ownership. Thus there is little support for the hypothesis that majority ownership by employees is a form of privatization that is to be avoided.[21]

In accounting for differences in economic performance during transition, our previous discussion points to the potential role of variables other than majority ownership levels. Hence we undertook a series of exercises which were designed to provide various extensions to the approach of Frydman *et al.* (1997). In one set of exercises, for some performance measures (for example sales growth), we find evidence that the preferred specification is one that includes measures not only of majority ownership but also of minority ownership. Furthermore, we find evidence that economic performance varies with the type of minority ownership. As such, these results support the view that, in accounting for differences in economic performance, it is not sufficient to identify the majority owners, and that sometimes more favourable performance may arise from decreasing the concentration of majority ownership and increasing minority ownership.

In other exercises examining differences in performance, the hypothesis that the joint effect of a vector of 'changes-in-ownership' variables on economic performance is nil, is always accepted. Nevertheless, occasionally, there is evidence that particular ownership transitions do have an effect on economic performance that is statistically significant. In particular, movements away from state ownership tend to lead to faster sales growth. As such, these results give mild support to the view that when investigating economic performance in transition economies, some attention might be paid to the ownership trajectory that the firm has followed (rather than just the current ownership configuration).

Future research might go in two directions. First, there is a need to explore the use of empirical approaches that are alternative to the empirical strategy adopted in this paper. In particular, in investigating the determinants of business performance, more standard strategies (such as estimating technical efficiency frontiers and production functions) need to be implemented (and their results compared to findings based on the approach used in this paper). Secondly, research might focus on identifying the different legal and institutional factors which may contribute to the discrepancy in results for even the same ownership forms among the transitional countries. Indeed, there is a limited volume of other research which points to the empirical importance of other factors in accounting for differences in efficiency. For example, in an important study, Weitzman and Xu (1994) find that, in China, economic efficiency may not require unambiguous property rights and that contracts may not need to be accompanied by the full gamut of legal institutions. The implication is that the optimal level of property rights may vary with the underlying propensity of the population to cooperate and that in cultures where cooperative traditions are strong (China) ambiguous property rights may work best. Also, as predicted by Horvat (1982), evidence for Russia (Jones, 1998) and for Bulgaria (Jones, Klinedinst and Rock, 1998) points to the important influence of employee participation upon business performance.[22]

Appendix: definitions of variables

Ownership

PRV Privatization dummy. Whether the firm was privatized in 1996.

Majority Ownership

MAJEE is a dummy variable for whether or not, in 1997, a firm's majority ownership group was employees. Analogous variables are defined for MAJMAN (management), MAJDOM (domestic outsiders), and MAJFOR (foreigners). The base case is MAJSTA (state).

Largest Minority

In Table 10.2, 16 particular forms of 'largest minority' are used in the sense that a group other than the majority owner owns between 15 and 50 per cent of the total capital share. Variables are defined for firms in which, for a given majority owner (employees, EMAJ; foreigners, FMAJ; managers, MMAJ; and outside domestic, DMAJ), there is another group which has a largest minority ownership stake (MIN). Thus for firms in which employees are the majority owner, large minority variables are included for foreigners, domestic outsiders, managers and the state – respectively EMAJFMIN, EMAJDMIN, EMAJMMIN and EMAJSMIN.

Majority Ownership Transitions

For firms which between 1995 and 1997 do not change their majority owner, a set of 'constant' ownership variables are included, for foreigners, domestic outsiders, managers, employees and no majority – respectively KMAJF, KMAJD, KMAJM, KMAJE and KMAJN (The base case is state majority ownership throughout the period).

For firms which do change majority ownership, firms which begin with majority ownership in foreign hands and ownership switches to domestic outsiders, managers, employees, and to no majority, the variables are F95D97, F95M97, F95E97, F95N97 respectively. Analogous variables are defined for other majority groups and other transitions. Since there were no switches to state ownership and no switches from no majority to either foreign or employee ownership, there was a total of 28 variables in this 'ownership dynamics' vector.

Firm Characteristics and Performance

AVPERF = average performance computed for some measure of performance using annual data over the period 1994–7, except for those firms which were privatized during that period in which case it is measured relative to the year of privatization

INIPERF = corresponding measure of the level of performance during the first year of privatization

Sales = annualized average growth in real sales

Exports to sales = annualized average growth in the ratio of exports to sales

180 *Privatization: Evidence from Estonia*

Labour productivity = annualized average growth in (real sales)/employment
Employment = annualized average growth in employment

Control (Dummy) Variables

TALLINN Dummy = 1 for firm located in Tallinn, the capital of Estonia
IND* = set of industry Dummies

Notes

1. For a survey of British economic thought on the effects of worker management and worker participation on enterprise performance, see Jones (1976).
2. For reviews, see Carlin and Landsmann (1997) and EBRD (1997).
3. Unfortunately, our data do not enable us to examine the effects of other potentially important factors that influence enterprise performance (such as employee influence). We focus on ownership because that is a focus of the current debate in transition economies.
4. There is also abundant empirical evidence which points to the superior economic performance of economic systems that are neither state-owned nor capitalist. For an important contribution on the better performance of the (former) Yugoslav labour managed economy, see Horvat (1969).
5. To illustrate some of these points, Ben-Ner and Jones (1995) have noted that ownership of an asset consists of two central rights – the right to control its use and to enjoy its returns.
6. However, there are few empirical studies that have looked at minority ownership when minority ownership stakes are 'large' – say, more than 10 per cent. For example, in the case of Japan, employee ownership stakes average less than 2 per cent (see Jones and Kato, 1995). For the potential benefits of managerial stakes see the executive compensation literature (for example, Asch and Warner, 1997).
7. Moreover, the links between majority ownership and control are expected to be diffuse. Thus, studies of firms in many transition economies have examined the implications of different ownership configurations for corporate governance and most conclude that, irrespective of ownership form, normally employee influence is quite limited and management influence is very pronounced (Blasi, 1994; Jones and Weisskopf, 1996). Hence, it is also potentially important to take account of the effects on enterprise behaviour not only of ownership but also of control. While we will endeavour to collect measures of control for use in future studies, in this paper, we follow the bulk of the literature and assume that our measures of ownership are adequate.
8. For more exhaustive accounts, see Mygind (1996, 1997).
9. For details of the way the sample was selected see Jones and Mygind (1998).
10. Based on two sample mean t tests, there do not appear to be any significant differences in the nature of the firms for which we have only partial information.
11. This definition of 'transition effect' is most appropriate when privatization is accompanied by other major economic reforms such as price liberalization.

12 Frydman *et al.* (1996) use data for 1990–93 for a sample of 185 firms in Poland, Hungary and the Czech Republic. Evidence is found both of a transition effect and, most importantly, of a privatization effect.
13 For example, by focusing only on dominant ownership at the end of the period, Frydman *et al.* (1997) thus attribute all performance effects of ownership to the dominant form of ownership at the end of the period under investigation (and thus implicitly assume that the form of dominant ownership does not change during the period of study).
14 At the same time, we recognize that the available data for Estonia do not enable us to investigate the effects on business performance of all variables which theory suggests are potentially important – for example employee control and different forms of incentives.
15 One shortcoming of our not having data before 1994 is that for firms privatized before then, we implicitly assume that the growth effect will be the same as for newly privatized firms.
16 While, for the reasons previously discussed, we do not focus on the transition effect, note that we nearly always find that the transition variables are statistically insignificant, including the reported case (where the base case is a firm in the service sector outside of Tallinn.)
17 For example, the F statistic in the model for growth in sales was 3.04.
18 For example, the F statistic for the exports-to-sales model is 3.02, making the joint inclusion of ownership variables significant at the 1 per cent significance level.
19 Again, the overall explanatory power of the labour productivity equation is very tiny.
20 Indeed, only in the growth of sales model does an F test reject the null hypothesis (at the 10 per cent significance level) that the joint effect of the large minority ownership variables *alone* on performance is zero.
21 Also see Mygind (1997).
22 There is also evidence that points to the important role of providing for incentive compensation arrangements for employees (for example, Jones, Klinedinst and Rock, 1998).

References

Aoki, M. (1995) 'Controlling Insider Control: Issues of Corporate Governance in Transition Economies', in Aoki M. and H.-K. Kim (eds.) (1995).
Aoki, M. and Kim, H.-K. (eds.) (1995) *Corporate Governance in Transitional Economies*, Washington: The World Bank.
Asch, B. J. and J. T. Warner, (1997) 'Incentive Systems: Theory and Evidence' in D. Lewis, D. Mitchell and M. Zaidi (eds.), *Handbook of Human Resources*, Greenwich: JAI.
Barberis *et al.* (1996) 'How Does Privatization Work. Evidence from Russian Shops', *Journal of Political Economy*, August: 764–90.
Ben-Ner, A. and Jones, D. C. (1995) 'Employee Participation, Ownership and Productivity: A Theoretical Framework', *Industrial Relations*, 34 (4): 532–54.
Bim, A., Jones, D. C. and Weisskopf, T. (1993) 'Hybrid Forms of Enterprise Organization in the Former USSR and the Russian Federation', *Comparative Economic Studies*, 35(1): 1–37.

Blasi, J. (1994) 'Russian Labor-Management Relations: Some Preliminary Lessons from Newly Privatized Enterprises', in P. B. Voos (ed.), *Proceedings of the Forty-Seventh Annual Meeting*, IRRA Series, Madison WI.

Blasi, J., Kroumova, M. and Kruse, D. (1997) *Kremlin Capitalism*, Ithaca: Cornell University Press – ILR Press.

Boycko, M., Schleifer, A. and Vishny, R. (1996) 'A Theory of Privatization' *Economic Journal*, 106 (March): 309–19.

Carlin, W. and Landesmann, M. (1997) 'From Theory into Practice? Restructuring and Dynamism in Transition Economies', *Oxford Review of Economic Policy*, 13 (2): 77–105.

Earle, J. S. and Estrin S. (1996) 'Employee Ownership in Transition', in Frydman *et al.* (eds), vol. 2, pp. 1–62.

Earle, J. S., Estrin, S. and Leshchenko, I. (1996) 'Ownership Structures, Patterns of Control and Enterprise Behavior in Russia', in S. Commander, Q. Fan and M. Schaffer (eds) (1996), *Enterprise Restructuring and Economic Policy in Russia*, EDI Development Studies, Washington, D. C.: World Bank, pp. 205–52.

EBRD (1997) *Transition Report 1997 – Enterprise Performance and Growth*, London: EBRD.

Filatochev, I., Grosfeld, I., Karsai, J., Wright, M., and Buck, T. (1996) 'Buyout in Hungary, Poland and Russia: The Financial Issues', *Economics of Transition*, 4(1): 67–88.

Fischer, S., Ratna, S. and Vegh, C. (1996) 'Stabilization and Growth in Transition Economies: The Early Experience', *Journal of Economic Perspectives*, 10 (2): 45–66.

Frydman, R., Gray, C., Hessel, M. and Rapaczynski, A. (1997) 'Private Ownership and Corporate Performance: Some Lessons from Transition Economies', *Economic Research Reports*, C.V. Starr Center for Applied Economics.

Frydman, R., Gray, C. and Rapaczynski, A. (eds), (1996) *Corporate Governance in Central Europe and Russia*, Budapest: CEU Press.

Horvat, B. (1969) 'Technical Progress in Yugoslavia', *Economic Analysis*, nos. 1–2: 29–57.

Horvat, B. (1982) *The Political Economy of Socialism*, New York: Sharpe.

Horvat, B. (ed.), (1975) *Self Governing Socialism: A Reader*, edited together with R. Supek and M. Marković, New York: Sharpe.

Jones, D. C. (1976) 'British Economic Thought on Associations of Labourers, 1848–974,' *Annals of Public and Cooperative Economy*, 47 (Jan./March): 5–36.

Jones, D. C. (1998) 'The Economic Effects of Privatization: Evidence from a Russian Panel', *Comparative Economic Studies*, 30 (2): 75–102.

Jones, D. C. and Kato, T. (1995) 'The Productivity Effects of Bonuses and Employee Ownership: Evidence Using Japanese Panel Data', *American Economic Review*, 85(3): 391–414.

Jones, D. C. and Mygind, N. (1998) 'The Nature and Determinants of Ownership Changes after Privatization: Evidence from Estonia', mimeo, CEES and Hamilton College.

Jones, D. C., Klinedinst, M. and Rock, C. (1998) 'Productive Efficiency During Transition: Evidence from Bulgarian Panel Data', *Journal of Comparative Economics*, 26: 446–64.

Jones, D. C. and Weisskopf, T. (1996) 'Employee Ownership and Control: Evidence from Russia', *Proceedings of the Forty Eighth Meeting of the Industrial Relations Research Association*, pp. 64–76.

Mygind N. (1997) 'Employee Ownership in the Baltic Countries' in Uvalić and Vaughan-Whitehead (eds.), pp. 49–79.
Mygind, N. (ed.), (1996) *Privatization and Financial Participation in the Baltic Countries*, Copenhagen: Copenhagen Business School, pp. 95–122.
Nuti, M. (1997) 'Employeeism: Corporate Governance and Employee Ownership in Transitional Economies', in M. I. Blejer and M. Škreb (eds.) *Macroeconomic Stabilization in Transition Economies*, Budapest: Central University Press, pp. 126–54.
Pinto, B., Belka, M. and Krajewski, S. (1993) 'Transforming State Enterprises in Poland', *Brookings Papers on Economic Activity*, no 1: 213–70.
Pohl, G., Anderson, R. E., Claessens, S. and Djankov, S. (1997) 'Privatization and Restructuring in Central and Eastern Europe: Evidence and Policy Options', *World Bank Technical Paper* no. 368, The World Bank, Washington DC.
Schleifer, A. and Vishny, R. (1997) 'A Survey of Corporate Governance', *Journal of Finance*, 52 (June): 737–83.
Sertel, M. (ed.), (1996) *Workers Enterprises: Alternatives in Privatization*, Elsevier Science.
Smith, S., Cin, B. and Vodopivec, M. (1997) 'Privatization Incidence, Ownership Forms, and Firm Performance: Evidence from Slovenia', *Journal of Comparative Economics*, 25: 158–79.
Uvalić, M. and Vaughan-Whitehead, D. (eds.), (1997) *Privatization Surprises in Transition Economies*, Cheltenham: Edward Elgar.
Weitzman, M. and Xu, C. (1994) 'Chinese Township Village Enterprises as Vaguely Defined Cooperatives', *Journal of Comparative Economics*, 22(2): 121–45.

11
Growth Theory and Transition Economies
Ivo Bićanić

11.1 Introduction

After almost a decade of 'transitioning' and 'transforming', it seems that for all the 27 transition economies, the first phase of economic transition is over. Decline in production has stopped for all of them and some have already experienced several years of economic growth. All have introduced markets and chosen a wide range of market structures and institutions to underpin them. Similarly, all have liberalized foreign trade but many have kept some form of restrictions on the capital account. Without exception, all have experienced major restructuring which has increased the share of services and small firms. Finally, all have experienced some degree of privatization, and through implementing very different mechanisms (which probably include all the possibilities available), have gained varied privatization experience. Thus the same basic common experience of the first phase has generated many different paths.

The variety and variations of transition paths generated by the first phase is very wide and includes a whole range of possibilities. Various circumstances, as well as the time span which has generated limited data set for a ten-year period, have already led to first attempts to identify transition path regularities, patterns, similarities and country-specific differences. Two approaches seem to dominate these attempts. The first concentrates on trying to recognize factors influencing the course and extent of economic transition, namely its determinants; the second takes a broader view by offering a theoretical explanation of the changes.

As a result, the range of interpretations on offer is already wide and with the blossoming of literature in both traditions this will likely increase. At one extreme are studies which concentrate on the dominance of the political process and the path dependency generated by the first elections (see Fish, 1998). The middle ground is held by papers using a wide range of economic indicators to measure both the extent and course of transition. These seek explanatory variables and suggest causes for it (see Cornia and Popov, 1998 or Aslund et al., 1996). At the other extreme are those studies demonstrating the success of some theoretical explanation. In this vein, most work has been done on demonstrating the validity (and thus providing justification) of 'Washington consensus' policies. Understandably, the most notable examples of this third kind of study come from publications in some way related to the international financial community (see for example, EBRD, 1998 or World Bank, 1996).

All these attempts appear to share at least three common features: the importance of non-economic factors, an optimistic approach, and a linearity of stages.

A discussion of transition optimism and transition linearity form the focus of this paper. However, because of the unexpectedly prominent role of non-economic factors and their place in the latter two features, it is important to note the main preoccupations. Among the non-economic factors, political ones dominate. Here the ideas of democracy with its implications of a multiparty political system, free and fair elections with public accountability, economic transparency and policies based on political consensus, have central place. They are considered to have as important a role as private ownership and market economy and form with them a 'transition trinity'. Notions of social capability have recently come to be included among political factors. Interestingly, these non-economic notions figure prominently even in papers coming from authors writing in the tradition of the economic mainstream, and where one would not normally expect them.

11.2 Transition optimism and transition linearity

Transition optimism and linearity are closely related to growth theory and their discussion merits great attention because of the rising importance of growth related issues for economies in transition. The importance of growth theory is seen on both the level of interpretation and policy advice. On the level of interpretation, we need to face questions related to growth paths and their possible convergence properties, issues involved in 'catching up' and reducing the 'lagging behind' developed economies as well as questions of 'falling behind'.

186 *Growth Theory and Transition Economies*

The determination of growth factors and their presence in transition economies and growth projections are also of obvious interest. On the policy level, issues of the existence of pro-active growth policies and their form and scope are central in the economic debates both of serious policy makers and their advisers and of the less serious participants with their Krugmanite policy entrepreneurs.

Growth theory related issues have a prominent place not only because of their role in the first phase of transition (and its interpretations) but even more so because of their importance in the coming second phase of economic transition.

For even though the second stage of transition will undoubtedly increase the variety and divergence of transition paths, they will all have one thing in common. Growth related issues will remain one of the few common economic features of all former socialist economies and, for most of them, will be the central economic issue. As Table 11.1 shows, regardless which of the four groups[1] of economies is chosen, growth related questions have centre stage. In addition to using GNP per capita in purchasing power parity (ppp) to indicate their current (and initial) lag, Table 11.1 also notes the number of years required by each group to achieve the current average of the 'Mediterranean' EU average GNP per capita in purchasing power parity (ppp) of 13 823 USD.[2] The number of years is calculated for three scenarios each of which assumes a 3 per cent, 5 per cent and 7 per cent stable growth rate over the period in question. The time required shows the magnitude of the economic task facing these economies if they are to reduce the lag and catch up. Even the unlikely, optimistic scenario at best requires a decade, while more probable scenarios require significantly more. The size of the growth challenge required for 'catch up' is perhaps best seen if one notes that the East Asian economies did not manage to achieve high growth rates over even such a long period. Of course, catching up with the average of the EU as a whole or its more developed part would take significantly longer than the period calculated in Table 11.1. Indeed, the question of the economic prospects of 'catching up' or at least 'reducing the lag' provides the only real justification (barring treating democracy as a public good of great value) for the large 'up front' social costs of transition. Falling living standards, rising unemployment, increasing uncertainty and expanding inequality can only be endured for a decade or longer in the hope that they will in the end lead to rising economic welfare for those enduring the costs. In this indirect way, growth related issues are important for the political considerations related to adjustment fatigue and derailment which were

Table 11.1 The economic lag of transitioning economies

	Unweighted average group1996 GNP per capita in ppp	Catch up time in years to EU 1996 GNP per capita in ppp Med average* at 3% p.a. growth	Catch up time in years to EU 1996 GNP per capita in ppp Med average* at 5% p.a. growth	Catch up time in years to EU 1996 GNP per capita in ppp Med average* at 7% p.a. growth
'North tier' economies[1]	6.984	23	14	10
'South tier' economies[2]	3.648	45	27	19
Western FSU economies[3]	3.633	45	27	19
Central Asian economies[4]	2.003	66	40	28

* 'Mediteranean, (Greece, Spain and Portugal) average 1996 GNP: 13.823 USD
[1] 'North tier' economies: Czechia, Estonia, Hungary, Latvia, Lithuania, Poland, Slovakia and Slovenia.
[2] 'South tier' economies: Bulgaria, Croatia, Moldova and Romania; data for Albania, Bosnia and Herzegovina, Macedonia and Yugoslavia do not exist.
[3] Western FSU economies: Belarus, Russia and Ukraine.
[4] Central Asian economies: Armenia, Azerbeijan, Georgia, Kazakstan, Kyrgyz Republic, Tajikistan, Turkmenistan and Uzbekistan.
Source: Author's calculations from Transition Report (EBRD, 1998).

mentioned above and are duly noted by economists through the prominent role of non-economic factors.

Under such circumstances it is understandable that transition optimism and linearity have a high value. What form do they take?

Transition optimism refers to the implicit assumption that the transition will succeed and that all the economies currently in transition and transformation will end up with modern mixed ownership market economies experiencing Modern Economic Growth (as defined by Kuznets[3]). Of course, economists are aware of the difficulties. The dangers, pitfalls and possible derailment are noted by an increasing number (see Blanchard, 1997); comparisons made among the two prevailing grand schemes of transition, that is the European and the Asian one (see Woo et al., 1997), or the relevance of the Latin American experience is discussed (see McMahan, 1996). But in spite of this, overall optimism remains prominent. In the paradigm, derailment can only be a result of applying mistaken policies or of an insufficiently determined or unenthusiastic application of proper policies. The basic ingredients of success are in the 'Washington consensus' recipe with its 'holy transition trinity' (of markets with transparency, democracy with accountability, and privatization with incentives). Research emanating from the international financial community must, for obvious reasons, be optimistic: those backing up policy advisers with their conditionality and financial muscle must not sow any seeds of doubt (see World Bank, 1996; or de Melo *et al.*, 1996). But even authors with a less vested interest in the transition project, who accept that the transition is a case of 'social engineering', do not doubt its ultimate success. In today's case, social engineering will succeed because in contrast to the preceding one, of designing and building socialism, it is based on translating and adapting and implementing the economic framework of already existing and successful capitalist economies (see Ellman, 1997).

There is equal optimism regarding growth prospects. The recommended 'Washington consensus' policy mix will, it is claimed, in the end lead to sustained high growth rates and with that to the dynamics of convergency and 'catch up'. The newly privatized sector growth and dynamics will eventually dominate the receding state sector and the whole economy will pick up. Two sector models generating the 'transitional U' have become standard (see Blanchard, 1997). The resulting high growth rates, it is claimed, will be a result not only of a cyclical upswing, restructuring and greater efficiency of privatized and especially *de novo* private firms, employment of abundant high quality human capital, but also of convergency mechanisms generated by the growth process as envisaged by the Solow-Swann Neoclassical growth model. This model, as will be explained later, generates convergency and with it, optimism.

The implied linearity is closely related to the optimism. It assumes that existing variations in transition paths are essentially variations around a path which is, in its economic fundamentals, the same (that is, common). Thus individual economies are at different stages of the same process. Those which currently lag behind will eventually, in their fundamentals, resemble the front runners of today; and furthermore, the front runners of today will eventually resemble in their fundamentals the most developed economies. Economies are viewed as being at different stages along the same path. The individual differences can and indeed do lead to variations but the underlying linearity remains.

As in the case of optimism, the theoretical basis for linearity is derived from mainstream economics and Solow-Swann Neoclassical growth models. Again, papers written under the auspices of the international financial community provide the best examples of linearity. Thus their seminal contribution, the *From Plan to Market: World*

Development Report 1996 (World Bank, 1996) divides transition economies into four stages: Advanced reformers, High-intermediate reformers, Low-intermediate reformers and Slow reformers.

11.3 Optimism, linearity and reality

These optimistic expectations and linear interpretations face two kinds of problems when confronted with empirical work. First, when taking a wider view they are quite out of step with both the historical record and more recent economic development. Secondly, there is an increasing amount of empirical literature on transitioning economies which casts a shadow on both notions.

The historical record shows, beyond any doubt, that generating Modern Economic Growth is not the rule, and that many economies have not succeeded in achieving it. From the very beginning, when Modern Economic Growth emerged in Western Europe in the late 17th century, matters were unclear. Economic historians still vehemently discuss the causes of both the industrial revolution and its location. From a growth and technology perspective, the case of China is most interesting since a more advanced economy than Europe in the 16th and 17th century never generated growth (see Mokyr, 1990). Looking at more recent periods we see that the growth track record is mixed. In Europe, together with the success of Germany from the mid 19th century, and Scandinavia in the late 19th and early 20th century (see Good, 1994), there have been notable failures in Eastern Europe (see Chirot, 1989 and Good, 1994) and the Italian and Iberian peninsula (see Tortella, 1994). On a wider scale, the success of the United States from the early 19th century must be viewed together with the failures in Latin America and South Africa in the late 19th and early 20th century (see Lewis, 1978). The most recent experience of post-World War II indicates that growth does not 'emanate' (or seem to 'trickle down') from those who are experiencing it. While Europe was enjoying its 'golden age' of convergence with the United States (see Crafts and Toniolo, 1997), Eastern Europe, in spite of massive efforts, was not 'catching up', and neither were the less developed countries of Africa and most of Asia. Indeed, more recent measurements show that the inequality of the world distribution of income is not only increasing, but increasingly becoming a twin peak distribution (see Jones, 1997). Furthermore historical experience, rather than pointing to long periods of stable growth, indicates that oscillations are more common. Periods of high growth are replaced by periods of slow growth (see Boltho and Holtham, 1992).

Empirical research has generated a voluminous literature on another important aspect of the growth process. Such work attempts to establish the presence of convergency, that is, to what extent the growth record of real world economies shows that the differences decrease over time and that the laggards/late comers/followers begin to catch up with the leaders.

Even though such literature does not include or address transition issues *per se*, it is relevant for economies in transition. The actual incentive for this body of research came either from a discussion of another linearity and optimism (namely that of the less developed economies generating Modern Economic Growth and catching up over time and, in this context, explaining the success of East Asian economies), or a discussion among growth theorists (the exogenous vs. endogenous growth debate). The reason transitioning economies were excluded was twofold. First, they could not use data from most presently transitioning economies for the simple reason that these economies did not exist as separate entities (22 of the 27 European transitioning economies were generated by the transition, see Bićanić, 1995). Secondly, the data which did exist was either unreliable and subject to 'ideological massaging', or incompatible since it was not based on UN national accounting. As a result, data from transition economies could not be used neither in cross-section work, nor in constructing time series for individual economies.

There is now a consensus among growth economists that empirical work on convergence clearly indicates several things. First, there is no general convergence. What convergence has been found is limited to two aspects of convergence in the most developed economies. Namely, it is now generally accepted, first, that a significant number of results show that the most developed economies seem to be converging among themselves (see Sala-I-Martin, 1996; or Crafts and Toniolo, 1996); and, secondly, that there seems to be convergence within the European Union as regional differences diminish, and in the United States as states converge (see Sala-I-Martin, 1996; and Barro and Sala-I-Martin, 1995). But beyond this, there is no consensus among economists. Recent studies point to increasing inequality among per capita income of individual economies on a global level (see Jones, 1997 or Pritchett, 1997). In spite of a lack of general convergence, some authors do find a structure emerging. In this empirical work, the 'Theory of clubs' or 'Twin peaks' theories have attained special prominence (see Quah, 1996a). As explained below, this approach seeks to define common growth paths for groups (clubs) of similar economies.

Certainly, the clear lack of convergence does not *a priori* support either the optimism or linearity on a general level, or transitioning economies specifically. The existence of clubs can even generate pessimism, if it is shown that transition economies are members of clubs not converging to levels of the currently most developed economies.

Regarding empirical research into growth in transitioning economies, researchers (and policy makers, but they are not of direct concern here) face additional problems. The first concerns the lack of available results. While some partial country studies exist, reliable comparative ones are still absent. But even the limited scope of the former show that a decade of growth experience of transition does not provide clear support for the linear and optimistic approach either. While the left hand side of the transition 'U' is now more or less known, the length of the trough and the steepness of the right hand side, which stands for positive growth rates, is unknown. Even if transition related war-torn economies, that is the Wars of the Yugoslav succession and those in the former Soviet Union, are disregarded, the record is ambiguous. To date, not a single economy in transition has yet generated sustained high economic growth rates. Poland was closest, but in 1998 growth faltered and for 1999 low growth is predicted. Thus for the most successfully growing economy in transition, the average yearly growth rate since the economy started growing is 5.3 per cent[4] (for the period 1992–8). The other 'flagship' transitioning economies have done even worse. The average yearly growth rates after the turnaround for Hungary is 3.0 per cent (period 1994–8), Slovenia 3.8 per cent (period 1993–8) and Czechia 2.2 per cent (period 1993–8). Regarding Croatia, the other economy with consistently high growth rates and a post-turnaround yearly average of 4.8 per cent (for the period 1994–8), its growth is a result of post-war reconstruction and the statistics are unreliable.

In all likelihood, the prospects of empirical research into transitioning growth and of reliable results will remain slender. There are at least two reasons for this. The first is data related, and the second methodological. Inadequate data is a feature of transition crises. The first part of the transitioning decade was a time of high inflation rates and falling production; neither provide a sound basis for empirical growth research. Thus, at best, there is in most cases less than five years of 'usable' data, which is not enough for reliable empirical work. The methodological problem is one which accompanies all broadly based comparative growth studies based on cross-section data. There is a great variety among the 27 transition economies, ranging from the poorest – Tajikistan and its 900 USD, to the richest – Slovenia and its

12 110 USD (both GNP per capita at ppp). The methodological problems of plugging data from such varied economies into the same regression analysis are well-known in growth theory. In the case of transitioning economies this is made even more serious by the complete economic collapse of some national economies. This collapse has not been restricted to war-torn economies (for example, Bosnia and Herzegovina, FR Yugoslavia, Georgia, Tajikistan, Azerbeijan and Armenia), but to others as well (Albania, Bulgaria for a short time).

As a result, the scope for empirical results is small. Long-term trends cannot be derived and the most recent experience is not encouraging, especially since the empirical results derived under different circumstances, countries and periods do not clearly support optimism and linearity but, on the contrary, quite substantially question it.

11.4 Optimism, linearity and growth theory

Because of the problems described above, the empirical study of growth in transitioning economies cannot have great 'mileage'. As a result, the importance of and reliance on growth theory necessarily increases.

The optimistic and linear approach to transition finds its strongest support in basic mainstream growth theory. The Neoclassical Solow-Swann model (with or without Ramsey optimizing households) is quite clear on both issues. The Solow-Swann model's 'world' generates only one equilibrium steady state growth path. This equilibrium steady state growth path is generated by the assumptions of well-behaved production functions and preferences, perfect competition, profit maximizing firms and welfare maximizing households. Furthermore, this path is globally stable so that, regardless of the economy's initial conditions, the economy converges over time to this one growth path which is common to all economies. Linearity is thus dealt with by the existence of a single steady state growth path, and optimism by the unavoidable convergence of economies to this path. The Neoclassical Solow-Swann model allows per capita GDP and per capita consumption to grow. Additional assumptions are required to enable per capita GDP and consumption to rise, while maintaining equilibrium steady state and stability. In particular, Harrod neutral labour augmenting technical progress is included, and this has the properties of undiscriminating manna from heaven.

The model's equilibrium steady state growth rate is determined by the exogenously given rate of growth of the population and exogenously given rate of growth of technical progress. While the exogenous fundamentals of the model remain unchanged, different values of variables lead to transitionary changes in growth rates. For example, an increase in saving rates does lead to a spurt of growth but it does not change the steady state growth rate.

The stability of this steady state growth is fundamental to this approach because it implies all deviations are transitory, namely that economies will converge to this path regardless of their initial position (and eventually reach it), which makes for both stability and optimism.

Optimism is further strengthened by the convergency properties of the model. The same assumptions about technology (encapsulated in well-behaved production functions with Harrod neutral labour augmenting technical progress) which generate one steady state path and stability also generate interesting convergency properties. Namely, the further any individual economy is from its steady state path the higher its growth rate will be. The convergency properties are part of the strong version of the Neoclassical Solow-Swann model drawn in panel (a) of Figure 11.1. Time is on the horizontal axis and growth rates on the vertical one (steeper paths imply higher growth rates). The steady state growth path is given by the thick line and the growth path of individual economies by the thin lines. The thin lines converge to the steady state growth path with reduced steepness, implying falling growth rates the closer they are to the thick line. The final optimism of the Neoclassical Solow-Swann model is that models can converge only from below, and optimizing Ramsey households guarantee that property.

In its strongest version, the Neoclassical Solow-Swann model assumes a common technology (production function) and common parameters which generate the steady state growth path and absolute convergency. Translated into an econometrically testable form, the rate of convergency was 2 per cent of the distance from the steady state path (see standard Neoclassical growth textbook Barro and Sala-I-Martin, 1995; and for an extensive discussion on convergence Sala-I-Martin, 1996). Economies more distant from this path had higher growth rates and quicker convergence speeds so that the speed of convergence decreased over time.

A weaker version of the Neoclassical Solow-Swann model had to be introduced to deal with the complexities of the real world and answer some of the criticisms leveled at the model in the 1980s. However, the main assumptions (well-behaved production functions and perfect competition, profit maximizing firms, welfare maximizing households as well as exogenous growth rates of population and labour augmenting technical progress) were retained, and with it, the model's main features. For the current discussion an important novelty was the variation

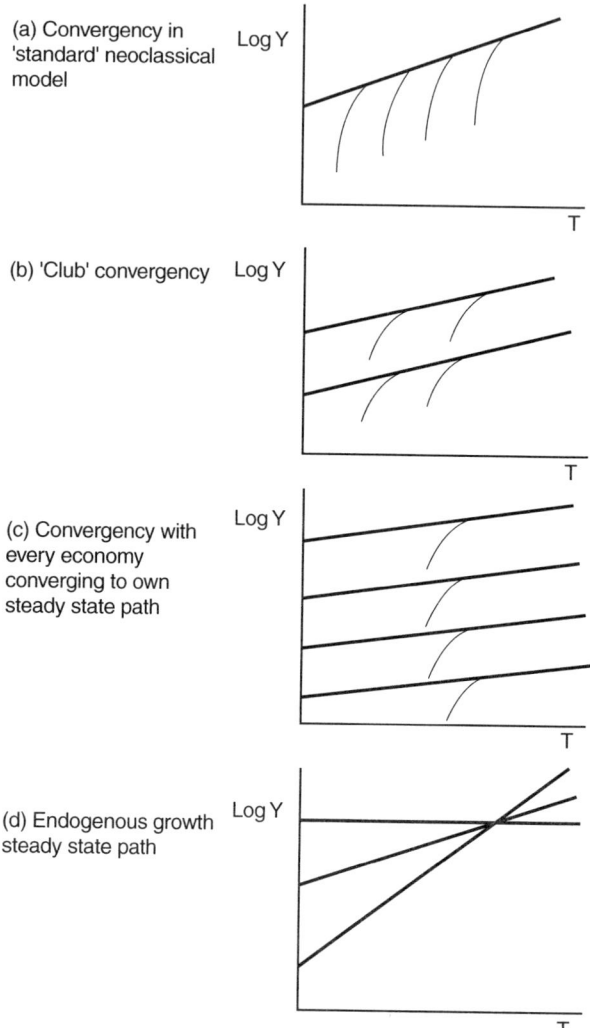

Figure 11.1 Convergency 'scenarios' of different growth model specifications

in parameters.[5] Thus for each set of parameters one steady state growth path can be derived, but due to common growth rates of the population and technical progress, all economies have the same steady state growth rates. The equilibrium growth rates are the same but the values of other parameters can differ. In this case, similar economies have similar parameter values and converge to a common growth path (again from below if Ramsey optimization is allowed), but economies with different parameter values converge to different steady state growth paths. The convergence properties of each individual path remain the same (namely, the more distant an economy is from its steady state path, the faster the convergence is for individual economies), but different for the system. The absolute convergency of the initial model has been replaced by conditional convergency. With conditional convergency, more developed economies can have higher growth rates and convergency speeds than individual less developed ones (if, for example, the more developed economy was further from its steady state path than the less developed one). All the economies converging to any individual steady state growth path are similar and are called 'a club'. This adaptation of the basic Neoclassical model has spawned an increasingly voluminous literature on the 'theory of clubs' and 'club convergence' (see Quah, 1996a). The increasing empirical literature identifies various numbers and types of growth-related clubs, depending on the approach. If only two clubs are identified, then the growth patterns are called 'twin peaks' (see Quah, 1996b). The situation is depicted in panel (b) of Figure 11.1. In the panel, the number of growth clubs has been arbitrarily reduced to two to keep the picture simple.

Once the neoclassical model has been 'opened up' in this manner, the number of clubs remains an open question. The opposite extreme from the initial model regarding clubs is to assume that every individual economy forms a one-member club. Empirical research along these lines has been done by Islan (1995). In this case, every economy has its own steady state growth path to which it converges in line with neoclassical rules: the further away the greater the growth rates. This situation is depicted in panel (c) of Figure 11.1. Again, to keep the picture simple, only four economies are depicted.

Introducing clubs into the analysis maintains a limited linearity but replaces the neoclassical optimism with fatalism. The limited linearity is retained because the steady state growth rates remain the same and the convergence properties remain for every equilibrium steady state growth path. Optimism is now replaced by fatalism in the sense that, while all economies still converge to the same growth rates, they do not converge to the same levels. The levels are different in individual clubs. Concerning the central variable of per capita consumption, even though all economies still converge to the same growth rate of consumption per capita, the level may vary. Individual economies are condemned to their clubs. For some economies, however, the levels they are converging to may on other accounts be quite unacceptable.

The issue of changing clubs then becomes very important but the possibility of changing clubs is clearly not generated by the model.

Fatalism is further strengthened by the role of pro-growth policies in the Neoclassical Solow-Swann model. The growth rates of population and labour augmenting technical progress are exogenously given and cannot be influenced, so that the steady state growth path is given, and the complete institutional framework underpinning the Solow-Swann 'world' is also assumed to be in place (see Solow, 1997). Under such circumstances, pro-growth policies have no place, in two senses. First, their scope is limited to a brief and transitory influence on growth rates. Secondly, there are no mechanisms on how to introduce them into the model.

For economies in transition, the above-described development of the mainstream Solow-Swann model is troublesome. For them the two most interesting features of the model, that is its linearity and optimism, were constrained. The linearity was limited and made questionable by introducing clubs, the optimism was dimmed by introducing types of convergency. Finally, fatalism was introduced by not providing a meaningful scope for pro-active growth policies designed to allow changing clubs and generating Modern Economic Growth.

Luckily, within mainstream economics since the mid-1980s a new type of growth models has started to emerge. These models attempt to introduce the growth generating process into the models and are commonly referred to as endogenous growth models. By using a richer (but mathematically less precise) description of technology, these models include many new issues and aspects. Most importantly, they replace decreasing returns, which are so fundamental in Solow-Swann, by constant or increasing returns and are thus often called AK models. In addition, as pointed out by Barro and Sala-I-Martin (1995), the parameters can sometimes include institutional variables (property rights, competitive conditions, size, and so on). Endogenous growth models are difficult to describe because of their variety – the central variables are various descriptions of technological progress, research and development, human capital, knowledge, increasing returns, and so on.

Regarding the central problem of growth in transition economies, two things are important. The first is that they generate equilibrium steady state growth paths with different long-term growth rates. This means that different economies can have different steady state growth paths, depending on the parameters of the model, and these parameters are in turn generated by policies. These circumstances are depicted in panel (d) of Figure 11.1. For simplicity, only three economies are shown and the different slope implies different growth rates. The second appealing aspect of these models is that growth factors are endogenous and thus can be changed and influenced by policy decisions. The model includes the causal links for the changes and as a result, in endogenous growth theories, there is room for active growth policies, which can lead to accelerated growth.

In this way, optimism is restored to the growth of transition economies: transition economies can generate high growth rates allowing them to catch up (but not converge because there is no convergence in these models, indeed the dynamics are rather poor), and achieve Modern Economic Growth. The analysis of the policy implications and generation of high growth rates is outside the scope of this chapter. But endogenous growth has another important aspect which makes it especially interesting for economies in transition. Equally importantly though, the optimism is limited. The 'world' of endogenous growth models need not generate high growth rates automatically. Policies need not be developed, yet there is room for failure. Success and failure enter on an equal footing. Growth potentials need not be realized; there can be errors in policy choice and policy implementation, derailments, barriers and a host of other obstructions which prevent high growth and can occur in transition economies.

The rich possibilities opened by interpretations of endogenous growth models has not gone unnoticed. Development economists seem to favour them, even though they point out that they still have a way to go for being applied in development theory (see Coricelli *et al.*, 1998), and researchers of growth in transition economies have also pointed to their advantages (see Gomulka, 1998).

11.5 Conclusion

With the completion of the first phase of transition, the most important aspect of the process concerns the issue of generating Modern Economic Growth. By the end of the 20th century this goal has not been achieved by any economy in transition. However, the dominating paradigm of transition in theory and policy is based on notions of linearity and optimism. The varied historical experience of growth, the recent experience and some implications of the modern growth theory cast a shadow on the optimistic and linear approach. Growth and 'catch up' are not inevitable.

The challenges of the second stage may likely show that the common features of the transition process diminish and the variety of transition paths increase. While for some, consolidation will be the main preoccupation, others will be primarily concerned with a second stage of transition, perhaps for some, even a third stage. Growth will, however, remain the common goal for all. In this respect, the growth theory developed since the 1980s is of special interest. It leads to limited optimism and linearity. But perhaps most importantly, by allowing a place for barriers and missed opportunities, it points to the complexities faced by economies in transition when attempting to generate Modern Economic Growth.

Notes

1 The four groups of economies are partly chosen *ad hoc*. This was unavoidable since, first, no generally accepted grouping exists; and secondly, the groups to a great extent coincide with groups identified in other social sciences (for example, geography). There are, however, differences. Thus the 'North tier' includes not only economies in the first group designated for EU membership (Poland, Czech Republic, Hungary and Estonia) but also other economies of a similar level of development and location which have gone through a similar transition path (Lithuania, Latvia, Slovenia and Slovakia). The justification for this group is thus not only the relationship towards the EU and EU support they receive, but also that the main transition task they face in the medium term is the consolidation and improvement of their existing path. The 'Southern tier' includes not only South-eastern Europe (Bosnia and Herzegovina, FR Yugoslavia, Albania, Bulgaria and Romania) but also Croatia and Moldova. These countries are grouped together not only due to geographical location, but also due to the transition track record (their transition crises was deeper and lasted longer, their economic disequilibrium larger and privatization slower than in the first group), and the medium term expectations. In all countries of the second group, the medium term will be dominated by a probable 'second transition', an experience they have either already partly faced or will experience. Finally, another common element of the 'Southern tier' is its relationship towards the EU and membership (with Slovenia and Hungary) of SECI. The third group includes the two largest European transition economies (Russia and Ukraine) as well as Belarus. Even though there are differences (for example, in privatization), the magnitude of the tasks facing them and their links justify grouping them together, since all of them face not only a second but perhaps a third transition as well. In the fourth group are the Central Asian economies. Even though they are different, the meager results of transition to date, their geographical position, achieved level of development and economic difficulties seem to justify putting them into a separate group.
2 This average (which has an unfortunate name since, in addition to Greece and Spain, it includes Portugal but not Italy or France) was calculated from the same source and has been chosen as a benchmark. It seems a more appropriate value then either the EU or OECD average, or the per capita income of some economies that those in transition quite mistakenly like to compare themselves to (for example, Croatia to Denmark).

3 Who defines it as '... a sustained increase in per capita or per worker product, most often accompanied by an increase in population and usually sweeping structural change' (Kuznets, 1966:1).
4 All growth rate data come from EBRD Transition reports for various years; the 1998 rate is an estimate.
5 The other main innovation concerns introduction of a larger number of factors of production (for example, human capital).

References

Aslund A., Boone, P. and Johnson, S. (1996) 'How to Stabilize: Lessons from Post-Communist Countries', *Brookings Papers in Economic Activity*, Washington DC, pp. 217–313.
Barro, R. and Sala-I-Martin, X. (1995) *Economic Growth*, Boston: McGraw Hill.
Bićanić, I. (1995) 'The Economic Causes of New State Formation During the Transition', *East European Politics and Society*, 9(1): 2–21.
Blanchard, O. (1997) *The Economics of Post-Communist Transition*, Oxford: Clarendon Press.
Boltho, A. and Holtham, G. (1992) 'The Assessment: New Approaches to Economic Growth', *Oxford Review of Economic Policy*, 8(4): 1–14.
Chirot, D. (ed.) (1989) *The Origins of Backwardness in Eastern Europe*, Berkeley: California UP.
Coricelli, F., di Matteo, M. and Hahn, F. (eds) (1998) *New Theories in Growth and Development*, London: Macmillan.
Cornia, G. and Popov V. (1998), 'Transition and Long-term Growth: Conventional versus Non-conventional Determinants', *MOCT–MOST*, 8: 7–32.
Crafts, N. (1995) 'The Golden Age of Economic Growth in Western Europe 1950–1973', *Economic History Review*, 48(3): 429–47.
Crafts, N. and Toniolo, G. (eds) (1996) *Economic Growth in Europe Since 1945*, Cambridge: Cambridge UP.
EBRD (1998) *Transition Report 1998*, London: EBRD.
Ellman, M. (1997) 'The Political Economy of Transformation', *Oxford Review of Economic Policy*, 13(2): 23–32.
Fish, S. (1998) 'The Determinants of Economic Reform in the Post-Communist World', *East European Politics and Societies*, 12(1): 31–78.
Gomulka, S. (1998) 'Output: Causes of the Decline and the Recovery', *CASE–CEU Working paper* no. 8, Warsaw.
Good, D. (1994) 'The Economic Lag of Central and Eastern Europe: Income Estimates for Habsburg Successor States 1870–1910', *The Journal of Economic History*, 54(4): 869–91.
Islan, N. (1995) 'Growth Empirics: A Panel Data Approach', *Quarterly Journal of Economics*, 110: 1127–70.
Jones, C. (1995) 'Time Series Tests of Endogenous Growth Models', *Quarterly Journal of Economics*, 110(May): 495–525.
Jones, C. (1997) 'On the Evolution of the World Income Distribution', *Journal of Economic Perspectives*, 11(3): 19–36.
Kuznets, S. (1966) *Modern Economic Growth*, New Haven: Yale UP.

Lewis, A. (1978) *Growth and Fluctuations 1870–1913*, London: George Allen and Unwin.
McMahan, G. (ed.) (1996) *Lessons in Economic Policy for Eastern Europe from Latin America*, London: MacMillan.
de Melo, M., Denizer, C. and Gelb, A. (1996) 'Patterns of Transition from Plan to Market', *The World Bank Economic Review*, 10(3): 397–424.
Mokyr, J. (1990) *The Lever of Riches*, Oxford: Oxford UP.
Pritchett, L. (1997) 'Divergence, Big Time', *Journal of Economic Perspectives*, 11(3): 3–17.
Quah, D. (1996a) 'Twin Peaks: Growth and Convergence in Models of Distribution Dynamics', *Economic Journal*, 106:1045–55.
Quah, D. (1996b) 'Empirics for Economic Growth and Convergence', *European Economic Review*, 40: 1353–75.
Sala-I-Martin, X. (1996) 'The Classical Approach to Convergence Analysis', *Economic Journal*, 106: 1019–36.
Solow, R. (1997) *Learning from 'Learning by Doing,'* Stanford: Stanford UP.
Tortella, G. (1994) 'Patterns of Economic Retardation and Recovery in South-western Europe in the Nineteenth and Twentieth Centuries', *Economic History Review*, 47: 1–21.
Woo, W. T., Parker, S. and Sachs, J. (eds), (1997) *Economies in Transition: Comparing Asia and Eastern Europe*, Cambridge: MIT Press.
World Bank (1996) *From Plan to Market: World Development Report 1996*, Oxford: Oxford University Press.

Index

'Agathotopia', 92, 98, 99
altruism, 34, 35, 39
  see also cooperation, *Homo reciprocans*
Asian exceptionalism and crises, 5
  see also income inequality
associationist socialism, xxvii, 5–7, 14n
  see also self-management; employee participation
Atlantic republicanism, 27–9
Austrian school of economics, 16, 24–5
  on entrepreneurship, 25

capitalism, xxiii, 1, 27, 103
  emerging, in Croatia, xxv
  return to in Yugoslavia, 135
  and Joseph Schumpeter on business cycle in, 13
  see also laissez-faire
co-determination, 21, 103, 156
  in transition, 103
collective ownership, 29, 133, 145, 153, 155, 156
  see also social ownership
command economy, 3–4, 6, 162
  roots, 6
convergence, economic, 185, 188, 190, 192, 193–5, 197
  club, 191, 195
  conditional, 195
cooperation, xxviii
  and culture, 178
  in dictator games, 41
  inter-firm, 109, 110–11
  in iterated prisoner's dilemma, 36, 45; and Robert Axelrod's tournaments, 36–7
  and notion of fairness, 41; and contrived social relations, 41–2; and egalitarian redistribution, 33, 42

  in public goods games 39–40, 45; and *Homo economicus* model, 39–40
  and 'tit-for-tat' strategy, 36–7; in dynamic social processes, 37–9; cyclical pattern, 38–9
  in ultimatum games, 40–1: and *Homo economicus*, 41
cooperative skills, 113, 114
corporate governance, 100n, 156, 164, 180n
corruption, 105
creative destruction, 5, 11, 13–14
cultural learning, 35, 37
culture
  and moral predispositions, 43–4
  and property rights, 178

decolonization, 22
democratic society, 18, 20, 22, 23, 28, 29, 33; Swiss canton, 17, 18; democratic market society, 20
  immigration policies in, 86–7
dictator(ship), 18–19; Adolf Hitler's Germany, 17, 18, 19, 23; Anastasio Somosa's Nicaragua, 17, 18, 19, 23

economic democracy, xxv, xxviii, xxix
  and Austrian economics, 16
  and Alvarado J. Velasco's reforms in Peru, 16–17, 24
economic growth
  AK model of, 196
  and democracy, 70
  v. efficiency trade-off, 3; and 'Euro-Sclerosis', 4; and revisionism, 4; and structural adjustment policies, 4
  endogenous model of, 196, 197
  and fatalism, 195–6
  and income inequality, 49

economic growth – *continued*
  long-term trends, 189, 192
  models, ix, xxii, xxxi
  policies, 186, 196, 197
  political economy link, 70
  scenarios, 191
  Solow–Swan neoclassical models, 188, 192–3
  theory, xxxi, 185; and transition, 185–6, 196, 197, 198
  and theory of clubs, 191, 193–5; and transition pessimism, 191
  in Yugoslavia, 124, 131, 139
  see also convergence; transition; 'Washington consensus'
economic systems, alternative, 3–6, 180n
  economic efficiency, 3–5
  see also capitalism, command economy; etatism; laissez-faire; market socialism; real socialism, self-management; socio-economic system; Soviet-type planned economy
economic theory
  four cells of, xxvii, 2
  and Branko Horvat, 2
  and John M. Keynes, 2
  and Karl Marx, 2
  and David Ricardo, 2
  and Adam Smith, 2
  and efficiency *v.* distribution trade-off, 3
egalitarianism, xxviii, 27–44
  and Atlantic republicanism, 27
  and capitalism, 27
  and democratic socialists, 29
  importance of economics, 33, 43
  Thomas Jefferson's, 28–9, 44n; and Alexis de Tocqueville, 28; and Karl Marx, 28–9
  and moral sensibility, 32, 43
  neo-Jeffersonian paradigm, 29–30; redistribution, 30
  radical, 27, 43
  and self-management, 104
  and socialism, 27
  and social preferences, 68, 69

egalitarian policies, programs, xxviii, 29–30, 32
  asset-based, 29, 33, 42
  concept of fairness, 31
  cost-effectiveness, 32
  and governance structures, 29
  and government production, 30
  insurance-based, 29
  moral case for, 27
  and moral sentiments, 43–4; roles of genes and culture, 35, 43–4
  opposition to, 33
  political viability, 30, 33
  status quo bias, 32
  support, reasons for, 35; insurance motive, 35; and 'reciprocal fairness', 35; and Social Security and Medicare, 42
  see also cooperation
egalitarian project, demoralization of xxviii, 31–2
  and incentive structures, 30
  and utopian yearnings, 27
employee ownership, 94, 99
  in transition economies, xxx, 99, 100n, 145–6, 147, 149, 153, 155–6, 158, 159, 163, 165; and context of restructuring, 158; and control, 155–6, 159; in Estonia, 168–9; and investment, 156; performance, 163; and participation, 163, 170; and productivity, 156; public policy, 159; and slowly-dying firms, 158; and 'Benn co-operatives', 159
employee participation
  and business performance, 163, 178, 180n, 181n
  and competitiveness, 105–6
  in control, 92, 93, 94, 95, 97, 98; effective, dominant, 96, 180n
  and W. E. Deming's quality movement, 103
  effective control, 96, 180n
  entrepreneurial control, 91–2, 95–6, 97, 99, 100n

enterprise types by degree of, xxix, 91–3, 97–9; critique of standard classification, 95–7
and firm's organization, xxix, 113–14
and flexibility of firms, 105, 114
and free-market approach, 105
in James Meade's 'Agathotopia', 99
and management paradigm, *see* management-decision making
in Mondragon cooperatives, 100n, 146
productivity impact, xxix, 92, 94–6, 100
public policy, support, xxix, 92, 95, 99–100
in returns, 92, 93, 94, 95–7, 98, 100n, 180n
and self-interest, 113
and system of '20 keys', 110
see also industrial democracy; workers' involvement
'end of history', 4
enlightenment
and alternatives to capitalism, 1
in economic theory, 1–2; origin, 1; Scottish and Adam Smith, 1
liberal, 27, 43
enterprise ownership, forms
and control, 165
in economic theory, 165
and performance, 162–3, 164–6
see also employee ownership, privatization
entrepreneurship
in 'Agathotopia', 99
Austrian school, 24
bureaucratic, 108, 112
and employee participation, 108
and laws of optimal participation, xxviii
lessons from Slovenia, 107–13
parental, 23–5
in producer cooperatives, 84
revival of, 106
two trajectories, 24–5; *see also* Mammon-developer capitalist
entry of new firms, promotion, 106, 107–8

and competitiveness of the Slovene economy, 108
and economics of self-management, 107
and Marshallian competition, 107
obstacles to in self-managed Yugoslav economy, 112
resistance to, 108
Schumpeterian inspiration, 108
equality of opportunity, 31
and cultural capital, 32
educational, 31–2
Estonia, *see* privatization
etatism, xxiii, xxv
'Euro-Sclerosis', 4

game theory and cooperation, *see* cooperation
genes and moral predispositions, 43–4
see also cooperation; *compare* culture
genetic learning, 35, 27
globalization, 113
grandfather clause, 17
see also parental involvement
Great Depression, 13
growth, *see* economic growth

Homo economicus, 35–6, 39–42
see also Homo reciprocans
Homo reciprocans, xxviii, 36–42
and egalitarian redistribution, 42
and notion of fairness, 40, 41
and opposition to welfare state policies, 42
in public goods games, 40
see also cooperation; egalitarianism; egalitarian policies; sharing institutions
Horvat, Branko
on crises in Kosovo, xxvi
on crises in Yugoslavia, xxvi
economist, xxii–xxiv, 2
on emerging capitalism in Croatia, xxv, xxvi
fusion of democracy and socialism, 1; and enlightenment, 1–2
on international trade theory, xxiv
and JUNASET group, xxv

Horvat, Branko – *continued*
  on labour-managed firm, xxiii, 7–9, 81, 130, 162
  and labour theory of value, xxiv
  life and work, xx–xxii
  and Marxism, x, xxii
  model of economic growth, ix, xxii, 130
  on neoclassical economics, x, xxii
  on neo-Ricardian theory, xxiv
  and normative theory, xxvi
  pedagogue, xxv
  political activist, xxvi
  political economist, xxiii
  on role of institutions, ix, xxiii
  on self-management, x, xxv, xxix, 5–7, 91, 102, 114, 130, 165
  and socialism, xxiii, xxiv
  and social ownership, 154
  on Yugoslav economic system, xxv, 13

Illyrian theory of the firm, xxiii, xxix, 8–9, 88
  applications, xxix, 80; *see also* immigration policy; joint-stock companies; producer cooperatives
  and cooperative rent-sharing, xxix, 80–2, 89n
  of labour-managed firm, 81; Illyrian disease of, 81
  and participation in returns, 97
  relevance, 88
  and self-management in Yugoslavia, 80, 88, 89n, 118
  Benjamin Ward's model, xxiii, 8–9, 89n
  see also labour-managed firm
International Monetary Fund (IMF) structural adjustment policy, 4
immigration policy, xxix, 86–8, 90n
  and Illyrian theory, 86–8, 89n; and Illyrian rents, 87
  and state as a citizens' cooperative, 87–8

income inequality
  in Asian countries, 60–1, 64–5, 69; and distribution of capital, 60–1, 69
  'augmented' (Simon) Kuznets' hypothesis, 50–2; analysis and findings, 54–68, 74–6n; testing 52–68
  and development policies, 69
  and economic growth, 45
  increasing, 31
  international differences, ix, xxviii, 48–52, 61–6, 73n, 105, 189; determinants, xxix, 50–2; regional, 54, 61–6
  Kuznets' (Simon) hypothesis, xxix, 48–50, 66–7, 68, 69, 73n
  and level of decentralization, 51–2
  and Arthur Lewis-type pattern of growth, 49
  measuring, 31, 44–5n; data issues, 52–3, 55, 58–9, 70–3, 76n; heteroskedasticity problem, 55; household surveys, 70–1
  and moral sensibilities, 32–3
  role of economic factors, 50
  and size of government transfers, 52, 54, 55, 59, 67, 69, 70, 71, 72, 74n; and population structure, 60
  and size of the state sector, 51–2, 54, 65, 68, 69, 72; in former socialist countries, 51, 52, 54, 55, 59, 65
  and social (public) choices, factors, 50–2, 61, 66–9; and distribution of assets, 69–70
  in socialist economies, 51, 52, 65, 73n, 76n
  and social preferences, 68, 69
  compare egalitarianism; egalitarian policies
industrial democracy, 91, 95; and productivity, 95, 97
  see also employee participation
insider ownership, 164–5, 167, 168
  see also privatization

institutions
  role of, ix, xxiii
  sharing, 33–4
investment, optimal rate of, xxii

joint-stock companies, xxix, 12, 92
  Illyrian aspect, 85, 86; as capitalist cooperative, 85–6, 88, 89n; *v.* producer co-ops, 86
  and participation, 21

Kuznets, Simon, inverted U curve, *see* income inequality; Kuznets' hypothesis

labour-managed firm, x, xxiii, xxvii, 7–9, 80–2, 89n, 97, 146, 156, 158
  and bureaucratic entrepreneurship, 112
  and capital market, 146
  v. capitalist firm, 7–9, 12, 82, 129, 162
  choice of technology, 11–12; and capital-intensity bias, 11
  and corporate governance, 156
  exit, 158
  'Illyrian disease', 81; and free entry, 81, 90n
  and information differentials, 7
  and investment, 11, 12, 130
  and labour hoarding, 8, 10, 158
  and labour productivity, 12
  macro-foundations, 8–9
  and macro-policy adjustments, 8
  and managerial functions, 7
  and new entry, 108, 112
  and optimizing function, 8–9, 12, 80–1
  performance, 156, 162
  and rent appropriation, 81–2
  in Yugoslavia, 112
  see also Illyrian theory of the firm; producer cooperative
labour-management, *see* self-management
laissez-faire
  and alternatives, 2, 3–5
  and economic efficiency, 3–5

economics, 3
  triumph of, 5
laws of optimal participation, xxviii
  first law of, 18–20
  and parental entrepreneurship, 23–5
  second law of, 21–3

Mammon-developer capitalist, xxviii, 24
management decision-making
  change in management paradigm, 103, 105–6; and revival of entrepreneurship, 106
  decentralization, 106
  and inter-firm associations, 109–11
  and managerial science, 107
  quality-based, 112, 113; and employee ownership, 112; and cooperative skills, 113; and workers' involvement, 111, 112–13
  and system of '20 keys', 109–11
  and traditional self-management model, 114
  and workers' participation, 114
market socialism
  Branko Horvat's *v.* Oskar Lange's model of, 14n
  and transition, 102–3, 104
  in Yugoslavia, xxv, xxx, 6, 118, 132, *see also* Yugoslavia
Marshallian concept of competition, 107
Marxism
  and economic reforms in Yugoslavia, 122, 125, 132, 139, 140
  Branko Horvat's, x, xxii
Mitbestimmung, 97
'Modern Economic Growth', 187, 189–90, 196, 197, 198
Mondragon system, 14n, 83, 100n, 146

neoclassical economics, x, xxii, xxviii, 24, 36
  and growth models, 188, 192, 193
  and international trade theory, xxiv

neoclassical economics – *continued*
  neo-Ricardian critique of, xxiv
  see also Homo economicus
'new competition', 106–7, 109

optimal states of society, *see* socio-economic system
outsider ownership, 154, 165
  see also privatization

parental involvement, *see* socio-economic system
participation, *see* employee participation; laws of optimal participation, self-management
social, *see* socio-economic system
participatory economy, *see* self-management
Peru, problem of Alvarado J. Velasco's economic reform, 16–17, 24
prisoner's dilemma, *see* cooperation
Phillips curve trade-off, 5
private sector, in transition economies, 148–9, 167
privatization, 147, 163–6, 184, 198n
  and capital markets, 147
  and *de novo* private firms, 163, 188
  and economic performance, xxx, 157, 162–3, 167, 169–76, 177, 178, 180n, 181n; and institutional factors; and participation, 170, 178
  and employee ownership, 99, 100n, 146, 149, 153, 155, 163, 176, 177; and control, 155–6; and ESOP, 153
  in Estonia, xxx; methods and processes, 166–7; ownership structures, 168–9; economic effects, 169–77
  and form of ownership, 163, 180; and control, 180n; preferred, 165–6
  insiders, 149, 153, 154, 165, 167–9
  and labour management, xxx, 145,156, 159; *see also* employee ownership, in transition economies; transition, and labour management
  lagging, in countries of former Yugoslavia, 149
  majority ownership, 153, 164–6, 168, 170, 173, 176, 177, 179, 180n; foreign, 173
  management–employee buy-outs, 105, 149
  Managerially Controlled Employee Owned Firm (MCEO), 155, 157
  managerial ownership, 154, 167
  mass, 149, 152, 153
  methods, xxx, 147–51, 159n, 166, 171
  minority ownership, 164, 165, 169, 170, 171, 173, 174, 175, 178, 179, 180n
  outsiders, 149, 165, 168
  in Russia, 163, 167, 177
  in Slovenia, 103, 105
  and state ownership, 173, 175, 177, 178
  theoretical case for, 164–6
  and transition effect, 169, 170, 180n, 181n
  in Visegrad countries, xxx, 163, 166, 177
  voucher, 149, 167
  see also economic growth; employee ownership; transition
producer cooperatives, 80, 83–5, 88, 89n, 145, 146, 155
  behaviour, 83–5
  capital intensity, 83
  v. capitalist firms, 83
  funds, securing, 83–4
  James Meade on inegalitarian, 87
  optimizing function, 84–5, 89n
  plywood, in the US, 83
  relative scarcity of, 83–4, 89n
  and transition, 145, 155
  and unions, 84, 89n
  see also Mondragon system
prisoner's dilemma, *see* cooperation
property rights
  and economic efficiency, 178
  in China, 178
  in labour-managed firms, 82

and redistribution, 29
temporary, contingent, 100n

quality movement, 103, 106, 107
  and industrial organization, 106;
  and 'new competition', 106–7
  introduction of ISO 9000, 107

real socialism
  economic stagnation, collapse, 11, 13
  income distribution, 51, 65, 73
  see also command economies; etatism; Soviet-type planned economies
reciprocity
  and concept of fairness, 40, 42
  motive for, 36
  and reciprocal fairness, 35
  see also cooperation; *Homo reciprocans*
regionalization of the class, ix
rent-sharing, cooperative, *see* Illyrian theory of the firm
restructuring
  and employee involvement, 109–10
  and employee ownership, 100n, 158
  and employment, 157
  and enterprise culture, 109
  and export competitiveness of Slovene enterprises, 109–12; and 'new competition'; and system of '20 keys', 109–11
  and future of employee participation, 111

self-management
  and accountability, 111, 115n
  and cooperation, inter-firm, 110
  as economic system, 6–7, 102, 118, 122–3, 125, 129, 180
  and economic welfare, 103
  and enterprise performance, 129, 180n
  and income distribution, 104
  and lack of creative destruction, 13–14
  and level of development, 102–3
  and loyalty, 113

  macroeconomic performance, 129–30, 180n
  in Peru, 16–17
  and privatization in Slovenia, 103, 105
  in transition economies, xxx, 104, 159; *see also* employee ownership
  in Yugoslavia, x, xxv, xxvii, xxx, 11, 12–13, 103, 111–12, 115n, 122, 125, 128, 129, 132, 133, 135, 145, 159, 180; *see also* Horvat, Branko; Yugoslavia
  see also associationist socialism; employee participation
sharing institutions, xxviii, 33–5
  sunay, 34–5
  and Talcott Parsons' *evolutionary universals*, 34
slavery, 22
social democratic model
  and evolutionary socialism, 6
  and Phillips curve trade-off, 5
social ownership, 6, 103, 121, 126, 133, 134, 135, 145, 149, 154
  see also collective ownership
socio-economic system
  and co-determination, 21
  and consumers' participation, 20
  degree of involvement, 18–20
  degree of participation, 18–20
  laws of optimal participation, xxviii, 18–23
  optimal xxviii, 17, 18, 24
  quality of involvement, 21–3; and decolonization, 22; and political democracy, 22; in slavery, 22
  unified theory of, xxxviii, 17–23
Soviet-type planned economy
  and income inequality, 51, 52, 65, 73n; and consumers' subsidies, 76n; and *nomenklatura*, 76n
  and 'third way', 104
  in Yugoslavia, 121–22
  see also command economy
system of '20 keys', 109–11;
  and efficiency, 110
  and employees' involvement, 110

'third way', 88, 104
  see also market socialism
Third World, ix, 4
'tit-for-tat' strategy, 36-7
transition, xxx, 145, 157, 159, 176-8
  and capitalism, 103
  and 'catching-up', 185, 186, 188, 197
  crises, 198n
  economic collapse in, 192
  and EU membership, 198n
  first phase of, 184, 197
  and free market system, 105; and workplace democracy, 105
  growth, xxxi, 184, 186, 188-90, 196, 197, 198
  growth rates, 187, 188, 191; and data/methodological, issues, 190-2
  Branko Horvat's critique of, xxv, xxvi
  and labour management, opportunities, xxx, 102-3, 145-7, 154-9, 165
  and labour productivity, 157
  linearity, xxxi, 185, 188, 191, 192, 197, 198
  and market socialism ('third way'), 102-3
  non-economic factors, role of, 185, 186
  'North tier' of, 198n
  optimism, xxxi, 185, 187-8, 191, 192, 197, 198; and 'Modern Economic Growth', 187, 189, 197, 198
  and ownership forms, preferred, 165-6
  paths, xxxi, 184, 186, 188, 197, 198n; and path-dependency, 185
  and restructuring, 157-8
  second stage of, 186, 198, 198n
  social costs, 186
  and social engineering, 188
  and social ownership, 154-5
  'Southern tier' of, 198n; and 'second transition', 198n
  'trinity', 185

  in Yugoslavia 140-2
  see also economic growth; employee ownership; privatization, restructuring, self-management,

Virginia Constitution, 28

'Washington consensus', 185, 188
  and 'transition trinity', 188
welfare economics, xxix, 103
  and economic systems, 104; and self-management, 103
welfare state, 33, 43
  opposition to, 42
workers' involvement, and modern firm's organization, xxix, 103, 105, 109, 110, 113-14
workers' management, *see* self-management
workers' participation, *see* employee participation
World Bank, 4

yeoman democracy, 28
Yugoslavia
  administrative market socialism (1953-62), 119, 121-3, 131; and introduction of self-management, 122
  administrative socialism (1945-52), 119, 120-1, 131
  associated labour concept, 125
  Basic Organization of Associated Labour (BOAL), 126, 127
  break with Soviet Union, 122
  collapse of, xxx, 139-42; and disintegration of economic system, 142; and elections, 142; and prospects for radical reform, 139-40
  Composite Organizations of Associated Labour (COAL), 126, 127
  contractual socialism (1973-88), 119, 125-7, 131, 132, 135; crises of, 132-3; deficiencies, 128-9; disintegration, 127-9
  degeneration of social ownership, 134

dominance of bureaucratic entrepreneurship, 112
economic crises, stagnation, 11, 120, 132, 135, 136, 141; and economists, 107
economic growth, 124, 131, 136, 139; and Soviet-type pattern of development, 131–2
economic performance, xxx, 11, 13, 104, 124, 129, 130–1, 135–8, 141
economic reform of 1965, xxvi, 119, 124, 141
economic reforms, xxx, 118, 120, 123, 124, 129–30, 131, 132, 139–42; and counter-reforms, 118, 125, 139; and political reforms, 140; and transition, 140
economic systems, periodization, 119
Enterprise Law of 1989 and return to capitalism, 135
entrepreneurship support, 107–8; new entry promotion, 108
failures of self-management system, 11, 111–12, 115n
first five-year plan (1947–52), 120–1
foreign debt, 135–6, 138
foreign trade, balance, 123–4, 135–6, 137, 141
Free Exchange of Labour (FEL), 127
government control, intervention, 123, 124, 128, 129, 132, 136, 137
group ownership, 124
hyper-stagflation, 136, 138
inflation, 124, 136–7, 141
inflationary expectations, 137
institutional changes, 141
labour and capital markets, 123, 127, 133, 134, 135, 140
Long Run Stabilization Program of 1982, 132–3

market socialism (1963–73), 119, 123–5, 133
'Mikulić Commission', 134
nationalism, xxvi, 11, 13; and ethnic tensions, 132, 140, 142
permanent reforms, 123
political crises, 132, 142; and stalemate, 133, 140
pooling of labour and resources, 126, 128
rational behaviour of agents, 128, 129
and real employee participation, 112
regional disparities in, 136, 138
Self-Management Agreements (SMAs), 125–7
Social Contracts, 125–7
social crises, tensions, 132, 138, 140
socialization of the countryside, 127
social planning, 127, 134
soft-budget constraints, 137
and Soviet-type planned economy, 122
stabilization policies, 138; shock-therapy stabilization program of 1989, 141
structural change, 131–2
systemic transformation, 119, 139, 141; and role of political/economic factors, 119, 122
transition, 140: and pre-conditions for, 140–41
unemployment, 136, 137–8; and underemployment, 138
wage v. accumulation dilemma, 128
workers' control, 125
Working Organization (WO), 126, 127
see also Horvat Branko; Illyrian theory of the firm; labour-managed firm; Marxism; self-management; social ownership